Sport and the
Literary Imagination

To Katharine, Tim and Richard

# Contents

# Acknowledgements

My thanks are due to the staff of De Montfort University Library, the British Library at St Pancras and Colindale, and to the many colleagues whose comments on drafts have helped shape the text. In particular I should like to record my appreciation of the thoughtful criticisms received at several conferences of the British Society of Sport History, and of the North American Society of Sport Historians, as well as from members of staff/postgraduate seminars at the universities of Loughborough, Southampton, Lincoln, Sheffield, Odense, and Aarhus over the past four years. My fellow historians at the International Centre for Sport History and Culture at De Montfort University have always been ready to give advice and support. Thanks are also due to Graham Speake, Sue Leigh, and Adrian Baggett at Peter Lang, and to their anonymous reviewer whose comments on the original proposal were so valuable. Finally, and not least in importance, my thanks to Katharine and Tim Hill for their skill in solving, among many other computer-related problems, the mystery of the hanging indent.

# Chapter One
# The Historicity of the Text: A Historian's Reading

'All good tales are true tales, at least for those who read them, which is all that counts.'[1]

This book has two main focal points. The *subject* focus is sport, and particularly how this feature of modern society has been represented in creative writing, especially novels. Its *methodological* concern is with the practice of the historian when dealing with imaginative literary constructions of this kind. The book is directed primarily at historians, though it is hoped that those whose business is literary analysis might find in it something of value. In the second emphasis, though, the book attempts to contribute to current debates about the nature of history and what its 'proper' concerns might be. This claim might provoke an initial suspicion among those who detect another book about 'theory'. To allay such fears I should note at the outset that I regard reports of the 'death' of history as premature, just as I see claims that theory is 'killing' the discipline equally exaggerated.[2] Teaching history for over thirty years in higher education, during which time I have worked with a great many historians of different persuasions, has led me to believe that most members of our profession still believe that 'doing' history is about reconstructing the past in as objective a way as is possible, and that whilst the outcome of this endeavour is not a perfect representation of the truth it is

---

1    Javier Cercas, *Soldiers of Salamis*, [trans. from Spanish by Anne McLean], (London: Bloomsbury Publishing, 2003), p. 161.

2    See Elizabeth A. Clarke, *History, Theory, Text: Historians and the Linguistic Turn* (Cambridge, Mass.: Harvard University Press, 2004), esp. Introduction, p. 1; and Keith Windschuttle, *The Killing of History: How Literary Critics and Social Theorists Are Murdering Our Past* (New York: First Free Press Edition, 1997).

nonetheless a worthwhile academic pursuit. In general, I agree with this view from the factory floor. As the historian Jeremy Black has recently put it: 'Far from being postmodernists or pomophobes, most historians get on with research, which they generally approach in an accretional fashion, and treat debates about pomo as self-referential, if not self-regarding, and of little relevance to the practitioner.'[3] I do not, personally, subscribe to the scepticism about 'pomo' to which Black alludes. Some of postmodernism's baggage can, to be sure, seem very strange to the empirically-minded historian.[4] But many of the influences that have come into history from theoretical sources have been invigorating, if only because at long last they have forced British historians out of the epistemological insularity they had inhabited for over a century, and caused them to think about the problems relating to knowledge creation that most other disciplines have been aware of since at least the nineteenth century. In this broader intellectual context I certainly do not believe that the historical method has been shown to be value-less. We in the profession should remind ourselves, however, that our subject is a slippery one, more slippery perhaps than the devotees of pure empiricism have admitted, and that the process of finding out is beset with problems of 'knowing'. Still, in the last analysis, the business of the historian is about trying to figure out what life was like in the past.

3    Jeremy Black, 'Past Lives of the Pomos, Proto-Pomos and Pomophobics', *Times Higher Educational Supplement*, 27 August 2004, 24.
4    What seems to irritate many conventional historians is the tendency of their 'postmodernist' colleagues to write in a rather abstract style that prevents their getting down to the 'real' history. This irritation will probably not be dispelled by the recent collection from Gabrielle M. Spiegel, *Practicing History: New Directions in Historical Writing After the Linguistic Turn* (New York: Routledge, 2005).

1

Since it is sport and the literary representation of it that forms the main subject matter of the book, it is fitting to begin the discussion with some thoughts on the subject. Sport is something that has interested a great many people in the past hundred or so years, and this being so it is not surprising that historians have found their way into it. What is surprising is that it has taken them so long. However, since the 1970s, initially in the United States, there has been a marked surge of interest in the place occupied by sport in society.[5] One consequence of this boom in sports studies is that the subject has gained a certain respectability. From the days when few academics considered sport a matter worthy of serious consideration – when, as the novelist Philip Roth once admitted, 'a certain snobbishness about the material [...] held my own imagination in check'[6] – we have now arrived at a point where students of sport are fairly common in the academy. It is now less likely that eyebrows will be raised when the academic study of sport is mentioned.

Sport is important not simply as a collection of practices – events of various kinds, the institutions and corporations that govern and sponsor them, and the people who are involved in them as athletes, administrators, and spectators. Beyond these relatively tangible and finite features, which have been the focus of much of what has been written over the past 25 or so years on the history of sport, sport also exhibits something that is less easy to pin down. This is the complex of ideas and images that surround sport and which are communicated through (though they do not necessarily have their origin in) the media: the newspaper press, radio, television, magazines and fanzines, books, films and photographs. Each has been implicated closely in sport. Newspapers, for example, have regularly given over a sizeable

5    See Richard William Cox, *British Sport: A Bibliography to 2000*, 4 vols (London:Frank Cass, 2003).
6    Philip Roth interviewed in George G. Searles ed, *Conversations with Philip Roth* (Jackson: University of Mississippi Press, 1992), p. 71.

proportion of their contents to the coverage of it.[7] At times of major international sporting events such as the Olympic Games or the FIFA World Cup those who do not like sport complain that it dominates the media, especially the television schedules. Even snooker, traditionally a participant rather than a spectator sport, has in recent years acquired a spectator following because of the clever way in which it has been adapted for television coverage. Through these branches of the media sport is taken into millions of homes, and carries with it many messages. The Olympic Games, for example, with the logo of five interlinked rings might encourage us to think of ourselves as part of a harmonious international community of friendly competitors, in spite of what we know from other sources about the amount of disharmony in the world, not least in the world of the Olympic movement. On the other hand, the World Cup might press home the message that some countries, once proud of their football traditions, have now been caught up and surpassed, much as the early industrialisers were overtaken by those coming later into the field. This message might encourage viewers to draw broader conclusions about the place of their country and its people in the world at large. Equally, though, it might not. Cricket, once considered the 'national game' in England – until this appellation was appropriated at some point in the twentieth century by the game of association football – has been linked with the idea of empire, and later of the Commonwealth. Cricket might have added a layer of cultural bonding to countries with a pre-existing shared background. For example, the attempts made by politicians to smooth over conflicts generated by the game at the time of the 'Bodyline' controversy of 1932–33 certainly underline a perception of the ability of sport to create deeper meanings and loyalties.[8] In fact, several studies of sport have in recent years paid attention to this relationship. In general they have indicated sport's potency as a shaper of identities of different kinds – religious, sexual, regional, ethnic, and

---

7    On average, in Britain, it has consistently been in the region of 15 per cent. See, for example, *Royal Commission on the Press 1947–1949: Report*, Cmd. 7700 (London: H.M.S.O., 1949), pp. 250, 253.

8    See Ric Sissons and Brian Stoddart, *Cricket and Empire: the 1932–33 Bodyline Tour of Australia* (London: Allen and Unwin, 1984).

14

especially national.[9] Taking this complex of ideas about sport together, it might be suggested that rather than seeing sport as something which has a fixed meaning, or at least a narrow range of meanings, it is actually something which communicates a large variety of ideas to those who follow it.[10] It is a rich assemblage of meanings, and the process through which those meanings are transmitted is an uncertain one. To put this point slightly differently, how people 'read' sport might vary from person to person and from place to place. But this system of negotiating meaning is important, for even the most active sport follower – s/he who plays, administers, and simply watches (and there are people who do all these things) – cannot 'know' sport more than fractionally by this direct involvement. For the rest, as it is with the process of 'knowing' generally, s/he is dependent upon what s/he is told through the various channels of knowledge that deal in sport. In short, how sport is *represented and mediated* to us is very important for what we understand sport, and by extension society, to be.

It is the process of representation, and the various mediations that accompany it, with which this book is in large part concerned. Historians of sport have been responsible for an immense growth of

9    For example see: D. Smith and G. Williams, *Fields of Praise: The Official History of the Welsh Rugby Union, 1881–1981* (Cardiff: University of Wales Press, 1980); G. Jarvie and G. Walker eds, *Scottish Sport in the Making of a Nation: Ninety Minute Patriots?* (Leicester: Leicester University Press, 1994); J. Sugden and A. Bairner, *Sport, Sectarianism and Society in a Divided Ireland* (Leicester: Leicester University Press, 1993); J. Hill and J. Williams eds, *Sport and Identity in the North of England* (Keele: Keele University Press, 1996); M. Cronin and D. Mayall eds, *Sporting Nationalisms: Identity, Ethnicity, Immigration and Assimilation* (London: Frank Cass, 1998); H. McD. Beckles and B. Stoddart, *Liberation Cricket: West Indies Cricket Culture* (Manchester: Manchester University Press, 1995); Jack Williams, *Cricket and Race* (Oxford: Berg, 2001).

10   The work of the anthropologist Clifford Geertz is relevant here. 'The concept of culture I espouse […] is essentially a semiotic one. Believing, with Max Weber, that man is an animal suspended in webs of significance he has himself spun, I take culture to be those webs.' Clifford Geertz, 'Thick Description: Toward an Interpretive Theory of Culture' in *The Interpretation of Cultures* (New York: Basic Books, 1973), p. 5. See also Sherry B. Ortner, 'Introduction', *Representations, 59* (1997), 1–13.

their particular branch of the discipline in recent years, but in all the work they have generated relatively little has been produced on the issue of representation and mediation. It has, on the other hand, been explored enthusiastically by academics in the related fields of sociology, media, and cultural studies. Their main emphasis, however, has been on television. In comparison there has been little on the coverage of sport by the newspapers or radio. Considering, for example, the amount of space devoted to sport by the daily and Sunday press, as well as the existence of a large specialist sporting press in Britain since the nineteenth century, it is astonishing that so few single studies, whether contemporary or historical, of this branch of the media exist. If, then, those parts of the media that reach the millions have received scant attention, it should not surprise us to learn that the less 'populist' parts, those which conventionally are not even referred to as 'media',[11] have been yet more neglected.

In this way the present book seeks, in a modest way, to open up new territory. Why has creative writing on sport been overlooked previously? Neglect might in part be a consequence of academic fashion, which like all fashion is often irrational and whimsical. But this in turn might also relate to the power structures of the academy, and the ways in which they either foster or militate against what is studied. A few words of comment and contextualisation are called for here to outline the various tendencies within the study of sport as they exist today, and to explain why opening up new territory might be necessary.

The academic study of sport in the early twenty-first century is an extensive (and sometimes profitable) business that takes many forms. This, of course, mirrors the increasing economic importance of sport in contemporary society, and therefore much of what passes for academic study is in fact a training of men and women for work in the sport industry: either as managers of sport (with qualifications in management, business, accountancy, law and so on) or as sport

---

11   'Print culture' is commonly used to describe a wide range of non-electronic products, though this term is rarely applied to the serious literature studied by academic literary critics.

professionals with skills in matters relating to the sporting body and the places where it performs. In both of these aspects the emphasis is on practical knowledge rather than academic analysis and discourse. Communications officers, for example, will be taught how to write a press release, how to organise and manage a media conference, and how to put the best possible interpretation on something that might otherwise reflect badly on the organisation that employs them. Subjecting a sportsperson's autobiography or a novel about sport to a close textual reading, as a means of trying to understand its effects, is not considered very 'relevant'. The spirit of Alistair Campbell, rather than of Jacques Derrida, tends to prevail in this environment. Quite simply, autobiographies and novels – literary representations of sport – are thought to contain little that is important to working in the business; unless, that is, the business is the commercial production of life histories, in which case teaching the winning formula might be the chief learning outcome.

In the recent past this provision of 'really useful knowledge' has been grafted on to a longer tradition of studying sport as part of the physical education curriculum. Some of the latter has now moved in to the study of the body (biomechanics, kinesiology, human kinetics), but part of it has maintained contact with a more purely academic interest in the history and sociology of sport. This area, which in spite of recent growth, is still the least prominent of the entire enterprise of sport study, has itself many fractions. Physical educationalists, because of their institutional traditions, often have a critical mass in university and college departments. Historians, sociologists and those from cultural studies rarely have. In their case they are usually to be found as individuals within 'mainstream' departments of history or other such subjects, who have taken up a study of sport because of personal academic interests, but who also have to work their passage in the department by teaching other parts of their discipline. Though they will combine nationally, and sometimes internationally, with like-minded fellows in learned societies, they lack a power base in their own institutions. This has had many repercussions within the academy's political structure. It has tended to reduce the impact of the specialism (sport), to make it harder for the specialism to cut a figure nationally, and thereby to win the respect of quality-monitoring mechanisms such as Britain's Research Assessment Exercise. This in turn affects the nature of work submitted, with sport historians being inclined either to moderate the amount of time they devote to their interest, or to tailor their interest to what it is assumed will count as more 'respectable' output in the right kind of publications.[12] For a variety of reasons, therefore, some to do with traditions and others to do with institutional pressures, the academic study of sport has taken on different forms, with different relationships to each other as well as to the academic mainstream.

## 2

We come, then, to the treatment of sport in creative/fictional writing, where the subject figures in various ways as a way of life, practice, idea, tradition, or metaphor that the writer plays around with in the course of the narrative. In America this is a fairly well-worked area. The Sport Literature Association has been in existence for some years for the very purpose of studying this process academically.[13] It has no

12  Douglas Booth has recently claimed that a more explicit discussion of methodology would help historians of sport to 'garner intellectual credibility for their field'. While I understand Booth's concern for 'credibility' his insistence on methodology as a means of achieving it could have a counter-productive effect in some circles. ('Escaping the Past? The Cultural Turn and Language in Sport History', *Rethinking History*, 8: 1 (March 2004), 103.)

13  Its journal *Aethlon: the Journal of Sport Literature* has been published biannually by East Tennessee State University since 1982. Other examples of American work in this field are to be seen in Michael Oriard's *Dreaming of Heroes: American Sports Fiction, 1868–1980* (Chicago: Nelson-Hall, 1982) and the special edition of the journal *Modern Fiction Studies* devoted to sport literature (33: 1 Spring, 1987). Sports sociologists inspired by the work of Norman Denzin have become interested in narratives, though this has usually resulted in an emphasis on personal narratives and life histories. See the special issue of *Sociology of Sport Journal* on this theme 17:1 (2000); also, for example, Fiona Dowling-Naess, 'Narratives About Young Men and Masculinities in Organised

real equivalent in Britain. There has been a notable lack of interest here in sport as a theme for the serious creative writer, and consequently a paucity of material on which the literary critic might work. The novels selected for treatment in this book are exceptional, therefore, in the British literary world. Equally, historians of sport in Britain have exhibited a similar disregard for the representation of sport in novels, poetry and drama. For this contrast between Britain and the USA there are three likely reasons, which say much about the relative positions of sport in the academy in the two countries. First, sport writing in America has traditionally been a more 'respectable' occupation; sports journalists have been accorded higher status that their British counterparts, a state of affairs partly accounted for by the emergence from their ranks of distinguished writers such as Paul Gallico and Ring Lardner, and also because established national figures such as Mailer, Hemingway, Roth, Updike and others have taken up sport, either in their journalistic forays or as the subject of their fiction. Roth's treatment of baseball in *The Great American Novel* (1973), a text in which the game provides both plot and metaphorical meaning, has nothing to match it in English literature. Second, and simply, the much greater population of sports studies academics in the USA has enabled bodies like the Sport Literature Association to sustain a critical mass of support. But, third, the greater opportunities available in America for academics to work as reporters, commentators and analysts in radio, television and the press, often at local level, has meant that they themselves have become 'sportswriters', if not necessarily writers of fiction (though some of their readers might disagree). In Britain, where none (or very few) of these factors apply, an added problem (which is also present in the USA) has assumed greater force. This is the academic question of whether the study of fiction is the job of the historian or the literary critic.

This brings us back to our earlier reflections on the nature of history. If we assume that historians *should* concern themselves with 'literary' sources, how then should they use them? Leaving aside for

Sport in Norway', *Sport Education and Society*, 6: 2 (2001), 125–42, and Jim Denison, 'Sport Narratives', *Qualitative Enquiry*, 2: 3 (1996), 351–62.

the time being the controversial matter of how far the writing of history is itself a *fictive* art[14] there appears to be no generally agreed line among historians on this question.[15] The question is partly clouded by some of the structural problems of the academy we noted earlier. The inter-disciplinary implications in the question have been plagued over the years by the influence in British universities of the single-subject department. Although this influence was less apparent in the post-1992 universities (where the multi-disciplinary course rather than the subject had often provided the organising rationale of study) recent developments in British higher education have served to swing the emphasis back to the subject, its supposed distinctive methodologies, and its corporate identity. Quality monitoring, with its discipline-based 'benchmarking standards' and research assessment focus, whilst not positively erecting an obstacle to inter-disciplinarity, has not exactly stimulated the pursuit of it. 'Benchmarking' in particular, which sets out the methods, skills, and content thought to define a subject's uniqueness, can be a conservative influence, turning academics back into the discipline rather than seeking eclectic liaisons with cognate areas. For this reason alone, therefore, it may well be that for some the question 'history and/or literature?' is never even put; each to her/his own becomes the order of the day.

But beyond these structural constraints there is a longstanding reluctance on the part of historians to take up 'literature' seriously. It is generally agreed that 'doing history' is different from 'doing literature', whether the latter activity means creative writing or the criticising of·creative writing.[16] It is evident not only among historians

14    See Alun Munslow, *Deconstructing History* (London: Routledge, 1997), esp. pp. 51–5; and the same author's piece in *Guardian Education*, 6 February 2001, 15: 'the emphasis now is less on history as a process of objective discovery and instead more and more of an acceptance of its unavoidably fictive nature – that is, its literary constructedness.'

15    Windschuttle, *The Killing of History* raises some interesting questions about the boundaries between disciplines when he talks about 'real historians' and 'genuine historians' (p. 4). Who is a historian these days? Must such a person necessarily inhabit a history department?

16    In a recent article Shani D'Cruze has raised this issue: 'Fiction is not history', she claims. 'Historians have long acknowledged the ambiguous nature of fiction

20

of sport but those in most other areas of the discipline. To be sure, historians, often when writing in more expansive mood, will refer to works of literature as indications of particular moods or mentalities, acknowledging that the creative writer can sometimes 'capture' the flavour of a period better than the historian.[17] The finely wrought historical novel can, as Robert Rosenstone has observed, bring 'the world alive in a way that historical writing never did'.[18] For example, Tracey Chevalier's subtle treatment of the status, religious and gender hierarchies in seventeenth-century Holland in *The Girl with a Pearl Earring* (1999) would certainly fall into this category. Would Chevalier's work, I wonder, seriously rate inclusion in a course on Dutch history, and if it did, how would it be studied? Historians who take up literary sources and scrutinise them with the same intensity as they would scrutinise their 'historical' sources are indeed few and far between. For those who have departed from the norm and essayed the literary turn, the work of the America scholar Michael Oriard, in two major books on the development of American sport, provides an example to follow. His concern is less the institutional forms in which sport was organised than the ways in which sport was presented to its public as a spectacle and experience. Representation is therefore Oriard's main theme. In analysing the process he eschews the methodology often loosely applied by many historians, which is what I would term 'reflection theory'; in other words the notion that the textual source

as historical "evidence".' ('"Dad's Back": Mapping Masculinities, Moralities and the Law in the Novels of Margery Allingham', *Cultural and Social History*, 1: 3 (2004), 256. Roland Barthes, however, questioned the supposed difference. See *Oeuvres Completes* (Paris: Editions du Seuil, 1994), p. 417. An interesting discussion of the relationship between history and literature is to be found in Linda Orr, 'The Revenge of Literature: A History of History', *New Literary History*, 18: 1 (1986), 1–22.

17   See, for example, Carolyn Steedman, *Dust* (Manchester: Manchester University Press, 2001) referring to the value of *Middlemarch* in providing 'better than any modern history of medicine Bichat's tissue theory (for example) and why it held sway until cell theory was established in the 1840s.' (pp. 99–100).

18   Robert A. Rosenstone, 'Confessions of a Postmodern (?) Historian', *Rethinking History*, 8: 1 (Spring 2004), p. 151.

being studied *reflects* an already existing social reality.[19] Drawing from work in cultural studies Oriard dispenses with assumptions about a correspondence between text and practice, and instead sees the experience as something inscribed in the text, and the text itself therefore having a degree of autonomy from the economic and social conditions of its production. In other words the text has the capacity to *create* meaning, as much as to *reflect* meanings construed elsewhere.[20] This approach, making use of inter-disciplinary influences, is one that might be applied to the study of literary sources with potentially great profit by historians, though it has by no means achieved general acceptance.


3


Leaving aside those historians who ignore (or treat very lightly) fictional sources, there is a large group of historians who adopt the 'reflectionist' method, using fictions as 'illustrative' of broader issues. How often for example has the fictional literature of Rider Haggard or Kipling been cited as evidence of popular enthusiasm for imperialism in late Victorian and Edwardian England; or the Grossmith brothers' Mr Pooter been offered as a characterisation of lower-middle class mentalities in north London in the same period? In other words, the literary text becomes a passive mediator of ideas and social mores, the origins of which are to be found elsewhere in society. The force of this

19    There is a clear discussion of this point in Gabrielle M. Spiegel, 'Introduction', Spiegel ed., *Practicing History*, pp. 1–31.
20    See Michael Oriard, *Reading Football: How the Popular Press Created an American Spectacle* (Chapel Hill: University of North Carolina Press, 1993); *King Football: Sport and Spectacle in the Golden Age of Radio and Newsreels, Movies and Magazines, the Weekly and Daily Press* (Chapel Hill: University of North Carolina Press, 2001). This point is made very well in Anthony Bateman, 'The Politics of the Aesthetic: Cricket, Literature and Culture 1850–1965', Ph.D. thesis, University of Salford (2005), pp. 6–7.

conventional wisdom then creates the further assumption that the literary text is of a lower order than the 'historical' source, and is in some sense therefore 'suspect' when set against other evidence because it is a product of the imagination. In fact, it is a common practice among historians – grounded, indeed, in the exercises we set first level undergraduates – to place the literary text against its historical 'reality' in order to judge the text's veracity as a source; as if the historical 'reality' is something produced without help from literary or other cultural products. Ian Carter's fine essay on Lewis Grassic Gibbon's *Sunset Song* is a clear example of this technique. It pays very close attention to the text but still insists: 'Novels can give us evidence that we cannot get from other sources, *but we must check the novel against other kinds of evidence before we accept it as an accurate account of what 'really happened ...'* (my italics).[21] This notion was clearly exemplified in a recent comment by Ian Kershaw, reviewing the controversial Hitler film *Der Untergang (The Downfall)*. Kershaw, a distinguished historian of Germany in the Nazi era, enunciated what might be taken as the orthodoxy in the profession on the use of fictional sources:

> I reminded myself as I entered the cinema that feature films, however good they are, amount to artistic constructs which are of their nature incompatible with strict historical accuracy. In this they differ from film documentaries. Factual accuracy is as important to the documentary as to the written work of history. A historical feature film operates differently in that it is not confined by rules of evidence. This does not mean that it is unable, if well done, to convey through its very dramatic power a substantial insight into reality.[22]

Leaving aside the faith that Kershaw curiously appears to place in the film documentary (a form notably artful and fictive, notwithstanding its attention to factual accuracy) his contrasting of history ('confined by rules of evidence') with art (imagination), raises issues about the nature of knowing which have been central to much debate about the nature of history in recent years. Kershaw offers here a clear example

21   Ian Carter, 'Lewis Grassic Gibbon, *A Scots Quair*, and the Peasantry', *History Workshop Journal: A Journal of Socialist Historians*, 6 (1978), 169.
22   'The Human Hitler', *Guardian (G2)*, 17 September 2004, 4–5.

23

of the historian's predilection for seeing a sharp distinction between on the one hand 'reality' - something that exists and into which 'insight' might be conveyed - and on the other 'imagination'. It is a blurring, if not an absolute breaking down, of the hard-and-fast distinction between these two categories, that this book is attempting.


# 4


There are of course historians whose attention to literary texts has been serious and detailed, and who have not been deterred by the fear of 'unreliable evidence'. One is Jeffrey Richards, responsible for a considerable body of work incorporating the texts of both literature and the cinema. In his study of public school fiction[23] (a book which provided powerful inspiration for the present volume) Richards examines the public school story and its historical development over the course of the nineteenth and twentieth centuries. *Happiest Days* is not heavy on theory (a feature which no doubt commends it to many historians) but Richards draws upon an amalgam of methodological influences to fashion an interesting approach: there is a nod towards the text as 'a mirror to the mind set of the nation', a healthy acknowledgement of the difficulty of ascertaining the influence exercised by popular fiction over the reading public, and, from the work of Joan Rockwell, a readiness to see literature as simultaneously social product and agent of social change. For Richards, then, the public school story is both a repository of contemporary mentalities, giving the historian access to the world beyond the text, and a text that

---

23    Jeffrey Richards, *Happiest Days: The Public Schools in English Fiction* (Manchester: Manchester University Press, 1988). A similarly fruitful analysis of public school culture is to be found in J.A. Mangan, *Athleticism in the Victorian and Edwardian Public School: the Emergence and Consolidation of an Educational Ideology* (London: Frank Cass, 2000). Mangan's reading of the 'sporting prosody' of the schools (see ch. 8) is especially revealing of the workings of creative writing as ideology.

has the capacity to represent the world to readers, and by doing so to shape attitudes of the day.[24] Thus the text *constructs* as much as it *reflects*.

Another indication of how creative literature might be handled by the historian is to be gained from considering the work of Arthur Marwick. Marwick has consistently taken up fictional texts as worthy of serious historical study. He is perhaps best known in recent years for his vigorous and unqualified defence of conventional historical method against what he sees as the vapid notions of 'postmodernists'. Some might regard his idea of the historian's art (or *science* as he would aver) as unduly conservative, and he certainly makes a clear distinction between history and literature.[25] To the notion, associated with the writings of such analysts as Paul Ricoeur and, in particular, Hayden White, that history is a form of story-telling in which the narrative strategies available to the historian determine to a degree what s/he is able to say, Marwick notes 'the total misunderstandings of such philosophers as Paul Ricoeur who insists that history is essentially the same as novel writing, and then draws absurd conclusions from this illegitimate contention.'[26]

Marwick has, however, no inhibitions about enlarging the corpus of historical sources. On what might constitute fit material for the historian his vision is panoptic, including films (documentary and feature) and novels. In contrast with the sledgehammer technique on display in his more polemical work Marwick's treatment of fictional literature shows immense perception and sensitivity, and provides a model to be followed even by some of his professed antagonists. Articles published over the past twenty years reveal a capacity for close textual reading which bring out the insights to be gained into a

---

24  Ibid., pp. 1–3, and Joan Rockwell, *Fact in Fiction: The Use of Literature in the Systematic Study of Society* (London: Routledge and Kegan Paul, 1974). 'My basic premise is that literature neither "reflects" nor "arises from" society, but rather is an integral part of it' (p. vii).

25  Arthur Marwick, *The New Nature of History: Knowledge, Evidence ,Language* (Basingstoke: Palgrave, 2001), pp. 11, 262.

26  Ibid., p. 263.

society and its mores from novels like John Braine's *Room at the Top* (1957), the 1959 film of which is regarded by Marwick as having wrought a profound historical effect on its times.[27] Here, then, is certainly not a historian who sees literature as merely 'reflecting' the conditions of its existence, nor of the cultural as something which is understood by being 'read off' from prior economic and social developments. The meaning is in the text, which in turn has the capacity to change meaning.[28] There is, nonetheless, a sense in which even Marwick's rigour has its limitations. For one thing, literary evidence still tends to be 'ghetto-ised'; it is assigned to the area of 'arts/culture' whilst for other subjects - race for example - conventional sources are deployed, as if the subject is too serious a matter for creative writing to be of much value. Also, there is a tendency to prioritise 'history' in its relationship with 'literature'. Marwick's establishing of his historical model of change, for example, before proceeding to the analysis of literature, rather underlines the latter's junior position in the relationship. There is, moreover, a residual sense of the literary text being treated as a historical document that can be pinned down and dissected on the laboratory table where it yields interesting information but assumes the role of a passive object in the historian's hands.[29] Nonetheless, in spite of these reservations, with Richards and Marwick we begin to approach the notion of what I would call the 'active text'.

27    Arthur Marwick, 'The Arts, Books, Media and Entertainments in Britain Since 1945', in J. Obelkevich and P. Catterall eds, *Understanding Post War Society* (London: Routledge, 1994), p. 185; 'one of those occasional products that illuminate a whole moment of change, and is, indeed, *in itself a component of change.'* (My italics.)

28    See in particular: Arthur Marwick, '*Room at the Top, Saturday Night and Sunday Morning,* and the "Cultural Revolution" in Britain', *Journal of Contemporary History*, 19 (1984), 127–52; 'Six Novels of the Sixties – Three French, Three Italian', *Journal of Contemporary History*, 28 (1993), 563–91.

29    These features are evident in Marwick's *The Sixties: Cultural Revolution in Britain, France, Italy, and the United States, c. 1958-c.1974* (Oxford: Oxford University Press, 1998).

# 5

This notion involves taking Marwick's approach a step farther. In other words, seeing the novel as a cultural artefact that is itself capable of producing 'reality' in the same way as other historical evidence.[30] It is endowed with an *ideological* function in the sense that the novel contains meanings that contribute to its readers' understanding of society and their own place in it. To put it bluntly, the novel is something capable of 'making sense' of the world,[31] and this attribute of literature is something that should be very important for historians.

Against the empiricist approach of Kershaw [32] which holds that careful scrutiny of the sources can take us to the reality of life in the past, is ranged a variety of positions which have as a common focus the questioning of the source/evidence, an emphasis on its indeterminacy of meaning, and doubts about the detachment from the evidence of the historian. Much of this stems from the work of the French philosopher Jacques Derrida whose theories have been both derided and praised, pretty much in equal measure. Few historians have delved into Derrida in any detail, although his technique of 'deconstruction' – of seeing a text, including a historical document, as something susceptible of varied meanings ('polysemic') – is clearly an important one for historians to grapple with.[33] History becomes in all this a created narrative, something that exists in the telling rather than in a past reality. It is (to revert to Ricoeur's point which so troubled Marwick) a form of literature. A recent pertinent illustration of these issues was provided by the historian David Wootton, reviewing a

---

30     See Raymond Williams, *Marxism and Literature* (Oxford: Oxford University Press, 1977), pp. 95–100.

31     A term viewed, incidentally, with great distaste by Marwick; see *New Nature of History,* p. 137.

32     See also Richard J Evans, *In Defence of History* (London: Granta Books, 1997).

33     On Derrida the obituary in the *Guardian,* 11 October, 2004, 21, by Derek Attridge and Thomas Baldwin, is very clear about his method. See also Anna Green and Kathleen Troup, *The Houses of History: a Critical Reader in Twentieth-Century History and Theory* (Manchester: Manchester University Press, 1999).

book by fellow historian James Sharpe on the eighteenth-century highwayman and English legend Dick Turpin. The Turpin legend is a perfect example of the process of myth making through various kinds of stories in which the myth is perpetuated. Whereas Sharpe's approach is to debunk the myth and tell us how Turpin the noble highwayman was in actuality a thuggish criminal – something that is no doubt true and verifiable from historical records – Wootton turns his attention not to the inaccuracy of the myth but to the importance of it as a social force. Thus, the story of Turpin's impossible ride from London to York, for example, which could never have taken place as a historical reality, is nevertheless seen by Wootton as a material product of its historical circumstances, something that people read about and enjoyed, and which fulfilled an important function in their lives. The significance of the story therefore lies in its being something that affected people and the way in which they thought about their world. Thus as Wootton argues: 'a book about Turpin needs to handle fiction with the confidence that it handles fact.'[34]

The most systematic applications of this perceived fluidity of literature and history are to be found in the New Historicist tendency of American literary/historical studies. In general historians have tended to be dismissive of these approaches, largely because their professed 'historicism' is seen as wanting in methodological rigour.[35]

34    David Wootton, 'The road is still open', *London Review of Books,* 3 February 2005, 21–2. The book reviewed is James Sharpe, *Dick Turpin: the Myth of the English Highwayman* (Profile: London, 2005). Wooton goes on to say: 'Sharpe could have been provoked by his subject into reinventing the idea of what history is: instead, his conclusion ... retreats into the old clichés that the business of the historian is to deal in facts.'

35    For example, Marwick, 'Six Novels' *Journal of Contemporary History,* 1993, 588. He makes a passing reference to 'the manner in which many literary scholars invent their history.' There is surprisingly no direct engagement with the New Historicism in *The New Nature of History.* Windschuttle, however, in *Killing of History* is pretty scathing (see pp. 16–19). There are dismissive comments also from Terry Eagleton, *Literary Theory: an Introduction* (Oxford: Blackwell Publishers, 1996), pp. 197–8. An interesting perspective is offered by Douglas Bruster, 'New Light on the Old Historicism: Shakespeare and the Forms of Historicist Criticism', *Literature and History,* 5: 1 (1996), 1–18.

A good deal of fuss - perhaps too much - has been made from both sides of the fence about the New Historicism, so that its value and influence has become overestimated. To place it in its context it is worth reminding ourselves that the New Historicism represented a 'historical turn' in literary studies in the 1980s, and that therefore what seemed innovative and enlightening to scholars brought up in the tradition of American New Criticism, with its circumscribed emphasis on 'the text', might appear less remarkable to historians. Furthermore, even its protagonists have declared their method as being nothing more than an eclectic blend of approaches, with certainly no overarching theory or party line.[36] Being properly cautious about New Historicism's claims, however, should not prevent us from assimilating some of its more useful techniques. Prominent within them is the technique of blurring the boundaries between what have conventionally been seen as the separate spheres of 'text' (literature) and 'context' (history), and the intertwining of them to form what Louis Montrose, in a famous phrase, has termed the 'textuality of history and the historicity of the text'.[37] It reminds us that historical documents are, when all is said and done, only 'texts', and that whilst they are not always texts in the same sense that literary creations are, there are times when the differences between the two are outweighed by their similarities. This duality accords with another of the New Historicism's key methodologies, associated with the work of Stephen Greenblatt, which emphasises the 'inseparability of [the meaning of literary texts] from the circumstances of their making or reception'.[38] The placing of literary creation in a material context in this way is of course not entirely new; it owes a strong debt to the influence of Raymond Williams.[39] It involves paying attention to a whole range of

36    See Catherine Gallagher and Stephen Greenblatt, *Practicing New Historicism* (Chicago: University of Chicago Press, 2000), pp. 1–4.
37    Louis A. Montrose, 'Professing the Renaissance: the Poetics and Politics of Culture' in H. Aram Veeser ed, *The New Historicism* (London: Routledge, 1989), p. 15.
38    Stephen J. Greenblatt, *Learning to Curse: Essays in Early Modern Culture* (London: Routledge, 1992), p. 9.
39    See Lucasta Miller, 'The Human Factor' [interview with Stephen Greenblatt], *Guardian Review*, 26 February 2005, 20–23.

influences that are brought to bear on literature, such as the control of the methods of production, the relationship between social power and the aesthetic values created by writers, and the 'voices' represented (and suppressed) in the literature available to the reading public. In all this one characteristic stands out, and that is the willingness to recognise, as one commentator has neatly put it, 'that the text is an event [...] part of the process of historical change, and indeed may constitute historical change.'[40]


# 6


The novels that follow are a personal selection. Readers' misgivings about my choice are therefore inevitable. Many will question the omission of Bernard Malamud's *The Natural,* for example, sunnily transformed into a well-loved film starring Robert Redford (1984). The absence of novels by John Updike and Don DeLillo, both of whom have brought sport into the forefront of their writing, will no doubt also prompt criticism. Some might even regret that *How Steeple Sinderby Wanderers Won the FA Cup* (1975), by the fine English novelist J.L. Carr, has not been included. Equally likely to provoke comment, and perhaps even some hostility, is the absence of anything about women in sport. There are, to be sure, plenty of gender issues to explore in the novels chosen, but none has as its central character a woman. The fact is that very few such novels exist.[41] In response to all

---

40    John Brannigan, *New Historicism and Cultural Materialism* (Basingstoke: Macmillan, 1998), p. 203.

41    Allen Guttmann writes interestingly about one of the exceptions, *Sport um Gagaly* (1928) by Kasimir Edschmid. He acknowledges that this fascinating novel 'remains little known even among *Germanisten*'. Allen Guttmann, 'Faustian Athletes? Sports As a Theme in Modern German Literature', *Modern Fiction Studies,* 33: 1 (Spring 1987), p. 30. On American sport novels about women see Michael Oriard, 'From Jane Allen to *Water Dancer*: A Brief History of the Feminist (?) Sports Novel', *Modern Fiction Studies*, 33: 1 (Spring 1987), pp. 9–20.

this my defence would be that given my aim, which was to examine in detail a limited number of texts (and to subject them to what literary people call a 'close reading'), there was only so much that could be included. Something had to give, and doubtless my own preferences took over in making the choice. Not that the selection was completely subjective and random. It was guided by five major considerations. The texts, firstly, had to deal with sport *in some form or another*; this of course did not mean that they had to be 'sport novels' in the sense of classic realist texts in which the subject and world of sport formed the centrepiece of the narrative. [42] In this respect the collection provides much variation – from Glanville's novel, which does more or less match up to the standard of sport 'realism', to Ford's reflective interior monologue in which sport operates as a metaphor. Second, the texts had to fall within a common period of time, and this is achieved by taking stories written in the second-half of the twentieth century; only the Lardner text misses this timescale, although the film adaptation that forms the major part of the chapter was distributed in 1949. Third, whilst confining myself to works in English, I wanted to have a degree of international comparison, and certainly to avoid a purely Anglo-centric perspective. Beginning with the Robin Jenkins novel serves to turn attention to a neglected Scottish writer, and the Roth-Ford-Keneally inclusion extends the coverage internationally. Fourth, there needed to be a variety of themes to which, as a historian, I could orientate the texts and relate them to other developments of their time; there is in the selection a mixture of issues to do with some of the central questions of later-twentieth century history – the nation and modernisation, gender, and ethnicity being among the more prominent, and as may be imagined with a variety of rich textual material there is a good deal of overlap between these themes across the chapters. Fifth, I wanted as far as possible to include stories that not only matched the aims of the book but which, in my view, had been unjustly neglected. Thus, whilst the titles of some of the novels

---

42    This is the definition of a sport novel used by Oriard (*Dreaming of Heroes*):
      'one in which sport plays a dominant role or in which the sport milieu is the
      dominant setting.' (p. 6). I find it too restricting.

discussed here will readily strike a chord in the reader's mind (*This Sporting Life,* for example) others might seem to have little connection to sport, whilst others might seem completely obscure. The Keneally novel included here, for instance, receives little recognition these days in the aftermath of the translation of *Schindler's Ark* into Steven Spielberg's enormously successful film (1993). All of the texts included have, however, received a degree of critical approval, and in some cases a great deal of acclaim. Each can therefore be classified as a 'literary' text of the kind that in Britain has received scant attention from students of sport, and on these grounds they therefore make up an appropriate body of evidence for the task in hand.

Besides a link with sport, the novels have another feature in common. They deal with what David Lodge has described as 'consciousness' – 'the dense specificity of personal experience.'[43] In the treatment of this, as in other aspects of their composition, there is considerable variety between the texts. In most of them the favoured technique follows what Lodge describes as 'post-modern', meaning something rather more literal than the usual connotations this term has today. In other words, they take a different approach in dealing with consciousness from that found in the 'modernist' novels of Joyce, Conrad, Lawrence, Woolf, and others. Authorial reflection in a third-person narrative gives way to a more subjective form of story telling. The characters' thoughts are transmitted through their dialogue and set within a discontinuous narrative that is often pieced together from fragments of evidence, almost as would a historian in attempting to reconstruct a subject. Philip Roth's *American Pastoral* is pre-eminently of this stripe, as the narrator Nathan Zuckerman struggles to make sense of Swede Levov's life: 'I kept waiting for him to lay bare something more than this pointed unobjectionableness, but all that rose to the surface was more surface' (23). Glanville too gives us Gerry Logan's life history from several points of view, privileging none; the author, moreover, is also a character in the novel. Robin Jenkins, on the other hand, assumes a story-telling style that seems

---

43    David Lodge, *Consciousness and the Novel: Connected Essays* (London: Penguin Books, 2003), ch. 1, esp. pp. 8–16.

old-fashioned by comparison, with an omniscient third-person narrator who stands outside the story. Hornby's approach is the complete opposite: true to its late-twentieth century origins the status of *Fever Pitch* as a piece of literature is enigmatic: is it fact, or fiction, autobiography or proto-novel?

Finally, a caution: this is a book by a historian, not a literary critic. It is neither a history of literature, nor an attempt aesthetically to evaluate the literary worth of the pieces included. The aim is simply to study literary texts as historical evidence.

# Chapter Two
## 'Mean, Drab Times': Robin Jenkins's
## *The Thistle and the Grail*

'The development of the novel', says Cairns Craig, 'is profoundly linked to the development of the modern nation.'[1] Communicating its narrative through a unitary language the novel plays its part in the process of the nation's being imagined, enabling individual readers to see their place in the national project by relating the individual fictional histories in the novel to the greater national narrative. Thus, in the nation building of the nineteenth and twentieth century in Europe and America, the great novelists – Balzac, Dickens, Tolstoy, Melville – performed a political service. It was not quite like this, however, in Scotland. Without either a unitary language or an independent state Scottish national identity was frail and confused. Scotland's most popular literary movement of the later-nineteenth century – the Kailyard – reflected this predicament. In the hands of writers like J.M. Barrie and Ian Maclaren 'kailyard' literature conjured a country of independent small towns in rural settings populated by whimsical characters drawn from a narrow band of society. Class divisions were fixed and events took place in a past sufficiently recent to be recognisable, but at the same distant enough to afford a sense of nostalgia as well as to remove any feeling of threat. Kailyard provided, according to one of its sternest critics, the Scots social-realist novelist George Blake, 'amusing little stories of bucolic intrigue, as seen through the windows of the Presbyterian manse'.[2]

---

1   *The Modern Scottish Novel* (Edinburgh: Edinburgh University Press, 1999), p. 9.
2   A kailyard is, literally, a cabbage patch. The term was probably first applied to literature in the 1890s. See George Blake, *Barrie and the Kailyard School* (London: Arthur Barker, 1951), p. 13. Ian Maclaren's *Beside the Bonnie Brier Bush* was immensely popular, especially in the United States in the early

Industrial Scotland, with its appalling poverty and urban squalor, found no place in this literature, an omission which (according to Blake) amounted to a 'national infantilism'.[3] The kailyard was an invented image of Scotland which bore little relation to economic and social realities but which nonetheless contributed powerfully to notions of Scottishness. It fed an appetite for 'tartanry' that was particularly hearty among Scottish émigrés, Not surprisingly it came under attack in the twentieth century. George Douglas Brown's *The House with the Green Shutters* (1901) is usually recognised as having occasioned the breakthough. Brown's stance was taken up in works such as Lewis Grassic Gibbon's *A Scots Quair* (1932–34) and Blake's *The Shipbuilders* (1935), Scotland's first serious industrial novel. Both directed their readers' attention to contemporary problems of Scottish life: the class struggle, industrial depression, unemployment, and the growing economic and cultural hegemony exercised by England. The Scottish Literary Renaissance of the 1920s onwards, in which Gibbon and Blake, together with novelist and critic Neil Gunn, the poet Hugh MacDiarmid, and critic Edwin Muir were leading figures, sought to elaborate not only a more authentic Scottish culture but a more truthful perspective on the Scottish predicament. Robin Jenkins, born in 1912, came to maturity in this intellectual environment.

1

It is therefore surprising to find, in a novel published in 1954 by a writer with this background, echoes of the kailyard. Only a year or two before English novelists like John Braine were beginning to explore issues that fused with a wider debate about the 'modernisation' of British society, Robin Jenkins published *The Thistle and the Grail*

twentieth century. See also Isobel Murray and Bob Tait eds, *Ten Modern Scottish Novels* (Aberdeen: Aberdeen University Press, 1984), p. 10.

3       Blake, *Barrie and the Kailyard School,* p. 9.

(1954).[4] In its style and characterisations it stands in marked contrast to the social realism of contemporary English writings in its seemingly determined refusal to confront issues of the day. But whereas Braine, Sillitoe, Storey and others grappled with the material problems of social class, gender and the prospects for the future, albeit often in a mood of pessimism, Jenkins turned his back on the present and, without ever becoming a historical novelist in the conventional sense of the term, recreated a recent past in which to explore Scotland's spiritual malaise. Brian Morton's phrase – 'the sheer old-fashionedness of his fiction' – admirably sums up Jenkins's style and content: 'Robin Jenkins's fate was to write at a time when the proper matter of fiction was supposed to be psychology, history and its illusions, or the nature of fiction itself, anything but questions of good and evil.'[5]

Robin Jenkins's considerable body of work is little-known outside his native country (and, some might say, not very well known in it). Yet he was a prolific and versatile author of some 30 novels written over a period spanning half a century from the early 1950s until his death in early 2005. He is capable of producing essentially Scottish themes, as in *The Thistle and the Grail*, or his last published novel *Lady Magdalen* (2003), which looks back with a rather modern eye on seventeenth-century Scotland to rue, among other things, the baneful influence of the kirk. In the same breath, so to say, he is capable of delivering enigmatic tales such as *Some Kind of Grace* (1960), part-detective story, part reflection on morality, set in Afghanistan where Jenkins lived for a time in the 1950s. An enduring theme in his writing has been the tension between the moral absolutes conceived by his characters and the social realities in which they live. Thus, in *Some Kind of Grace* the character McLeod drives himself to physical and psychological extremes to discover a truth which, for some, might conveniently have been left uninterrogated. James Graham, in *Lady Magdalen*, pays the ultimate price for high-minded ideals. The social totality in which Jenkins seeks to work has led to his being compared with the realist writers of the nineteenth century, though

4    All references are from the Polygon edition, Edinburgh, 1994.
5    Brian Morton, 'Goodness in a Fallen World: The Fate of Robin Jenkins' *Scottish Review of Books*, 1: 3 (2005), 8–9.

Cairns Craig has questioned the extent to which his 'realism' can be taken.[6] As another critic has said: 'Jenkins's novels [...] do sometimes present an extremely peculiar world.'[7] There remains an element of the unreal or magical in his stories, evident in the humanist novels *The Cone Gatherers* (1955) and *The Changeling* (1958), which critics see as his major works of his early period. It is there to a degree in *The Thistle and the Grail*, which by comparison with Jenkins's other works of the same period has received scant attention. This is surprising when it is considered that it is the one work in which Jenkins, a Scottish writer *par excellence,* addresses himself to a central feature (possibly *the* central feature) of Scottish popular culture in the twentieth century: association football. While remaining mindful of the fact that there were Scottish people, and even Scottish *men,* who knew nothing about this game,[8] it is nonetheless the case that football, as well as being one of the country's major cultural exports, was a site upon which Scots defined themselves as a nation. Scotland's footballers, perhaps only slightly less gloriously than its writers, philosophers and engineers, had gone forth and spread their influence throughout the world, and in particular to the world of England.

The historical curiosity which in the early twentieth century gave Britain four separate football associations in one state assured for Scotland an independent institutional framework in which to develop its major game.[9] How far the game was able to retain a Scottish autonomy, however, is questionable. The establishment of association football as a successful spectator sport in Britain during the late-nineteenth century owed a great deal to the Scots. Though the 'modern' game was given organisational form in England the Scots could with some justification claim that they perfected the *art* of

6    Cairns Craig, 'Robin Jenkins: A Would-be Realist', *Edinburgh Review* (106), 12–22.
7    Edwin Morgan, The Novels of Robin Jenkins, *The Listener,* 12 July 1973, 58.
8    See, for example, Ian Jack 'Not so much a religion, more a way of life', *Guardian Review,* 31 May 2004, 3.
9    See Pierre Lanfranchi, Christiane Eisenberg, Tony Mason and Alfred Wahl, *100 Years of Football: the FIFA Centennial Book* (London: Weidenfeld and Nicholson, 2004), p. 64.

football: in particular the technique of passing the ball between co-ordinated forward players ('the passing game'), rather than relying on a series of isolated dashes by individuals. The arrival in England of the skilled 'Scotch professors' in the 1880s was crucial to the commercialisation and professionalisation of the game there. Preston North End's early successes owed much to them, and the club long maintained a Scottish connection.[10] By the time of the First World War there were few clubs in the main English league that were not similarly dependent on a cadre of Scottish professionals. In the inter-war years some of the leading performers in English football – Alex James and Hughie Gallacher are the two outstanding examples – were Scotsmen renowned for their ball skills, tactical acumen, and bravery. This feature became more yet more prominent after 1945. What this meant was that the relationship between the two countries had assumed the nature of coloniser and colonised. English clubs drew on Scottish footballers to maintain the flow of quality players, and in turn Scottish clubs became a net exporter of football talent for most of the twentieth century, financially reliant of transfer fees to maintain their existence. It reduced Scotland to the position of a client sporting economy. In this way the business of football in Scotland came to mirror some aspects of the national economy. In Scotland itself only the two Glasgow clubs – Rangers and Celtic – were able to compete in the football labour market with English business. In spite of this unequal relationship, however, the achievement of Scottish players and the success of the national team – especially in matches against England – meant that Scottish supporters were able to invest great pride in their football traditions, and to convince themselves that their small country had a leading place in a sport of increasingly worldwide proportions. However, the contradictions in this perception were evident in the scene of one of Scottish football's greatest triumphs – the 5-1 defeat of England by the renowned 'Wembley Wizards' of 1928. Eight of the so-called 'wee blue devils' whose victory assured

10  See Tony Mason, *Association Football and English Society 1863–1917* (Brighton: Harvester, 1980), chs 4 and 7. The professionalism of English clubs, adopted in the later 1880s, forced Scottish clubs into the same process in an effort to prevent the wholesale English poaching of their players.

them a place in Scottish popular memory for the remainder of the century were currently playing their football in English club colours.[11]

National pride in the face of English economic superiority was also present in the lived culture of Scottish football. Alongside the religious and ethnic sectarianism that bred internal loyalties and hatreds, especially between the two big Glasgow clubs, there was nonetheless a fierce sense of the greater national unity and identity. This was never more evident than in the behaviour of Scottish supporters in great number during the biennial visit to London for the England-Scotland international match. It assumed the character of an 'invasion' with a symbolic 'taking' of the capital city. Scottish fans asserted their presence, often rudely and always noisily, in the football ground and on the streets of the West End after the match, and in doing so were using football to remind the metropolis and seat of government of Scotland's place in the national polity.[12] For writers seeking to explain Scottish identity in the twentieth century – and few Scottish writers have managed to avoid this issue – football is clearly a major subject of concern, though the fact seems to have escaped most of them.

11    See John Cottrell, *A Century of Great Soccer Drama* (Newton Abbot: Sportsman's Book Club, 1972), pp. 47–51. Strictly speaking one of them (Nelson) played for Cardiff City, in the English League. The Scottish clubs represented were Queen's Park, Hibs and Glasgow Rangers. For a succinct discussion of these and wider issues see Richard Holt, *Sport and the British; a Modern History* (Oxford: Oxford University Press, 1990), pp. 253–62. Also, R. Cox, D. Russell and W Vamplew eds, *Encyclopedia of British Football* (London: Frank Cass, 2002), pp. 278–80.

12    See the work of H.F. Moorhouse on the links between nationalism and football in Scotland; for example, 'Repressed Nationalism and Professional Football: Scotland versus England' in J. Mangan and R. Small eds, *Sport, Culture, Society: International Historical and Sociological Perspectives* (London: E.F. Spon, 1986), pp. 52–9; 'Blue Bonnets over the Border: Scotland and the Migration of Footballers', in J. Bale and J. Maguire, *The Global Sports Arena: Athletic Talent Migration in an Interdependent World* (London: Frank Cass, 1994), pp. 78–96. By contrast see Tom Nairn on Scottish sporting enthusiasm in *The Break-Up of Britain* (London: Verso, 1981) – 'How intolerably vulgar! What unbearable, crass, mindless philistinism!' (162). See also, Chalmers Anderson, *Association Football: Scotland v. England 1872–1946* (Edinburgh: C.J. Carsland, 1947).

The national preoccupation with the game is, however, Jenkins's concern, and it lies at the very heart of *The Thistle and the Grail*. It is of course primarily a male obsession through which Jenkins attempts an analysis of the 'mind' of Scotland, though he shows that it is one that might affect women as well through its pervasive influence in the life of the community. Jenkins takes the national concern down to a local level to tell the story of a minor football club – Drumsagart Thistle Junior FC (the 'Thistle') – and its attempts to win the national Junior Cup competition (the 'Grail'). 'Thistle', of course, stands symbolically for Scotland, whilst the 'Grail' might equally be read symbolically as a quest by the people of Scotland for salvation, of either a religious or a secular kind. The narrative covers a season in the life of the club and its supporters. During this time a miraculous transformation from sporting despair to the pinnacle of success takes place. Starting as a team of no-hopers the Thistle proceeds to win the cup, the club's exploits provide a source of growing interest and eventually pride in the community it represents, and a sense of achievement – however transitory – is bestowed on the people of Drumsagart. Football success appears to have brought the community together and provided it with a sense of purpose.

Nowhere is the dependence of the community on the outcome of the football better illustrated than in the elaborate arrangements made to communicate the result of the fifth round tie. The Thistle are drawn away in far Aberdeenshire to Forgie Bluebell, a powerful team with three internationals. The fare to go and watch the match was 'too much for dolemen' (189) especially coming as it did only two days after the Hogmanay celebrations. Since the torment of having to wait to learn the result on the return of those fortunate to have journeyed to Forgie is too terrible to contemplate, the stay-at-homes devise a plan. It is decided to pay for one of their number, Archie, to travel to the match on condition that he leaves the ground at intervals of fifteen minutes to telephone reports on the state of play back to the others. A committee is formed to orchestrate a scheme. They commandeer a kiosk, appoint a former bookie's runner, Jock Saunders, 'an expert with the telephone' (191) to occupy it, and on a 'filthily, scandalously, brutally wet' afternoon (191) assemble to await the call. At one point the scheme appears to have foundered through the intervention of the local police sergeant, who insists that the kiosk be kept clear for 'general use' (195). A little later, approaching full time in Forgie, a moral dilemma is posed when a widow woman needs to telephone the hospital about her sick daughter:

> 'If she phones', muttered another to his friend, 'do you see what's going to happen? Archie will be told the number's engaged, he'll not wait because he'll be in a hurry to catch the bus hame, and we'll not get the result at all.' (202)

The policeman is unimpressed with the men's urgent requests that, since the ninety minutes are almost up, the woman should wait: 'Five minutes of this poor woman's worry causes me more concern [...] than if you'd been waiting ninety years to hear how many times a chunk of leather was kicked between a couple of posts' (202). But, to general applause, the woman agrees to wait, and after further delays that stretch the collective patience almost beyond endurance the necessary information is passed on – a win for the Thistle. To Jock's disgust the men cheer as the woman, whose news about her daughter has been less uplifting, makes her way home. On this juxtaposition of joy and sadness one of the novel's great comic scenes ends, in pathos; the temporary elation brought by a football result contrasted with the enduring misfortune and poverty suffered by many of Drumsagart's inhabitants.

In spite of the eventual glory enjoyed by the club, *The Thistle and the Grail* is not in any sense a mere fable of success. Through the people of Drumsagart it presents a jaundiced view of Scotland and its inhabitants. The publisher's blurb of the Polygon edition (1994) describes the book as 'one of the finest comic novels produced in Scotland this century', but Jenkins has a depressing tale to tell in an atmosphere which, in the last analysis, is as gloomy as that created in Lewis Grassic Gibbon. To be sure the matches are finely reported – nowhere more so than in Thistle's contest with Carrick Harp, 'a memorable and historic game ... [t]he Angel of Football, in which all believed but few had ever seen, was hovering over Tara Park that afternoon.' (172)[13] – and the characters richly drawn with, in many cases, a surface comic appearance, but on reflection there is little to admire in the human landscape portrayed. Alec Elrigmuir, the centre-forward whose signing sparks the club's revival, is a dream of a footballer but as a person he is dim-witted and dominated by his bossy girlfriend Mysie. Turk, the centre-half who alongside Alec provides the backbone and inspiration of the team, is a repulsive drunkard who beats his mother. Two of the club's loyal supporters are aged and infirm, the diseased Tinto and a cripple, Crutch Brodie. The local publican, Sam Malarkin, is a predatory homosexual with designs on the star centre-forward whom he attempts to proposition: '"I am not understood in Drumsagart" said Malarkin wistfully, and put his hand on the young man's shoulder' (110). The novel is peopled by such flawed characters.

At the centre of the story is Andrew Robertson, the club president, a good man misunderstood and almost brought down by the grotesqueries that surround him. He is despised as a failure both by his fellow citizens and by members of his own family. His father is a dyspeptic ILPer from the days of Jimmy Maxton and Red Clydeside, whose own secular grail has been unrealised. Socialism has failed to provide Scotland's salvation, but in his father's eyes Andrew has sold out to capitalism by becoming the manager of a biscuit factory, pushed by his acquisitive wife into a life of middle-class respectability. He has also committed the irredeemable sin of not having fought in the war. His father had preached against it, and this gave Andrew's conscience some reassurance as he earned good wages in munitions work. But his brother Gavin had been killed. Father and son are by these circumstances alienated from each other, as is Andrew from his fellow citizens by social class. His dedication to the club, and to ensuring its success, is genuine, and accompanied by many small unobserved acts of kindness, but the labours he devotes to it are appreciated only with the coming of success, which ironically brings

---

13    It was no doubt this passage that drew from the reviewer in the *Times Literary Supplement* on the book's publication the comment: 'Mr Jenkins's real gift is for describing football matches.' ('Small Town Life', 18 June 1954, 389) - a clear case of being damned by faint praise.

about a hardening of his own character. Faced with the break-up of an unstable marriage and estrangement from his son, he decides to follow his wife's desires, and decamps to the posh resort town of Helensburgh for a life in the pay of his wealthy brother-in-law. But the hope of a better future fades; there is no life for the better. The only grail left for him is the success of the Thistle, which he pursues with a grim purpose, bending the rules when necessary. When the Thistle's progress to the semi-finals of the Cup competition is halted by a 3-2 defeat to Muirvale Athletic the compliant Andrew Rutherford, whose attempts to rub along with everybody have previously been met with disdain, now emerges in ruthless form. Having 'seen the unpleasant side of folk' (261) he now sets his face to achieve his own, and the Thistle's, ends:

> It was the president who resurrected hope. At the first committee meeting after the defeat he reminded his fellow members that it was possible, without magic, to have the tie replayed [...] If they could prove that any player of the team which had beaten them had been at the time ineligible [...] then they could protest to the Association, which would order an enquiry and the tie would be replayed '(258).

A player of doubtful provenance, whose status had been unsuccessfully contested by many other clubs, is identified and Rutherford orchestrates an unscrupulous campaign against him. Any scruples his fellow committee members might have at underhand dealings are brushed aside; one of Rutherford's allies, Angus Tennant, sums it up: 'I'd deal with the Deil himself if it would get us back into the Cup. All's fair in love and war; this is war' (265). Ironically, by abandoning (or at least reducing) his expectations of what humanity is capable Robertson finds that he is finally accepted into the community. But having bestowed on it the grail of football success, and thereby being acclaimed a local hero, Robertson realises that the prize is a fleeting one; in the aftermath of victory, as the Thistle team takes to the open-top bus to parade its trophy through the streets, Rutherford

> sat amidst that busload of familiar men, noticing how happiness had purged them, as it had purged him, of all characteristic meanness and selfishness. This really was how men were, how they would wish to be always if circumstances allowed them.' (289)

There is no lasting solace in football, though it is capable of providing brief epiphanies. It is perhaps the only hope for Scotland, since spiritual solace in the form of religion has made no impact. Jenkins, like many novelists of twentieth-century Scotland, targets the kirk and its Calvinist traditions as a pernicious influence on Scottish society. In *The Thistle and the Grail* the young minister, Mr Lockhart ('lanky, with uncouth elbows and knees') (37) wants to lead a religious revival: '[W]e have become in Scotland a race of pagans, we who used to die for our religion [...] Football is their religion now' (42–3).Rutherford can find nothing but distaste for a man whose outward piety is tainted by double-dealing and spiritual conceit. He recalls his father's summary dismissal of the kirk: '[it] has always kowtowed to money and position, and always will' (47). Lockhart's vain aspirations to bring devotion to Drumsagart (aspirations not shared by his more sensible wife) come to grief in the local pub, his chosen venue for the start of the revival. In the 'Lucky Sporran', where all the town's rivalries, personal and sectarian, are assembled, Lockhart's mission immediately hits the rocks, mainly in the form of the old atheistical miner Tinto Brown, risen from his sickbed to seek warmth and company in the pub: 'I need a change from girning weans and the stink of my own decay' (210). Sight of the heathen Tinto instantly undermines the minister's resolve, even before Tinto unleashes a tirade on him:

> What your kind's been saying for centuries has been the curse of Scotland and the whole world. When was there a war you didn't bless? [...] You all ken I'm a damned sight nearer my Maker than any one of you. If He's what your kind hae represented Him to be, when I meet Him face to face there'll be mony things far frae complimentary I'll hae to say to Him; and then, nae doubt, wi' your sanction and to the sound of your hallelujahs, He'll whistle up His son, young Christ, to strangle me wi' His bare hands for all my sins. Till then, leave me in peace. (212)

Tinto's intervention arouses a confusion of argument that detracts from the purpose of the meeting, not that Lockhart is in any state to continue. 'Physically, morally and spiritually shocked' (212) he is unconsoled by the landlord's offer to re-convene for better luck on another evening. '"No". The minister's voice was low, but the agony in it made the publican pout. "No, we shall not be lucky any night"'" (213). Lockhart is defeated and retreats into the safety of his manse where domesticity, confirmed by the love of his wife and the birth of their first child, offers a buffer against the harsh impieties of the outside world. There is a shell-shocked quality about his final appearance in the story, which contrasts with Rutherford's newly-acquired character of steel.

3

The outstanding characteristic of *The Thistle and the Grail*, and what marks it out from both *This Sporting Life* and *The Rise of Gerry Logan* as a 'football' novel, is the contrast Jenkins presents between the narrative world created in the book and the time of its publication. Contrary to the claim made by Manfred Malzahn *The Thistle and the Grail* seems decidedly – determinedly, one might even say – *not* to be a novel of the 1950s working class. There is something significantly old-fashioned about its historical setting which leaves no face of the Second World War and the subsequent economic upturn and social-democratic consensus that the conflict brought about.[14] The characteristic markers of post-war society, such as the coming of full employment and 'affluence', or urban regeneration through the creation of new towns, are conspicuously absent from the text. It may well have been that, in the early 1950s, the Scots were less receptive to the 'new Elizabethan' mood of optimism than were people south of the border, though Scotland did share to an extent in the general economic prosperity of the post-war years; the desperate prospect of industrial decline raised by George Blake's novel of 1935 had come to

---

14  Manfred Malzahn, 'The Industrial Novel' in Cairns Craig ed., *The History of Scottish Literature, volume 4, Twentieth Century* (Aberdeen: Aberdeen University Press, 1989), pp. 229–42.

seem a bad memory.[15] Jenkins makes no explicit attempt to date the events portrayed in *The Thistle and the Grail* but at the same time the story is consciously distanced from the present in which his readers received the novel. Through constant references to poverty, ill-health, unemployment, socialism and 'the war' ('Gavin lay buried in France') (34) and threats of a new one, he places it in a time that has all the characteristics of inter-war Scotland. The Great War was a recurring trope in Scottish novels of the inter-war period – a 'defining boundary of their narrative horizon.'[16]

In establishing this historical circumstance Jenkins gives his novel a form that belies the ideas at the heart of his text. Indeed, it adopts, beguilingly and with heavy irony, some features that are characteristic of the 'kailyard' tradition.[17] Thus, Jenkins presents us with Drumsagart as the kind of place peopled (in Tom Nairn's words) by '"small-town" characters given to bucolic intrigue and wise sayings'.[18] Though, contrary to the semi-rural context of the kailyard Drumsagart is an industrial town of 'miners, steelmen, and paper-makers' (68), its landscape is nevertheless a fair one – wide pavements, flowerbeds and trees grace its main street, where the great tower of the Town Hall dominates the view: '[E]xiles in America and Australia were known to close their eyes and see that tower constant against the shifting sky' (33). At the centre of the town is the kirk, marked by a particular icon of Scottish independence in the form of the sixteenth-century archway with its sentry box, popularly thought to have been installed 'in Covenanting times when church services were held in defiance of the law and armed sentries had to be posted' (34). It is another image for émigrés, one of the main consumers of kailyard literature, to bring to mind. But from within these images Jenkins conjures a far from comforting vision of a place where the

15    See K.J. Lea, *A Geography of Scotland* (Newton Abbot: David and Charles, 1977), pp. 68, 72–4, and chapter 5 for post-war industrial development in Scotland.

16    Cairns Craig, *Out of History: Narrative Paradigms in Scottish and English Literature* (Edinburgh: Polygon, 1996), p. 34.

17    See David Daiches ed., *A Companion to Scottish Culture* (London: Edward Arnold, 1981), pp. 196–7.

18    Nairn, *Break-Up*, p. 158.

chiliastic faiths of both religion and socialism have evaporated. His use of kailyard imagery is revealed as ironic, as in his description of the town's Mercat Cross, a heritage artefact installed in imitation of an original thirteenth-century cross. But the design has been declared spurious by 'a well-known historian', and the sanctity of the place, initially assured by a council prohibition on sitting and spitting on the steps of the cross, has been defiled by the consequences of industry: 'the unemployed had increased to such an extent that the benches provided in the main street were no longer sufficient. So the Cross had become an accepted forum; the steps of granite made convenient seats for men hardened by life's kicks' (48). And it is the game of football with its transient pleasures that holds the people together in a sense of purpose. 'These are mean drab times' (150) says one character, uttering what is perhaps the novel's central theme of despair.

*The Thistle and the Grail*'s intensely Scottish ambience is above all anchored in its being a novel about football. It was one of the rare occasions on which Jenkins took up this subject in his work, and yet, as one of his critical admirers has reminded us, 'he is more than a sociological writer'[19] and his treatment of football serves a metaphorical purpose. What could be a more appropriate context, therefore, in which to set the story than the inter-war years, a time when football in Scotland had its firmest grip on the public imagination? This was the time of record crowds at Hampden and Ibrox, and of the memorable victory of the 'Wembley Wizards' against the old enemy, an event that carried far more emotional freight for Scottish fans than its sporting significance warranted.[20] The period was the high peak of

---

19    Moira Burgess, 'Robin Jenkins: A Novelist of Scotland', *Library Review,* 22; 8 (1970), 410.
20    See Cottrell, *Century of Soccer Drama,* pp. 47–51; Chris Nawrat and Steve Hutchings, *The Sunday Times Illustrated History of Football* (London: Hamlyn, 1998), p. 41. The record attendance for a British league match of 118, 567 was set on 2 January 1939 in the match at Ibrox between Rangers and Celtic. 149,547 had attended the Scotland-England international fixture at Hampden in 1937. The win at Wembley was remembered for longer than the match itself – a contest between the bottom two teams in the Home Championship of that year – merited. But the important thing was that it was a win of ample proportions (5-1) against England.

Scottish football achievement, never matched after 1945. After the war there had seemed briefly a prospect of continuity with the glorious years, with a period of success in the late 'forties, and in 1950 an invitation for the national team to participate for the first time in the FIFA World Cup finals in Brazil. The invitation was refused[21] and shortly after the novel's publication Scottish football, for so long obsessed with its own internal rivalries and its inhabiting of a world where victory in the annual match against England was considered to bestow the title 'masters' of the game, was made aware of another world. It came in the form of the Hungarian football team, which in November 1953 had defeated the English heavily on their home ground at Wembley. Some twelve months later the Hungarians inflicted a similar, if slightly less emphatic, defeat on Scotland at Hampden. However, in the summer of 1954 the Scots had competed in the finals of the World Cup in Switzerland and had been made to realise that their football was hopelessly antiquated by comparison with their opponents. Uruguay (the holders) had defeated them 7-0. These events signified the end of both countries' long-cultivated myth of their superiority, based on their position as founders of the game. 'Waverley', the football correspondent of Scotland's biggest daily newspaper, had witnessed in the defeat of England in November 1953 a foretaste of what was to come for the Scots. A year later, when Hungary visited Glasgow, he invoked the spirit of past Scottish heroes – Wallace, Bruce, Rob Roy, Burns, Stevenson, and Livingstone – to 'make the Scots' blood boil' and create a 'Hampden Bannockburn'. But Scotland lost 4-2, and the only consolation in the result came from the relative narrowness of the defeat compared with the score against England.[22] Whilst England rallied from the shock of 1953 and won the World Cup in 1966, Scotland never did recover its assumed former greatness. There is, therefore, a certain irony in Jenkins's celebration

1928 compares in some respects with the victory of Scotland over England, recently crowned world champions, at Wembley in 1967.

21   The qualifying matches had been played in the British home championship, and because Scotland had not won it outright the Scottish F.A. decided that its team could not honourably take part. A case of *hubris*?

22   See *Daily Record and Mail,* 26 November 1953; 6, 7 and 9 December 1954. Hungary had beaten England 6-3 in November 1953, and 7-1 in May 1954.

of Scots' pride in their football at the very point when this shaper of their identity as a nation was to evaporate, probably for all time.

## 4

This was a sporting instance of the greater threat that many intellectuals felt existed to native traditions in twentieth-century Scotland. The Scots appeared to have lost their national purchase, and become impoverished as the country faced the subordination of its culture to an English or even American dominance. Cairns Craig has noted this 'sense of impending extinction [that] has never been far from the awareness of Scottish writers in the twentieth century.'[23] It is a theme brought out in George Blake's *The Shipbuilders*, published some twenty years before Jenkins's novel but closer to it in spirit than many a novel of the 1950s.[24] The sense of Scotland's decline, depicted by Blake in Leslie Pagan's tour of the desolate Clyde shipyards, and when the riveter Danny Shields sees, in the novel's final passage, 'the red lights of the Night Scot hurry away across the bridge towards the South' (265) is echoed in the work of Jenkins. It is in this context that Jenkins faces the challenges of modernity, and seems, like Blake, to find little hope for a Scottish future. The novel signifies this in a small though important way in the destiny of Andrew Robertson's son, Gerald, whose relationship with his father has never fulfilled Andrew's emotional expectations. The boy has been pulled between his father's sentimentalism and his mother Hannah's strict materialsm and gradually veers to the latter. Gerald's being taken away to Helensburgh (a substitute for England?) by his mother seals the end of the bond between father and son, and when in the moment of Drumsagart's Cup victory Gerald is offered the chance to accompany Andrew back to the town to enjoy the celebrations he refuses: '"No. I

23    *History of Scottish Literature,* vol 4, p. 1.
24    George Blake, *The Shipbuilders* (Edinburgh: B & W Publishing, 1993).

50

want to go home"' (288). Gerald has been the one central character whose presence in the story betokens a future. His rejection of Drumsagart thus provokes the thought of where 'home' is, and what the 'future' holds. Where the English writers Storey and Glanville engage with the problems of the post-war world Jenkins refuses to countenance them and turns his readers' gaze backwards; but not in order to derive comfort from the memory of a confectioned Scottish identity in the manner of the kailyard, for *The Thistle and the Grail* is not by any stretch of the imagination a comforting text. Rather, Jenkins appears to want us to see the country's fall, the point of convergence of all the circumstances that destroyed national hope, the site where the battle for the future was lost and football took over. It is his particular representation of the idea of 'escape' from a dissatisfaction with contemporary Scotland – seen also in the work of other novelists of the 1950s and 1960s, as well as in some of Jenkins's own later writings – into an unattainable Eden.[25] At some point in the early twentieth-century Scotland lost its heroic qualities and became a place where only football – 'the mysterious masculine sacrament' (63) – had the capacity to consume the spiritual faculties of its inhabitants. In this respect *The Thistle and the Grail* is a deeply pessimistic book. As Andrew Robertson reflects to himself when driving a group of supporters across the moors to a match:

> Scotland was a country where faith lay rotted like neglected roses, and the secret of resurrection was lost. We are a drench, miserable, back-biting, self-tormenting, haunted, self-pitying crew, he thought. This sunshine is as bright as any on earth, these moors are splendid; why are not the brightness and splendour in our lives? Seeking them, here we are speeding at fifty miles an hour to see what – a football match, a game invented for exercise and recreation, but now our only substitute for a faith and purpose. (166)

---

25   See Glenda Norquay, 'Four Novelists of the 1950s and 1960s', in Craig ed., *History of Scottish Literature*, pp. 259–76.

# Chapter Three
## 'Acting Big': David Storey's *This Sporting Life*[1]

'Course I strutted about. They expected it. I couldn't help it. I walked in front of these people now, and I felt a hero. They wanted me to be a hero - and I wanted to be a hero. Why didn't she see that?' (162)

David Storey's 1960 novel *This Sporting Life*, together with Lindsay Anderson's adaptation of it for the cinema in 1962,[2] is part of a discourse about the condition of Britain that had become pervasive by the late 1950s. Both novel and film derive from varied literary and artistic influences, but by far the most immediate and compelling, and certainly the most apparent, was the social realism that had come to prominence in British literature and film making in the 1950s and early 1960s. Alan Sillitoe, John Braine, John Wain, Stan Barstow, Keith Waterhouse, Tony Richardson, Lindsay Anderson, and Karel Reisz were among the major exponents of a genre that focused on English life and mores - specially in the north of England - at a time of economic, social, and cultural change, which has often been characterized as the 'affluent society'.[3] Not surprisingly, the genre's preoccupation

---

1   All page references to the novel are from the 1962 Penguin edition (Harmondsworth: Penguin Books Ltd, 1962). References to both book and film are used in this chapter, though this should not be taken to imply that the two texts are regarded as interchangeable. The film is far more faithful to the novel than many other cinematic adaptations of books, yet it has its own emphases and unity. It is, however, felt to be justified to draw freely from the two texts where they both deal with the same theme.

2   Lindsay Anderson , dir., *This Sporting Life* (London: Independent Artists, 1963).

3   See Stan Barstow, *A Kind of Loving* ( Harmondsworth: Penguin Books, 1962); John Braine, *Room At The Top* (Harmondsworth: Penguin Books, 1959); Erik Hedling, *Lindsay Anderson: Maverick Film-Maker* (London: Cassell, 1998); John Hill, *Sex, Class and Realism: British Cinema 1957–1963* (London: British Film Institute, 1986); Penelope Houston, *The Contemporary Cinema.* (Harmondsworth:

with the condition of Britain drew on a range of characteristic themes, including local identity, power relationships, affluence, gender, and, of special importance in all instances, the insidious problem of class relationships and privilege.

In John Braine's ambiguously entitled *Room at the Top*, the theme of class was handled in a most abrasive form, with the ambitious and amoral Joe Lampton presented as an upwardly mobile, working-class young man, impatient to throw off the shackles of a deferential upbringing. In Lampton, a man obsessively aware of the social hierarchies that impeded working-class talent, Braine offered a new anti-hero. He was the antithesis of the well-bred, courtly member of the officer class, a persona well recognized by filmgoers as the stock-in-trade of 1950s war films. Indeed, Braine made the contrast explicit in the two figures of Lampton and his adversary Jack Wales. Both had seen active service in the war, been captured in battle, and made prisoners of war. Wales, however, distinguished himself by escaping; 'it will be noted', mused Joe Lampton in a moment of self-reflection,

> that Lampton [...] made no attempt to escape, but devoted his attention to his studies, passing his main accountancy examinations whilst actually a prisoner. This proves [...] that he possesses an admirable pertinacity of purpose, since it must have been extremely difficult to study under prison camp conditions. It does not, however, say much for his manhood or patriotism.[4]

David Storey's position in relation to the rest of the British social realist school was an ambivalent one. To be sure, he converged with the others through a variety of paths. Artistically his work emphasized physical power and the social class relations in which it was exercised. In some respects his probings of working-class masculinity are comparable to those of Sillitoe in the more celebrated *Saturday Night and Sunday Morning*. Sociologically, Storey embodied the perspective

Penguin Books, 1963); Gavin Lambert, *Mainly About Lindsay Anderson* (London: Faber, 2000); Alan Sillitoe, *Saturday Night and Sunday Morning* (London: Pan Books, 1961); John Wain, *Hurry On Down* (London: Secker and Warburg, 1953).

4    Braine, *Room At The Top,* p. 149.

of the deracinated 'scholarship boy' evoked in Richard Hoggart's *Uses of Literacy*[5], a figure who typified many of the exponents of the realist school. Storey's educational achievement and intellectual ambition had partially freed him from his northern working-class roots and enabled him to stand back from the object of his art. Nonetheless, in spite of his detachment from the region, Storey's art has a pre-eminently 'northern' quality. His writing articulated a gritty realism characteristic of the genre, adding to it an element of primitivism: 'the words', said his anonymous reviewer in the *Times Literary Supplement*, 'rattle like flint arrow heads.'[6] But what Storey chose also to explore marked his work out from other writers of the genre. Although *This Sporting Life* has plenty to say about social class – it is essentially a study of a working-class man – it also succeeds to a greater extent than other examples of the genre in foregrounding issues of gender and gender relations. Where Sillitoe had cast in Arthur Seaton the drinking, fighting, and fornicating working-class male, Storey offers a more subdued, although no less physical, Arthur Machin. But in Mrs. Hammond, he brings into the centre of his narrative a finely drawn female character, as he had also done in *Flight Into Camden*, published in the same year.[7] Arthur Seaton's women are more marginal. Sillitoe's purpose is to define the boundaries of Seaton's power in a world of factory discipline and 'authority'. Storey places Machin in sport - after work, the main site of 'maleness' - where, increasingly throughout the novel, he comes to perceive the tensions between what is expected of him as a man and the shallowness of conventional

5    Richard Hoggart, TheUses of Literacy: Aspects of Working-Class Life, with Special Reference to Publications and Entertainments (London: Chatto and Windus, 1957).
6    *Times Literary Supplement (TLS)*, 11 March 1960, 157.
7    The central character of Margaret Thorpe in *Flight Into Camden* (London: Longmans, Green, 1960) is a remarkably sensitive one for a male novelist of this period. For Storey's treatment of Margaret's social and gender predicament, as well as his portrayal of the sex scenes, the novel deserves to be recognised as an early statement of feminism. See James Campbell, 'A Chekhov of the North', *Guardian Review*, 31 January 2004, 20–23. Campbell accurately says of *Flight Into Camden* that it is 'a feminist novel, written a dozen years before the genre became established.'

masculinity. Storey's text thus looks back to and draws inspiration from critiques of flawed masculinity to be found in popular crime fiction and, at the same time, anticipates issues brought out in the later 1960s by the women's movement. It might even prefigure, in certain respects, the 'crisis of masculinity' of the 1990s. The novel and its film version were received generally with critical applause, although both have now passed into neglect, if not oblivion.[8] When *This Sporting Life* is remembered, it is not as a great novel. The *Times Literary Supplement* reviewer might have been right when he of she suggested that in striving for social authenticity, Storey had sacrificed 'literature'.[9] The purpose here, however, is not to examine the literary credentials of Storey's writing but to direct attention to a text that contributes to the discourse of decline and modernization in 1950s and 1960s Britain and, therefore, to argue for its relevance as a source for historians and sociologists.

1

*This Sporting Life* portrays the career of a rugby league player, Arthur Machin (in the film, he becomes Frank Machin). Although hardly a historical novel as conventionally understood, it is nevertheless a history of a life, or at least a reflection on a changing awareness of self over time. Machin narrates a period of some ten years of his life, from a young player making his way into the rugby league team, through a phase of success, and to the eventual onset of his physical decline when the sporting life draws to a close. The sport is aptly chosen. Storey had shown promise at it as a youth and was, for a time in the early 1950s, a professional player, although he failed to make the grade to regular first-team football. More significant than authorial

---

8    Charles L.P.Silet, *Lindsay Anderson: A Guide to References and Resources* (London: George Prior, 1979); Elizabeth Sussex, *Lindsay Anderson* (London: Studio Vista, 1969).
9    *TLS,* 11 March 1960, 157.

experience, however, is the sport's symbolic status. Rugby league is synonymous with class and gender. It is the archetypal 'working-man's game'.[10] It is noted for its sheer physicality – fast running and hard tackling are its hallmarks. Until changes in its financing inspired by the Murdoch media corporation in the 1990s, most of rugby league's players were semi-professionals who earned modest wages from the game and were required by the league regulations to be employed in a respectable job.[11] Thus, work and sport were linked, and because of this, the rugby league players remained close to their community. The game had little of the glamour of professional soccer. In the film, Machin mildly rebukes an admirer who describes him as a 'star': 'There are no stars', he says, 'that's soccer.' The very hardness of the game and the absence of embellishment mirrored the communities in which it flourished in Britain – essentially the towns and villages of Lancashire, Yorkshire, and Cumberland in the north of England, all centres of the heavy industries of coal mining, steel, and chemicals.[12] Although some clubs were based in the metropolitan

10  Tony Collins, *Rugby's Great Split: Class, Culture and the Origins of Rugby League Football.* London: Frank Cass, 1998); Geoffrey Moorhouse, *At the George: And Other Essays of Rugby League* (London: Sceptre, 1990); Karl Spracklen, '"Playing the Ball": Constructing Community and Masculine Identity in Rugby: An Analysis of the Two Codes of League and Union and the People Involved', Ph.D. thesis, Leeds Metropolitan University, 1996.

11  Paul Blackledge, 'Rational Capitalist Concerns: William Cail and the Great Rugby Split of 1895' *International Journal of the History of Sport*, 18; 2 (2001), 35–53; Tony Collins, '"Noa Mutton, Noa Laaking": The Origins of Payment For Play in Rugby Football' *International Journal of the History of Sport*, 12; 1 (1995), 33–50; Paul Greenhalgh, 'The Work and Play Principle: The Professional Regulations of the Northern Rugby Football Union 1898–1905' *International Journal of the History of Sport*, 9; 3 (1992), 356–77.

12  T.C. Barker and J. R. Harris, *St Helens: A Merseyside Town in the Industrial Revolution* (Liverpool: Liverpool University Press, 1954); N. Dennis, F. Henriques and C. Slaughter. *Coal Is Our Life: An Analysis of a Yorkshire Mining Community* (London: Eyre and Spottiswoode, 1956); Brian Jackson, *Working-Class Community: Some General Notions Raised by a Series of Studies in Northern England* (London: Routledge, Kegan and Paul, 1968); Clancy Sigal, *Weekend in Dinlock* (London: Secker and Warburg, 1960).

areas of the north – Leeds, Bradford, Manchester, and Hull – the quintessential rugby-league town was a small place where people knew each other and where local civic leaders could exercise a close influence over people's lives. The film immediately establishes the juxtaposition of life and sport. In two early scenes, Anderson cuts from hard physical play to hard physical labour, with Machin seen as a faceworker in the cramped conditions of a coalmine.[13] Moreover, rugby league was a business. Ever since its formation as a sport in the late-nineteenth century, as a breakaway movement from the middle-class dominated rugby union, it had assumed a commercial orientation with the spectators a principal element of the game. The commercial relationships that governed the sport reproduced those present in work. As Storey shows, employers buy labour power through wages. The rugby players are commodities who symbolize the power of their employers. The sport has a different ethos from that of middle-class amateurism, where playing for the love of the game is its own reward. Machin, as a professional player, finds exhilaration in rugby, but he also seeks profit. For such men, the sporting life is a life of taking hard knocks to achieve material rewards and status in the community.[14]

In these communities, sport is what men do; indeed, it is the apotheosis of working-class manhood, one of the great driving forces of male society. Hoggart, in his intuitively perceptive way, claimed that in the intimate world of male sociability based around work and

13  In the book Machin is an engineer working at his own lathe, a skilled worker like the face worker in a mine although less obviously doing 'hard' work, which is presumably why Anderson made the change.

14  Richard Holt, *Sport and the British: A Modern History* (Oxford: Oxford University Press, 1989); J.A. Mangan, *Athleticism in the Victorian and Edwardian Public School: The Emergence and Consolidation of an Educational Ideology* (Cambridge: Cambridge University Press, 1981); J.A.Mangan and J. Walvin, *Manliness and Morality: Middle-Class Masculinity in Britain and America 1800–1940* (Manchester: Manchester University Press, 1987); Karl Spracklen, '"When You're Putting Yer Body On T'line Fer Beer Tokens You've Go'a Wonder Why": Expressions of Masculinity and Identity in Rugby Communities', *Scottish Centre Research Papers in Sport, Leisure and Society*, vol. 1 (Edinburgh: Moray House Institute of Education, 1996).

58

pub, 'sport vies with sex as the staple of conversation'.[15] Sport was watched, read about, discussed, gambled on, and imagined to an extent that excluded most other aspects of life. The male sporting hero (there were few female ones until the later twentieth century) was admired by men of all ages as a paragon, the happy warrior who all would wish to be.[16] Being a successful sportsman, that is, earning one's living by playing, was a state that most working-class males would willingly trade for other forms of wage labour. Not being good at sport could be compensated for by being an avid spectator, but not liking sport ensured marginalization in male society. It was a mark of not being a 'proper' man. In this respect, working-class society shared a characteristic with the culture of the public school, where those who eschewed the sporting life were viewed with suspicion.[17]

Machin is good at sport. He is a big man who revels in his physical power. Before the start of a match:

> I was suddenly happy, relieved, full of air. I didn't put it down to anything at that moment; I used it to encourage myself. Afterwards, I recognized it as preliminary feeling of power. I was big, strong, and could make people realize it. I could tackle hard and [...] really hurt someone. I was big. Big! It was no mean elation. (22)

Later, during a match:

> this big character comes round the blind side every time there's a scrum. He carries the ball loose. All I do is stand in his way, and he's never looking. I get my shoulder under his jaw and he goes down like a child. I start counting the times he comes round this way. Fourteen. I've hit every part of his face. The fifteenth time they carry him off. How thick can you get? This shows I'm good at defensive play. (33–4)

15    Hoggart, *Uses of Literacy,* p. 91.
16    Richard Holt, 'Heroes of the North: Sport and the Shaping of Regional Identity.' in Jeff Hill and Jack Williams eds, *Sport and Identity in the North of England* (Keele: Keele University Press, 1996), pp. 137–164.
17    Mangan, *Athleticism,* ch. 4.

In another match:

> I found myself in an opening and suddenly thought I might even reach the line. I went straight for the full-back, and when he came in I gave him the base of my wrist on his nose. The crack, the groan, the release of his arms, all coincide with a soaring of my guts. I moved in between the posts keeping my eye on the delight of the crowd as I put the ball down. (41)

Throughout book and film, there is an attempt to recreate the physical as the text reaches into the sensuous aspects of sport. Unlike an 'objective' academic study, *This Sporting Life* does not stand outside its subject. Sport and pain are not analysed but described in an existential statement of what it is like to be in the sporting life. The camaraderie of the changing room with its naked bodies and infantile horseplay emphasizes this through the physical proximity of male companionship, the world of sport literally stripped bare. Even the unnamed town has a physical presence. Nature, in the form of the weather, is never far away; it establishes a mood, affects the senses. In later scenes of the film and book, nature and the physical are brought together as an ageing Machin, seeking to deny his advancing years, desperately tries to keep up with the game:

> A shape came towards me in the gloom – I glimpsed the fierce and brilliant whiteness of its eyes and clenched teeth through its mask of mud, flashing with a useless hostility. It avoided my preparations to delay it, veering past out of reach. I put my foot out, and as the man stumbled took a swing with my fist. I missed, and fell down with a huge sound from the crowd. The man recovered and went on running. He ran between the posts. Frank picked me up, the mud covering my tears. Where's the bleeding full-back? I wanted to shout. But I could only stare unbelievingly at my legs which had betrayed me. (252)

Anderson films this scene as Machin defying nature's attempts to reclaim him, like some primitive beast out of its time being pulled back into a primeval swamp.

# 2

Footballers are public figures who, as Machin constantly avers, 'act big.' He performs his role in the public spaces of the severely circumscribed working-class world – factory, pub, dance hall, and, of course, sports field – by scoring tries, taking his ale, signing autographs for kids, driving a big car, singing in the pub. In such places, he becomes a shared commodity, representing for his admirers a vicarious escape from the mundane. He is, of course, exceptional. He does things that most will never experience. He is, however, still close enough to the everyday world to be 'one of us.' He fulfils an idealized reflection of self. He is at ease in these local surroundings, where he knows the protocols. By contrast, in the completely different social milieu of a middle-class restaurant where other codes of masculinity apply, he is without bearings; he is unable to 'act big' in these surroundings and, in trying to do so, only manages to make a fool of himself and embarrass those around him. The difference is that masculinity in his own society depends crucially on exerting a physical presence and, when necessary, solving problems by recourse to violence. In this way, Machin resolves, early in the narrative, the major problem of securing his place in the team against cynical competition from others. In a trial match, he finds that he is being deliberately starved of the ball by another player in his own team:

> I waited three scrums to make him feel relaxed and also to get the best opportunity. I kept my right arm loose. His face was upside down, his eyes straining, loose in their sockets, to catch a glimpse of the ball as it came in. I watched it leave the scrum-half's hands and his head buckled under the forwards' heaving. I swung my right fist into the middle of his face. He cried out loud. It hit him again and saw the red pulp of his nose and lips as my hand came away. He was crying out really loud now, partly affected, professional pain, but most of it real. (39)

This action is concealed from the referee, who dismisses the wrong man for the offence (to the delight of the crowd whose 'response reached a crescendo – far more than it would provide for, say, the burning of a church'). It is, however, seen by the trainer who dismisses

Machin's claim that he was being deliberately deprived of the ball: 'Nobody lakes (plays) that game here.' 'Not now they don't', retorts Machin (40). The film shows Machin shadow-boxing in front of his mirror, daily recreating himself as the hard man. It also has him, as a young man attempting to break into the rugby-league team, deliberately picking a fight with the club captain as a way of proving himself. He does this, moreover, in a crowded dance hall, a public place where the players are being hailed as local heroes. Such ideals of masculinity are manufactured and passed from one generation to the next, as young boys learn to be men through sport. Physical strength is prized as a virtue in contrast to other traditions of sporting behaviour, which emphasize 'fair play' and the building of 'good character'. In this respect, Machin's choice of reading is revealing. It is the cheap American novelette or biography, the kind parodied by Hoggart [18], usually featuring a boxing hero and dealing in simplistic gender roles and the objectification of women as 'samples'. Machin is a role model for his young admirers on the terraces who seek his autograph. He is also a man who is influenced by the crude images of masculinity that he reads about in his cheap pulp fiction – *Tropical Orgy* and *Blood on the Canvas* or the authentic *Somebody Up There Likes Me*, the autobiography of American boxer Rocky Graziano:

> I sat at the bar and got out *Tropical Orgy* - a moonlit night on a tropical sea, and Capt. Summers had just some on deck after leaving his sample 'fully satisfied and utterly contented' in his cabin down below. (97)

In some respects, the novel *This Sporting Life* works through the same kind of situations and plot progression encountered in this popular romantic fiction where, among other issues, gender ideologies are constructed and confirmed as part of a 'natural' order of things. But Storey parodies this genre by dislocating its neat connections and exposing its fallacies. Sporting success does not bring happiness, love does not conquer all, women do not always conform to men's ideas of them, loose ends are rarely tied up, and life is going nowhere.

18    Hoggart, *Uses of Literacy,* pp. 210–13.

Machin's laconic narrative ends pretty much where it began: 'I had my ankles strapped, got dressed, and put my teeth in' (253). The narrative provides no resolutions. Above all, the ideals of masculinity, the strutting and the acting big, the theatre of working-class manhood, all these are shown to be flawed ideals.

# 3

The narrative of *This Sporting Life* is a self-reflective one, developing Machin's gradual realization of the hollowness of his position. Once attained, sporting heroism is an empty prize. Storey portrays nothing worthy of admiration. Machin's life becomes a struggle to release himself from the cultural cage in which he is trapped. He likens himself to an ape, and this becomes the central simile of the text. He grows to despise those who admire him, for whom he is required to act big. They have created an ideal that is false both for themselves and for those admired:

> I wanted a bit more than a wave. I wanted to have something there for good: I wasn't going to be a footballer for ever. But I was an ape. Big, awe-inspiring, something to see perform. No feelings [...] I was paid not to have feelings. People looked at me as if I was an ape. (163-4)

It is in his relationship with a woman that Machin's masculinity is put to the test and found wanting. This has nothing to do with sex, success in which is the conventional measurement of masculine prowess. It has, however, everything to do with understanding women and being able to bridge a divide between the sexes that is created and re-created daily through countless forms of separation in work and play, driving men and women apart. Women are culturally defined as mothers:

> Mothers, mothers. Always mothers. Women are never anything but mothers. There's never a wife been born yet. I hate all these bloody mothers and their stinking brats. Can't women ever be anything without kids, kids, all the time?

You're not just animals. Mrs Hammond – she's a woman. Somewhere she's a woman. (209)

When Elsie, the wife of Frank Miles, the rugby club captain, announces that 'we are expecting another' the new baby's prospects are immediately set in this cultural divide. 'What do you want this time, Frank?' asks club director George Wade. 'Another doctor, or a nurse for a change?' Elsie is complicit in the exclusion of her own sex. 'Oh, it better be a girl this time. I want a bit of company myself in the house' (220). The sporting life is, of course, the quintessential instrument of female exclusion, for women have no part in the football.

Machin has an affair with his landlady, Mrs Hammond, a withdrawn, desiccated, self-pitying woman. In her psyche is stored all the toil and pain of working-class life. She is seeking to expunge the shame of a failed marriage, ended not in divorce (an exceptional occurrence in this social context and time) but in the suicide of her husband. The circumstances are mysterious, but he seems to have lost the will to live. The event leaves her guilt-stricken and suspicious of any relationship with a man. At the same time, she is caged in a confining domesticity, caring for her two young children, taking in a lodger to make ends meet, and keeping alive the memory of her dead husband through the ritual daily cleaning of his boots, which are permanently in the fireplace. Nobody could be farther removed than Mrs Hammond from the glamorized, sexually submissive image of woman conventionally associated with the masculine gaze, which is the image featured in Machin's novelettes. Yet, this is what provides the fascination for Machin. He wants to bring her back to life, to arouse in her some spark of emotion for him. All his efforts to establish a real relationship, shorn of the customary expectations of a society in which gender roles are rigidly performed, come to nothing.

Machin's masculinity is framed by other equally sour representations of men. There is, for example, Johnson, Machin's mentor, the football scout who discovers him and secures his trial game with the club, who is used by Machin and then discarded once his value has gone. Johnson is a solitary man, who appears not to have had a job or a wife and whose social existence depends on his tenuous attachment to the football club. Johnson is called 'Dad' by Machin, who little realizes the filial role he fulfils in Johnson's world view. Machin's success compensates Johnson's failure, and of all Machin's admirers, Johnson is the one who most desires the glory reflected by the footballer. It is a woman, Mrs Hammond, who first expresses revulsion at Johnson's form of masculinity, reminding us that images of men are reproduced as much through female as through male 'common-sense':

> [to Machin]: The way he treats you - ogles you.
> He looks at you like a girl [...] He's never had a job in his life [...]
> I've got eyes. Just look at his hands. He's never done a day's work. He's got awful hands. They're all soft. (30-1)

Johnson is neither a 'man's man' nor, it seems, a 'woman's man'. After a visit from Johnson to Machin's digs for a cup of tea, Mrs. Hammond instructs, 'Leave that Johnson's cup on one side. I'll wash it out later myself – scald it' (29). Alongside Johnson, also vying for Machin's attention, is the local employer and football club director, the aptly named and sexually ambiguous Weaver, whose oleaginous insincerity is beautifully captured in the film by the actor Alan Badel. It is Weaver who combines the themes of gender and power. He manipulates Machin, using his influence in the boardroom to bring about his signing against the wishes of a rival director, Slomer. The signing-on scene starkly exposes the power relationships in football. Machin thinks he is being clever, holding out for and getting a bigger-than-usual signing-on fee. In reality, Weaver has engineered the deal already, irrespective of Machin's stance, and at his capture, Machin notes, 'Weaver shook my hand softly and looked right into my eye with a kid's delight at a new toy' (57). However, the implication of sexual affection belies fickleness. Weaver tires of his protégé and becomes an enemy. Machin is in danger of losing his place at the club unless Slomer adopts him. In these ways, the position of the hero is uncertain. Physical strength is no weapon against the power of money; the footballers are the playthings of Olympian forces beyond their control, just as the security of their working-class fans can be dashed by the changing fortunes of capitalism. The best tactic is to be a trimmer – to 'float' – like the solid captain Frank Miles, whose name is always on the team sheet because he takes no side and makes no enemies; he represents a dull but contented domesticity with his wife, children, and small house. But the power exercised by Weaver and Slomer is out of its time, representing a local jurisdiction under threat from the forces of change and modernization. At the funeral of Slomer, the whole town turns out to honour one of its local grandees, but the occasion is a valediction for a civic identity about to be lost. Machin and George Wade encounter a shadowy stranger who fleetingly places the funeral in its historic context. 'It's the end of a way, you know […] With Slomer gone', the man told him, 'you'll find all the big combines finding it easier to move into town. We'll become like all the other big towns - socialist, impersonal, anonymous' (228–9).

Machin's emotional quest is not successful. His relationship with Mrs Hammond comes to nothing. Even their sexual relationship is a perfunctory one – 'We didn't do it very often' – and the first sexual encounter little more than a rugby scrum: 'All the time', says Machin, 'I reminded myself of the ugliness of her face, of her terror. I was half stunned by her lack of excitement' (96). There is nothing in Machin's cultural upbringing as a man to help him solve this problem. She remains cold, unnerved by his success, the material consequences of which (motor car, new clothes) represent a luxury with which her austere respectability cannot cope. The trappings of affluence often evoked a sense of prodigality in working-class women at this time, but as Richard Holt has noted, there was an additional fear for Mrs Hammond – that is, these things lowered her to the position of a 'kept woman'.[19] At a critical point in their relationship, this issue crops up and Machin expresses his frustration in violence: 'I cracked her hard across the face' (143). This becomes further proof to her that his attentions are nothing other than a means of fulfilling his own emotional desires, another facet of acting big. When Machin suggests that his material gifts give her and her children pleasure, she explodes

19    Richard Holt, 'Men and Rugby in the North: David Storey's *The Changing Room* and *This Sporting Life*', *Northern Review*, 4 (1996), 115–23.

into a tirade that has more than a suggestion of dissatisfaction with the empty slogans of contemporary politics[20]:

> Pleasure, pleasure, pleasure! You say pleasure! You standing over us! Like a bloody lord and master [...] You made us enjoy anything we ever had. You made us. (176)

Mrs Hammond spirals into depression and, like her husband before her, loses the will to live. 'I've every reason to believe she wants to die' says the doctor treating her (232). The object of Machin's quest has eluded his grasp. Or as Machin himself puts it on another occasion, 'I felt like a big ape given something precious to hold, but only squashing it in my big, clumsy, useless hands' (162). In a striking scene in the film, Anderson represents Machin's loss in a wordless but visually powerful image in which the actor Richard Harris, framed in Mrs. Hammond's small house, becomes ape-like, painfully attempting to break out of the cage in which he is imprisoned, unable to find the emotional contact he desires.

## 4

There are two aspects of Storey's work to emphasis in conclusion. One concerns his engagement with the discourses of decline and modernization. Here, the novel's strength lies in the critique it offers of 1950s ideas of masculinity and gender relations. It was a time of some softening of old attitudes that generated a vision of a more domesticated male. Equally, however, many women felt marginalized by contemporary notions of domesticity, which also became a target

---

20    The principal Conservative theme in the British general election of 1959 was 'You've never had it so good,' attributed to the prime minister of the day, Harold Macmillan. It encouraged the electorate to return the Conservatives to power with the promise of continuing the material prosperity enjoyed in the previous few years.

of hate for some 'angry young men'.[21] Moreover, there was much about gender that remained in the sediment of 'common sense', and it is remarkable how little the issue of gender figured in political debate of either right or left. Storey's novel probes questions of masculinity, its idealization through sport, men's visions of women, and the plight of the woman as mother in an unusually sensitive and perceptive way. Mrs Hammond, the character through which most of these matters are raised, is both a more central and a more finely drawn one than we find in Storey's social realist contemporaries. By contrasting Mrs Hammond with the images of women drawn from the fictional writing which forms Machin's daily reading matter, Storey points up Machin's powerlessness to deal with real gender relations and, thus, perhaps the failure of men in general to influence this aspect of social relations. There is a sense that men are simply victims of a their own cultural construction, but at the same time, in Machin's growing self-awareness and reflexivity, there is also a suggestion that change might come through the awakening of the individual.

The other aspect is methodological. Texts like *This Sporting Life* tend to be approached as touchstones of particular ideas, movements, and epochs when used by sociologists and social historians.[22] They are, however, often wary of placing too much credence on 'unreliable' imaginative literature and, conventionally, seek to 'test' the fiction's value as a historical source by measuring its verisimilitude against the actual historical record. Quite apart from the question posed by some nowadays[23] of just what the 'actual historical record' might amount to,

21    Lynne Segal, 'Look Back In Anger: Men in the Fifties', in Rowena Chapman and Jonathan Rutherford eds. *Male Order: Unwrapping Masculinity* (London: Lawrence and Wishart, 1988), pp. 68–96.

22    Colin Griffin's interesting and penetrative analysis of proletarian fiction provides a good example of the historian's conventional approach to creative literature. He tends to see the literary creation as an "expression" of the author's "experiences." (Colin Griffin, 'The Means-Test Man Revisited: Proletarian Writers and the Social Psychology of Unemployment in the Nottinghamshire-Derbyshire Coalfield in the 1930s' *Transactions of the Thoroton Society of Nottinghamshire*, XCIX (1995), 113–20.

23    See Alun Munslow, *Deconstructing History*. (London: Routledge, 1997).

68

there is also an assumption implicit in this approach of a hierarchy of value in historical sources: 'proper' sources at the top, 'fictional' accounts at the bottom. What has been discussed in this essay presents a challenge to this traditional thinking and attempts to restore to the novel in question not merely the attention that it merits but a methodological seriousness. At roughly the same time that David Storey was writing *This Sporting Life*, three sociologists were conducting an ethnographic study of a Yorkshire mining town that may have been the unnamed one of Storey's fiction. In fact, it was 'Ashton', the name which Dennis, Henriques, and Slaughter gave to Featherstone, a town chiefly known to outsiders by the renown of its rugby team. The study was not well received. Its conclusions were pessimistic ones, confounding the expectations of contemporaries about both the recently nationalized coal industry and the prospects for the material and spiritual life of the inhabitants of Britain's 'affluent society'. In particular, the authors of the study pointed to the cultural poverty of life in Ashton and especially to the way in which the domination of work and leisure by male employment brought oppression and exclusion to women. *Coal Is Our Life* was one of many studies carried out at this time into communities of different kinds.[24] They constitute a distinctive and keenly anthropological moment in the evolution of British sociology and represent a characteristic part of that discipline's contribution to the debate on modernization. The ethnographic work of Dennis, Henriques, and Slaughter, although it seeks an objective appraisal of life in a working-class community, complements Storey's imaginative recreation of the same milieu and its cultural cage, converging with it to introduce a pessimistic critique about the nature of society. In this respect, both texts have their value as 'sources' for the period; neither one stands above or below the other. The literary text is not passive, a mere reflection of other social processes. It plays an active and important ideological role in the

---

24    A.H. Birch, *Small Town Politics* (Oxford: Oxford University Press, 1959); Margaret Stacey, *Tradition and Change: A Study of Banbury* (Oxford: Oxford University Press, 1960); P. Willmott and M.Young, *Family and Kinship in East London.* (London: Routledge Kegan Paul., 1957).

creation of the entire social and cultural 'experience'. In this sense, *This Sporting Life* acts as a text that simultaneously exposes, in imaginative form, the ways in which masculinity is culturally constructed in society and contests the commonsense, everyday practice of being a man in a particular stratum of society.

The key device Storey employs to do this is sport. To what extent is the novel 'about sport'? It has been said of *This Sporting Life*, as of other fictions in which authors have deployed sport in a metaphoric role to deal with other issues, that it is not a novel about sport. Indeed, it was the very point agreed on at the outset by Anderson and Richard Harris in the making of the film. Although Harris was attracted by the rugby, 'neither he nor Anderson saw it as a film about sport'[25], and yet, it is in so many ways a film and a book about sport. It does not, of course, deal with the internal organization or the economics of sport; and the relationships that develop between sportsmen, although they figure to some extent, are not central to the narrative. Moreover, there is nothing here on sport to compare, for example, with George Eliot's detailed explication of tissue theory in medicine in *Middlemarch*.[26] But the novel is a reflection on cultural effects of sport and the ways in which sport is absolutely central to any understanding of masculinity in the society portrayed in the text. It is not about sport in any sense of documenting a sporting life, in the way that Brian Glanville portrayed the changes taking place in association football in the late 1950s and early 1960s.[27] What it does is to engage with its society, with the prevailing ideologies of the historical moment of the 1950s – in particular the discourses of class and gender. Sport gives *This Sporting Life* its distinctive, perhaps unique, position as a text that offers a critique of hegemonic heterosexual masculinity from the

---

25   Michael Feeny Callan, *Richard Harris:A Sporting Life* (London: Sidgwick and Jackson, 1990), p. 75. The point was affirmed by Anderson himself in an article written shortly after the film appeared. See Lindsay Anderson, *Never Apologise: the Collected Writings,* (ed. Paul Ryan, London: Plexus, 2004), pp. 90–98.
26   Carolyn Steedman, *Dust* (Manchester: Manchester University Press, 2002), pp. 99–100
27   Brian Glanville, *The Rise of Gerry Logan* (London: Martin Secker and Warburg, 1963), and see ch. 4.

point of view of a dominant heterosexual male. In this way, *This Sporting Life* attempts to strip bare sport's central place in the cultural construction of gender. It is a pessimistic text, offering the reader/ viewer nothing to be admired or valued. This is a mighty challenge to the orthodoxy of male working-class culture in this particular era. It explains why neither book nor film, for all the critical praise they received, elicited much popular affection. The film did not do well at the box office, despite its subject and the presence of well-known actors. The rugby-league authorities, moreover, were alarmed by the film's portrayal of the sport as brutal and disowned it.[28] Yet, the issues that Storey and Anderson subject to such caustic examination have not gone away with the passing of the particular historical circumstances that provide the context for Storey's narrative. Indeed, in some senses, they have become a stronger feature of contemporary global society. For example, with freedom of contract, commercial sponsorship, media fees, and the negotiating power of the sportsperson's agent, the opportunities for a small group of elite sportsmen and women to exploit the adulation they enjoy from their public seem boundless. Although contemporary hero worship might be moderated by new characteristics – the 'new man' persona, for example, of David Beckham or a new frankness about the dark side of the hero's life and a willingness to reform[29] - there is still much of the old masculinity around, and admiration essentially remains the response that the media constructions of heroes demand. It was this relationship between the admirer and the admired that David Storey was so anxious to explore and to dismiss. It is an aspect of the role of sport in society that academic analysis of sport – in other respects, so rich in recent years – has singularly failed to grapple with and that imaginative writing has

---

28    I am grateful to my colleague at De Montfort University, Dr. Tony Collins, for providing me with this information, which is drawn from the Rugby League archives.

29    Tony Adams, *Addicted*. (London: HarperCollins Willow, 1999); David Beckham, *My World* (London: Hodder and Stoughton, 2001); Elaine Showalter, 'They Think It's All Over' *New Statesman*, 12 August 2002, 24–6. See also Garry Whannel, 'Sport Stars, Narrativization and Masculinities' *Leisure Studies*, 18; 3 (1999), 249–63.

equally turned away from. The mysterious stranger at Slomer's funeral, musing on the impending changes to the town, notes the large crowds that 'wound up Market Street towards St. Teresa's […] "Just look at that," he said. "There won't be any more funerals where half the town lines the streets to watch the passing of a man they hardly knew […]" He flicked his gloved fingers. "We'll have a football team."' George Wade's retort, 'And thank God for that (229)', is perhaps the sentiment of the common man. The implication is: what is wrong with football, its heroes, and its values? They give the place a focus and an identity. But the response might equally well be: what is right with them and what kind of future do they offer to anybody? Modernizing Britain, it is implied, is a project that requires changes to many things, not least of which are the assumptions and relationships ingrained in sport.

# Chapter Four
## 'You are up against mean, small-minded men': Brian Glanville's *The Rise of Gerry Logan*

'The central character, Gerry himself, was a Scottish inside forward, based [...] on Danny Blanchflower [...] the footballer had to be untypically intelligent, as well as an accomplished performer.'[1]

Looking back in his autobiography *Football Memories* on some fifty years of involvement with the game, the football writer Brian Glanville recalls much pleasure mixed with some regrets. The pleasure is largely in the game itself, at both the recreational level, where Glanville himself played for many years, and at its very highest peak of performance, where he had long experience of reporting. Among the regrets is a persistent sense of disappointment with British football: always in need of reform, never quite achieving it, never quite discarding a parochialism born of being 'first in the field'. Above all Glanville regrets the game's continuing working-class associations, exemplified in its players, managers, and supporters, at their most distasteful when supporting England in the late-twentieth century. 'An alienated underclass that could express itself only through violence. A miserably untalented subspecies.'[2] In company with this there is a contempt for the way the game was run. For many years after it first developed as a modern sport in the 1880s control of professional football was vested in small-minded businessmen whose vision was circumscribed by their own ambitions and jealousies.[3] For

1    Brian Glanville, *Football Memories* (London: Virgin Publishing, 1999), p. 170.
2    Ibid., p. 265.
3    See the view of another 'moderniser' – Alan Hardaker, secretary of the Football League during a period of immense change (1957–77) – in Alan Hardaker, *Hardaker of the League* (London: Pelham Books, 1977), esp. ch. 9 where he

a game he clearly loves Glanville seems to have reserved a residual snobbishness.


# 1


Where it originates is difficult to place; in part perhaps from his own middle-class, public-school background, and in part from his early career as a sportswriter.[4] This took him to Italy at a time in life when many of his contemporaries were going off to university. It gave him a cosmopolitan vision from which British football always looked insular. He reserved a particular contempt for some sections of the newspaper press, and deplored the fact that British writing on sport lacked the quality to be found in America. Several examples were to be found there of writers who bridged journalism and serious fiction.[5] This was Glanville's purpose, to establish a style ('idiom') that would embrace a readership broader than that of the stereotyped British tabloid press. He built up an impressive portfolio of football reporting during the 1950s and also found time to write fiction – to create an 'idiom' lacking in British writing. His first novel, *The Reluctant Dictator*, was published in 1952, and in 1956 a novel set in Florence – *Along the Arno* – which was 'somehow a sad novel for a young man to have

ascribes the failure of his modernising scheme 'The Pattern of Football' to the 'selfishness and shallow thinking' of club directors (p. 97).

4    It is interesting to compare Glanville's reminiscences with the rosy nostalgia of the older and also public school-educated Geoffrey Green, the association football correspondent of the *Times;* see *Pardon Me For Living* (London: George Allen and Unwin, 1985). See also Brian Glanville, *People in Sport* (London: Secker and Warburg, 1967).

5    See Glanville, *People in Sport*, pp. 15–28. He instanced Red Smith, Damon Runyan, A.J. Liebling and Ring Lardner as writers capable of finding an 'idiom' which reached all types of readers. 'British sports journalism is still looking for an idiom … still waiting for the columnist who can be read by intellectuals without shame and by working men without labour.' (p. 15).

written', according to the review in the *Times*.[6] His journalism came increasingly to reflect on the state of the game. In *Soccer Nemesis*, written in the aftermath of heavy defeats of both England and Scotland by overseas opponents between 1953 and 1955, he expressed a low opinion of the management of the British game, especially for its reaction to the defeat by Hungary in 1953. 'Never was the inadequacy of most British managers and directors better illustrated than by the way they now reacted. It was at once decided that British footballers had been surpassed – the self-abasement was sudden and extraordinary – because they did not do enough training [...] [t]he reflection that what was wrong with British training, and had been wrong for years, was its quality rather than its excessive quantity scarcely occurred to anyone.'[7] It is an outlook that colours his first novel on sport (arguably the finest of his fictional writings), *The Rise of Gerry Logan* (1963).

Glanville's coming of age as a sportswriter coincided with a time of apparent decline in British sporting achievement. This in itself was just one aspect of a perceived decline of Britain in the world generally. The 1950s brought a mixture of fortunes on the athletic field. On the one hand there were national triumphs such as the ascent of Everest and the recovery of the cricket Ashes, both of which occurred to the accompaniment of much triumphalism in 1953. They were followed within the year by Roger Bannister's achieving the first sub-four-minute mile.[8] It was also a period of success in middle-distance running; the names of Pirie, Chataway, Ibbotson and Johnson gave Britain prominence on the world athletics stage. But as against this there was dismal failure to record. In the 1952 summer Olympics, for example, only one gold medal was won (in show jumping) whilst performances by British competitors in the 1956 Games were only marginally better. Worse still was the seemingly sudden decline of British soccer. This was the more difficult to comprehend for fans

---

6    *The Times*, 9 August 1956, 9.
7    Brian Glanville, *Soccer Nemesis* (London 1955), p. 182.
8    See John Bale, *Roger Bannister and the Four-Minute Mile* (London: Routledge, 2004).

encouraged to believe through the sports pages of their newspapers that the English and Scots were the world 'masters' of the game. Defeats at home for both England (1953) and Scotland (1954) by Hungary, and the results of British teams in all three World Cup competitions during the decade disposed of that particular myth. The standard of British play against foreign opposition was often mediocre, and on occasions, as in England's 1-0 defeat by the USA in 1950, or Scotland's 7-0 defeat by Uruguay in the 1954 World Cup finals, the experience was nothing less than humiliating.[9] The sense of decline in sport chimed with a growing mood of pessimism among the nation's opinion formers about Britain's ability to compete with its main rivals in more important areas of life. The late 1950s and early 1960s produced an intensifying self-doubt about economic performance, business efficiency and the level of professional competency in public affairs which created calls for 'modernisation'. The application by the British government to join the burgeoning EEC in 1962 was perhaps the most dynamic response to all this, and the application's summary rejection at the insistence of the French was all the more disillusioning.

In sport and leisure these developments were reflected in the response of the Central Council of Physical Recreation (CCPR), the only truly 'national' organisation representing British sport at that time. In late 1957 the Council set up a committee chaired by Sir John Wolfenden, Vice-Chancellor of Reading University, to inquire into a broad area of sport, games and outdoor activities. Its brief was 'to make recommendations to the CCPR as to any practical measures which should be taken by statutory or voluntary bodies in order that these activities may play their full part in promoting the general welfare of the community'. The Wolfenden Committee's report, published in 1960, was, in the words of one commentator, 'a watershed in the development of sport policy'.[10] Its main recommendation was

---

9    The exception was the remarkable performance in the 1958 World Cup of Northern Ireland, with an unusually good side built around Gregg, Blanchflower, McIlroy and MacParland.

10   Barrie Houlihan, *The Government and Politics of Sport* (London: Routledge, 1991), p. 87. For the Wolfenden report itself see Central Council of Physical Recreation, *Sport and the Community* (CCPR: London, 1960).

for the setting up of a Sports Development Council, which eventually became reality in 1965 with the creation of the Sports Council, an organisation that has strongly influenced public policy on sport ever since. But important as this was, it should be recalled that Wolfenden ranged over a number of other issues and its tone revealed much about the state of thinking on sport and leisure in the late 1950s. The central concern of the committee was 'the general welfare of the community', and was informed by a familiar idea of the 1950s that although leisure time had increased it was not always being put to good use. For example, much emphasis was placed on 'the Gap' (so-called), which occurred when young people left sports participation at school and did not immediately continue in adult sporting organisations. On this Wolfenden's concerns, prompted in part by the expected ending of national service, tied in closely with those explored at the same time by the Albemarle Committee[11] with a link between the youth service and the various bodies responsible for sports and games being suggested. In other respects Wolfenden's position reflected many of the views about the function of sport in society that had emerged from the schools – especially the public schools: that sport was a basic human need, that it promoted health, that it encouraged admirable qualities of self-discipline, endurance, self-reliance and determination, and that it might also inculcate moral and aesthetic sensibilities through 'sportsmanship' and the appreciation of 'the poetry of motion'.

Wolfenden linked sport firmly with modernisation, and Glanville's football novel is part of this same discourse. It was published at a critical point in time; not only was Britain's position in the world at large the subject of intense debate, but the nature of professional football in England was itself undergoing important changes. Two events in particular had profound repercussions. In 1961 the maximum wage system, which had been in existence since the 1890s and which had pegged players' earnings to a point a little above those of skilled workers, came to an end. A short while later, in 1963, the equally longstanding 'retain and transfer' arrangements, which had effectively

---

11    Ministry of Education, *The Youth Service in England and Wales* (London: HMSO, 1960).

restricted labour mobility by giving to the clubs the right to decide when a player could change his employer, were also terminated.[12] Significantly, 'retain and transfer' was held in the law court to be 'in restraint of trade'.[13] These changes, which came about as a result of campaigns by a labour force which was both better organised and more astutely led than in the past, were also influenced by a keener awareness of the state of football overseas. The closed mentality that the British game had possessed for over half a century was being exposed to new practices, commercial and tactical, from continental Europe and South America. They brought a realisation that other countries organised the game of football differently and played it better. There was much to learn from them. The defeat of England by Hungary at Wembley in 1953 was the singular event which had begun the process of awakening, in which the 'masters' were now 'pupils'.[14]

## 2

As in David Storey's novel, Glanville in *The Rise of Gerry Logan* (1963) covers a phase in the life of a sportsman – in this case a professional association footballer.[15] It tells the story of a man's rise, through a combination of exceptional football skills and an unusual

---

12    See Dave Russell, *Football and the English: A Social History of Association Football in England 1863–1995,* (Carnegie Press: Preston 1997), chs 6 and 7.
13    The legal challenge to the retain-and-transfer system was made by the Newcastle United player George Eastham. With the support of the Professional Footballers' Association Eastham won the right to transfer to Arsenal. See George Eastham, *Determined to Win* (London: Sportsman's Book Club, 1966).
14    See Tony Mason, '"I doubt if they will lose at all": Looking Back On England versus Hungary 1953'; Peter J. Beck, 'Losing Prestige On and Off the Field'; England versus Hungary 1953–54'; Ronald Kowalski and Dilwyn Porter, 'England's World Turned Upside Down? Magical Magyars and British Football'; and Jeffrey Hill, 'Narratives of the Nation: the Newspaper Press and England v. Hungary, 1953' in *Sport in History*, 23; 2 (winter 2003–04), 1–60.
15    All references are from the Hodder Paperback edition, London, 1970.

perceptiveness and determination, from the working-class districts of Glasgow to international football fame. The story is a fragmented one, told by turn from the perspective of the leading characters – Logan himself, his wife Mary, fellow players and managers, and the detached observer Brian, a figure clearly based on the author himself. The timescale of the narrative is indeterminate, loosely covering the period from the late 1940s to the early 1960s, and only a few clues are offered to locate the observant reader more precisely within this era. Whilst only lightly 'historical', therefore, *The Rise of Gerry Logan* nonetheless deals with a time of profound importance in the development of British football, and works dramatically to convey a feeling of impending change. It is a story of a quest – both personal and institutional – that is only partially fulfilled at the novel's end, where the reader is left uncertain as to what the future holds and where doubt is cast on any lingering notion of 'progress'.

Logan aspires not only to improve himself as a player, and thereby to acquire material rewards and adulation, but to *understand* the game, to treat it as an intellectual challenge, something to be worked upon, studied, and developed, rather than a job to be performed according to established conventions grown increasingly weary and outmoded. The novel's opening passage, written from the perspective of the (as yet unnamed) observer establishes Logan's *difference*:

> It was the openness of the face that struck me most, more even that its intelligence. Openness, in the sense of wanting to know, was what really set it apart from all the other faces in that dressing-room. They were heavier, of course, hadn't the same friendliness, the unexpected welcome, but above all, they were closed, they didn't aspire. They knew what they knew, and that was enough; they knew it at twenty-five, which was *his* age, they'd know it at thirty-five, and they'd know it still - no more, no less, at forty five. (9)

Logan is plainly both intelligent and ambitious. He seeks change and improvement for himself and for the knowledge he professes, and he possesses a cold single-mindedness which permits him to focus on his objectives. Though Scottish he appears to lack any strong sense of regional pride, as if this form of identity is a legacy of the past that he must discard if he is to progress. For Logan Scotland is intimately associated with economic depression and the banal sentimentality of working-class masculinity. He shares with his mother a revulsion for it.

> He [Logan's father] was proud of it, but it never meant a thing to me, and as for my mother she came from a village in Renfrewshire and she'd always hated the whole city. Glasgow to her meant a hard life and ugliness and unemployment and drunkenness and for me she wanted something different. (22)

He despises the provincialism that was the distinguishing feature of British football culture, and sees first London and then Europe as the focal point of his universe.

Gerry Logan also sees football in Britain as being in the grip of small-minded and selfish individuals whose vanity is fed by the petty authority they wield. This comes to the fore when he is transferred to a leading metropolitan club and encounters directors who through an irrational combination of jealousy and spite work to undermine the position of an intelligent and far-sighted manager; 'I knew they were full of their own importance, I knew they liked interfering, I knew they were mean, I knew they'd ponce on the club for everything they could get, especially in bottles. What I didn't know was the lengths they'd go, not when we were losing, but when we were *winning*' (54). Above all is the feeling that professional football is a trade consigned by social and intellectual snobberies to a lowly position in the hierarchy of British sport. Comparing the position the game enjoyed in Italy Logan claims: 'In Britain, soccer was something for the peasants; playing cricket for money was just about all right, but if it was football you played, people turned their noses up at you' (136).

In this respect Logan embodies the forces of change and the novel's feeling for history. But, in spite of his innate intelligence and a thirst for knowledge and understanding, he is a cold, unemotional character, self-obsessed and unable to sustain relationships. His story is in a certain respect the story of the slow dissolution of his marriage to Mary, a tolerant, conservative woman whom he has rescued from an earlier unhappy marriage. She bears Logan two children and follows him from club to club through his playing career until eventually her patience gives way. He has treated her with little affection, and when she discovers what she has long suspected – that her husband is having an affair with a singer – she leaves him. This central theme in the story ensures that Logan arouses little sympathy from the reader, and his ambitions similarly draw a cool response, embodied in the detached observations of the newspaper reporter Brian, the voice of common sense.


# 3


At the centre of the novel is Italy. Logan's search for improvement brings him into contact with continental Europe, just as Britain's modernising project led to application for membership of the Common Market. To a great extent the novel deals in the problem of assimilating the outside world to Britain's new post-imperial status. Europe – at least western Europe – had become a counterpoise to America in a new world order. Italy acquired a reputation for smartness and 'chic' in clothes, cars and food, the epitome of a 'cool' Continental style.[16] Through Logan Glanville provides a further narrative to those already being told in the early 1960s about the experiences of real-life footballers who had migrated to Italy in the footsteps of Eddie Firmani and John Charles. Firmani was transferred from Charlton Athletic to Sampdoria (Genoa) in 1956, and in the following year Charles, a player of greater renown, left Leeds United to play for Juventus (Turin). The terms of Charles's contract with Juventus were, by British standards of the day, extremely lucrative, and prompted *The Times* to offer the prescient observation that 'it may one day prove a lever to greater incentives and rewards for the footballer at home'.[17] Charles's experience in Italy was, according to most accounts, relatively happy and successful. He was remembered

16    Dick Hebdige, 'Towards a Cartography of Taste 1935–1962', in B. Waites, T. Bennett and G. Martin eds, *Popular Culture: Past and Present* (London: Croom Helm, 1982), ch. 9.
17    20 April 1957.

warmly in Italy for many years afterwards as a skilful and effective player, as well as a courteous man.[18] Far less satisfying were the experiences of those who followed his example. Jimmy Greaves, Denis Law and Joe Baker – all celebrated players in Britain – adjusted to neither the football conditions nor the cultural life of Italy. The brief time they spent in the country in the early 1960s was unsettling and bitter. Theirs was a story told from a traditional British perspective of the dangers to be encountered 'abroad'. Greaves, for example, had attempted to withdraw from his contract with Milan before even moving to Italy, though the attractions of the money he was to earn there ('the lure of the lira') eventually prevailed. His stay of only four months was one dominated by stories of stifling, defensive football and ruthless club discipline, against both of which Greaves the ingénue 'natural' instinctively rebelled. 'I quickly discovered that they treat footballers like schoolchildren in Italy'.[19] Greaves, who later confessed to alcoholism, was to date its onset from his time in Italy.[20] A resolution of these problems was found in a return to the 'normality' of the British game after the strange customs of a foreign land.[21]

18  See the obituary by Glanville in the *Guardian*, 23 February 2004, 32. The same was true of the Aston Villa centre forward Gerry Hitchens, who played in both Milan and Turin in the 1960s. Hitchens's stoical approach to Italian football – 'they pay me well, I do my best; I can't do any more' – endeared him to both fans and reporters. (Brian Glanville, 'Shropshire Lad in Turin', *New Statesman*, 14 December 1962, 15.) John Charles (with Bob Harris), *King John; The Autobiography* (London: Headline Book Publishing, 2003) was written shortly before the author's death; it emphasizes the wealth surrounding Italian football culture at the top level, but is complimentary about the game and its administrators. Looking back Charles harboured no grudges, even though his own marriage foundered during his time in Italy.
19  Jimmy Greaves and Reg Gutteridge, *Let's Be Honest* (Sportsman's Book Club, Newton Abbot, 1973), p. 62.
20  Jimmy Greaves, *This One's On Me* (Readers Union, Newton Abbot, 1979), p. 14.
21  Little had changed almost 30 years later when Ian Rush spent an unhappy season in Turin with Juventus. See Ian Rush, *My Italian Diary* (with an introduction by Brian Glanville. London: Arthur Barker, 1989), which includes an interesting chapter by Rush's wife. She claimed that, in spite of all the difficulties the couple faced in Italy, it had been a learning experience if only

Glanville knew the world of Italian football and portrays it in a far from complimentary image. To anyone nurtured in the ways of British football Italy was a febrile system. Even the resilient Logan admits: 'I think in those early months I'd have gone home, if it wasn't for the travelling' (132). He consoles himself with the belief that he is broadening his mind. Italian football at this time represented for aspiring footballers what the country's past had meant for eighteenth-century travellers on the Grand Tour: the opportunity to witness the pinnacle of human artistic achievement. In the contemporary case, however, it was not the fulfilling spiritual experience of the Grand Tour so much as a coming to terms with a rigid commercialism that might signal the future. It was in Italy that the game of football had developed to its fullest extent in Europe. It was the first country to import talent from elsewhere on a systematic basis, and the first country fully to explore the commercial (as against professional) aspects of the sport. This produced, however, a football culture of regional loyalties and personal feuds, fed by a voracious and fickle press. Its club politics combined a Machiavellian ruthlessness with echoes of the fascist past. Commercialism was epitomised in the notorious *catenaccio* style of play (originally devised in Switzerland as the 'verrou' form of defensive play) which inspired a fear of losing: 'all was caution and destruction', says Brian, 'the one unforgiveable sin, defeat' (110). Indeed fear – of crowds by referees, of club presidents by players, of their rivals by club presidents, and of the press by almost everyone – seems the abiding sentiment. All of this reaches its apotheosis in Rome, to where Logan is transferred by his English club, much to Brian's dismay. He describes the place as 'a beautiful old whore', 'a surrealist city' which would, he opines, 'fascinate [Gerry], but I wondered if it might not also destroy him'

because it made them realise how good a place Britain was (p. 146). Greaves's problem with drink also afflicted the talented Swedish footballer Lennart 'Nacka' Skoglund, who played with great success in Italy for ten years. (See Niels Kayser Nielsen, '"Nacka" Skoglund: a Swedish Soccer Player as a Welfare-Nationalistic Myth' in J. Bale, M.K. Christensen and G. Pfister eds, *Writing Lives in Sport: Biographies, Life-Histories and Methods* (Aarhus: Aarhus University Press, 2004), pp. 179–89.

(100). His arrival at the airport sees him physically drawn into the vortex of Italian football life:

> Gerry was borne away from me in the throng of vice-presidents, directors, clamorous hangers-on; among them gleamed the Cyclops monocle of Vice President Guadenzio, Bacchanalian as ever, all things to all men. As they swept him off, Gerry cast a glance at me over his shoulder, in apology and mock-appeal. His whole predicament in Rome was summed up by this moment; how little one could do to help him. (103)

In Rome Logan discovers that his club has little chance of big success. Many of the players are of a mediocre standard, and much depends on his own efforts on the field. Although he adapts well to the different routines and rhythms of Italian football, and works at learning the language, there are matters outside his control that influence his fate. These relate largely to the power relationships within the club, and particularly to the enmity that exists between the president, who has been the inspiration behind the acquisition of Logan, and one of the vice-presidents, Montico, who is challenging for power. In some respects the situation is one that Logan has encountered before in the dissembling of the directors at his previous club. Italian methods are far more unscrupulous, however; as Logan himself admits '[b]y comparison, Pyke and Dawson at Chiswick had been amateurs' (145). In the hope of discrediting the president, Montico works to secure Logan's failure. The more Logan fails on the pitch, and the more the club's fortunes will decline, and the greater will be Montico's chances of achieving his goal. 'He'll try to create a climate', says one experienced Roman observer, 'in which Logan *can't* succeed. Through the *consiglio direttiva*, through the other players, above all through the newspapers. Warn Logan to be careful' (124). Logan is too perceptive to be unaware of such manoeuvrings, but wrapped up as he is in football matters, he fails to see the trap set for him. It involves a scandal with a young, publicity-seeking actress, with whom Logan is photographed in a nightclub. The story provokes a storm of moral outrage. Brian's fellow reporters in the newspaper office gather around to pour scorn:

> "*Ecco il tuo Loggan!* Now we can see what he is! *Un donnaiolo!* A womaniser! *Un bel pezzo di mascalzone!*" and from every corner they came crowding;

Mengalvio, in shirtsleeves, Franzini, the little Fascist, Campello, strutting like a peacock; the boxing editor, the Third Division football correspondent, flocking round me to savour the moment of truth, the recognition, the unmasking of a charlatan, grinning, eager to confront me with his perfidy. (157)

Even Brian acknowledges a certain disappointment, 'as if I had been proved right when I was still hoping to be proved wrong; as if something still remained of the schoolboy hero-worship; the footballer hero who didn't smoke, didn't drink, and was happily, sexlessly, married' (158). The affair, whilst it is responsible for Logan's departure from Rome, brings to the fore flaws in Logan's character which have previously been only partially revealed.

His self-obsession, together with his suspicion of domesticity, creates a growing gulf with his wife. The scandal brings this to a point where she threatens to leave him. For Mary, Rome has meant nothing more than an enclosed and marginal existence as a soccer wife in a charmless masculine world. 'As for the men, they made me sick, it was their conceit that really got me, they seemed to think they'd only got to look at any woman - even the ugliest of them - and she'd fall into bed with them, she'd be so flattered' (171). Though this is not a world to which Logan himself warms it is one that nourishes his ambitions. Italian football has none of the working-class conventions of Britain. '... in Italy', says Logan, 'a footballer was a sort of hero to everyone, not just the working classes – everybody. Trastevere [his club] had supporters who were princes and millionaires and actors and writers, and when you met them, it was very stimulating ... you felt you were giving them something, at the same time they were giving something to you' (136). Mary begins to recognise her husband's growing vanity, his belief that his innate wit and sharpness can be put to effect in a post-football career as a media star. In her conventional way she fears for a future based on pretence, on the 'daydreams I knew he had of not being just a footballer, but being a great writer and a great intellectual as well. Gerry was very intelligent and clever, but because he was so eloquent, he could make people think he was cleverer than he was. But he couldn't keep up with them, he hadn't the education, and I was afraid he would overreach himself' (171). It is in the hope of restoring his relationship with Mary that Logan seeks a transfer to Milan, where he plays for a further two years, for a different club, before returning to England. But the inevitable rift is only delayed.

Logan, in contrast to Mary and her rejection of the whole experience, believes that Italy has made him into a better and wiser person who is able to see things in a new way. As Logan's career develops into a further phase of football success with his new English club the story clarifies the contrast between Mary's conservatism and Logan's embracing of change and the exploration of new horizons. Logan represents the new breed of footballer, determined to escape the life that had beckoned his predecessors after retirement, in which even for famous players there were limited opportunities: remain within football as a manager, have a ghost-written column for the national press, become a small businessman, shopkeeper or publican. Danny Blanchflower, upon whom the character of Logan was modelled, succeeded for a time in creating a new position, as a writer for the *Observer*. In some ways Logan's ambitions are to be admired for their questioning of tradition and the search for new experiences. Mary's narrative, however, provides a critical perspective on this emerging world where she sees shallowness and false values prevailing. The gradual dissolution and eventual bitter ending of the marriage can be seen not only as the divergence of two lives but of different systems of values.

The return to Britain takes Logan to London, to a club (Borough) with a proud history. 'They were like the aristocrats of football' (178). His career begins to develop outside football. Not surprisingly, perhaps, the media, and the ways in which the world is *represented*, come to occupy a prominent place in the story. The media, once seen by Logan as peopled by smug press journalists with inflated reputations and local reporters whose dependence on the clubs has been too close to allow for criticism, now has a new branch: television. This was the medium so skilfully exploited by the footballers' trade union in its campaign for reform in the early 1960s.[22] Glanville's portrayal, however, gives it another, less benign aspect. In Professor

---

22   See Jimmy Hill, *Striking for Soccer* (London: Sportsman's Book Club, 1963).

Hodgkinson, a philosopher who appears on the programme 'The Brains Trust', and who befriends Logan, there is a hint of the logical positivist A.J. Ayer, who at this time had declared his love of football and his loyalty to Tottenham Hotspur. There is a sense in this of middle-class intellectual patronage of the working-class man, taken up by the world of entertainment so long as he suits its purposes. Through his contacts in the press Logan finds his way into television. But he is unaware of the way he is being used, and persuades himself that he is a good performer (186). 'I got a lot of letters through being on the television, and I had an impression I was building up a following, which was something I liked, because when I made these appearances, I didn't feel I was just standing for myself, I was representing all the *other* professional footballers.' (186) He is presented on arts programmes as the voice of common sense. Logan feels that he is making a statement about a profession previously subjected to snobbery – 'I wanted to show the public we weren't just morons, with our brains in our boots' (186). Like virtually all professional footballers of this (or any other) era Logan possessed little in the way of formal education, though the fact that he has an enquiring mind, and has actually *read* something marks him out for television producers as a new form of working-class autodidact. From a different perspective, however, his performances seem commonplace, dependent on a few banal clichés drawn from a limited reading of Ernest Hemingway and an insistence on portraying football as his university of life. His utterances are an embarrassment to those not blinded by the medium's glare. The dispassionate Brian voices his scepticism of Logan's belief in his new-found status: 'Could one really be right while everyone else was wrong, crying the Emperor's Clothes?' (198). Logan's wife, Mary, is more direct: '... the more famous he got, the less I admired him. When I saw him on the television, giving out his ideas on this, giving out his ideas on the other, I wanted to shout at them all, "Can't you see through him? How can you let him take you in?"' (217)[23]

---

23    Danny Blanchflower, Glanville's model for Logan, had appeared on the *Face to Face* programme on BBC television, interviewed by John Freeman, in March 1962. The programme was dismissed by Arthur Calder-Marshall in his review

Mary Logan, who has tried to provide decency and good sense in Logan's life, is rejected. Gerry has never shown much feeling for his wife, and has been distant from his children. The domesticity that binds families together has never had much purchase in Logan's psyche, and now that he has convinced himself that he is an artist needing freedom to express himself family ties seem all the more like shackles. Mary finally leaves him and agrees to a divorce. She 'with her insights and her bitterness, her righteous grievance' (249) quietly disappears back to the provinces, while Logan consolidates a longstanding relationship with a woman from the world of entertainment. She, as befits her job as a stage performer, is inscrutable behind surface smiles and cosmetics – 'show-business gloss' as Brian describes it (248). Her partnership with Logan seems to possess all the emotion of a business venture. It symbolises the new alliance that football itself is about to forge with the media.

# 4

In his discussion of media sport stars Garry Whannel draws attention to the narrative form of this novel, noting that Glanville 'mimics the form of the rise-and-fall biography'.[24] There is no doubt that Glanville draws upon a variety of contemporary non-fictional techniques of representation, but the effect of this amalgam is to create a far from conventional narrative. The fiction becomes both a condition of and at the same time a challenge to the methods of story-telling that are a major part of sport discourse. The use of biographical reporting, as in the telling of Logan's life story, gives Glanville's text a verisimilitude

in *The Listener* as a way of bringing in new viewers. 'This amiable Ulsterman had nothing to say to me that mattered much', wrote Calder-Marshall, adding with obvious irony, 'the Captain of Spurs sat in the same seat as C.G. Jung and Dame Edith Sitwell.' (22 March 1962, 528)

24  Garry Whannel, *Media Sports Stars: Masculinities and Moralities* (London: Routledge, 2002), p. 62.

88

which adds to its intended social realism. There is a near-documentary approach to the reconstruction of the world of sport[25] evident most plainly in the reportage of the various voices that tell the story of Logan's career. Glanville's placing of himself – a real person – as a character in the story is the most extreme form of this striving for authenticity. Moreover, Actual footballers are introduced into the narrative – Alfredo Di Stefano, for example, is one of Logan's opponents in the climactic European Cup final which Borough narrowly lose – and there are many other references in the text to similar figures. The fictional world is furthermore reinforced by a 'real world' of football. This might be regarded as a flawed dramatic technique but it is highly effective in establishing the character of Logan as an outstanding player who had achieved his position through skill and sportsmanship. Equally, however, the voices are presented in an overlapping chronology, and the absence of a unified authorial narrative introduces conflicting interpretations and perspectives on the life in question. The autobiographical voice (Logan's) is only one of several, thus giving his version of events a critical counterpoint at each turn. This, in a sense, might be thought offer a more realistically 'truthful' account (and certainly a more taxing one for the reader) than the conventional biographical technique itself is capable of providing. It disturbs by posing questions, and asking ultimately what the 'truth' about Gerry Logan is.

Also, there is no 'fall' as such. The novel lacks an obvious denouement. Whereas Arthur Machin's laconic tale in *This Sporting Life* ends on a down beat – he is going nowhere and, as yet another match ends, 'I had my ankles strapped, got dressed, and put my teeth in' (253) – Logan refuses to accept the slow unwinding of a career. In what might be seen as a deluded attempt to deny the passing of time, he is still restlessly planning for new challenges, seeking to stretch out his playing days for a few more years, and dreaming of perpetuating his celebrity in television at the point when age eventually forces him to leave the game. The reader is left to imagine Logan's future, and to

---

25    The same 'realist' technique is evident in his later football novel *Goalkeepers are Different* (London: Hamish Hamilton, 1971).

take a view on the moral choices to be confronted. If 'fall', then, is largely absent 'rise' is undoubtedly central to the novel. It is, however, a process crucially treated with irony. There is achievement in abundance in football, especially in the match when Logan's club plays in the final of the European Cup – 'it seemed to me the climax of my whole career' (234). His ability and on-field demeanour are beyond question, evident to all, and these qualities more than equip him for conventional sporting heroism. Glanville, a working newspaper man in two countries, was familiar with the literary conventions used to construct sports stars in the media. At the time his novel was published the British press had traditionally assumed a respectful stance towards famous sportsmen, writing about them in the papers or in autobiographies (most of which were 'ghosted' by sport journalists) as figures to be admired. They were known by their deeds on the field of play. The strengths or weaknesses of their inner selves were left unexplored. Success in sport was held to be evidence of self-discipline and motivation, and successful players were presented to their reading public as models of virtue, according to accepted stereotypes such a 'working-class professional', 'amateur gentleman', and so forth.[26] It is, however, Glanville's purpose to explore the nature of this heroic status in fiction. Logan is beyond reproach as a hero in sport, but moral questions are posed about his life. What *value* has he derived from a life devoted to change and modernisation? What contribution has he made to other people's lives? The answers to these questions are less than satisfactory. As a man he is exposed as someone less than heroic. His self-obsession and single-mindedness might gain respect but will not claim the affection necessary to cast him, like the north-east's hero Jackie Milburn, as the 'good man'.[27] Rather, he is placed alongside other fictional creations of the period – Arthur Seaton and Arthur Machin, for example – for whom the term 'anti-hero' seems

26 See Whannel, *Media Sports Stars,* esp. chs 7–10. Sometimes the star was difficult to place in a category; see Jeffrey Hill, '"Brylcreem Boy": Inter-textual Signification in the Life of Denis Compton', in Bale, Christensen and Pfister, *Writing Lives in Sport*, pp. 171–78.
27 Richard Holt, 'The Legend of Jackie Milburn and the Life of Godfrey Brown', *Ibid.,* pp. 157–70.

the more appropriate designation. In this sense the novel raises questions about the portrayal of sportsmen in the popular media.

His status is further brought into question by the transition Logan seeks to make. What distinguishes the character as a moderniser – his desire to remove from football the aura of the 'working-man's game' and project himself and the sport in a new guise – simultaneously raises doubts about what modernity will bring. In this novel Glanville captures, through Logan's experiences, the dissolution of an old regime, a slow fragmentation of a traditional culture – the culture of a nation, perhaps, as much as the culture of a sport – taking place under essentially foreign pressures. There is also present in the text a strong sense, though it is suggested rather than defined, of a new order about to come. It is symbolised in the removal from the narrative of Mary, who has provided its moral centre. Without her a rootless and possibly amoral future beckons. In this respect the novel shares with many of the sociological studies of 1950s Britain a sense of unease about the effects of change. [28] Glanville's critique of all this is sharp, but ambivalent. He has few regrets about the passing of the old ways, but neither does he embrace the inchoate new world. If the small-minded men who have controlled the semi-commercial capitalist era of football are swept away in the changes to come in football, so much the better. But if they are to be replaced by self-sustaining egotists like Logan, who trade their sporting heroism for a spurious kind of celebrity, the future will be one of dubious worth. In the end, it seems, Glanville almost develops a nostalgia for the system he has begun his novel by attacking.

---

28    See, for example, N. Dennis, F. Henriques and C. Slaughter, *Coal Is Our Life: An Analysis of a Yorkshire Mining Community* London: Eyre and Spottiswoode, 1956); Richard Hoggart, *The Uses of Literacy: Aspects of Working-Class Life with Special Reference to Publications and Entertainment* (London: Chatto and Windus, 1957); M. Young and P. Wilmott, *Family and Kinship in East London* (London: Routledge and Kegan Paul, 1957).

# Chapter Five
# Men, 'A Boy's Game', and America: Richard Ford's *The Sportswriter* and Philip Roth's *American Pastoral*

It is often claimed that sport exercises a greater influence in the American imagination than it does in the European.[1] Sport's ability to combine the spirit of free enterprise with a striving for success is seen as giving it a central place in the notion of the American dream.[2] The routine observations of sports figures, usually renowned coaches, about the nature of sport have passed into the language as essential 'truths' about life: 'nice guys finish last' (Leo Durocher) or 'winning isn't everything – it's the only thing' (Vince Lombardi). Moreover, the deeper intrusion of a business ethos into many American sports has ensured, it is said, that they enter into the life of ordinary citizens more readily through the medium of radio, television and film than would be the case in a society where (as in Britain, for example) voluntary association has been a principal agency for sporting activity. Above all, perhaps, these influences have helped to nurture a male camaraderie, providing a common ground on which men may come together to define their gender.[3] Whatever doubts one might have about the validity of this thesis it certainly seems to be substantiated if viewed from the perspective of literature. The willingness of serious American writers to explore their chosen themes through the practices of sport has undoubtedly been greater than that of their European counterparts. As we shall see in this chapter the work of America's

---

1    Gordon Burn, 'The Games Writers Play', *Guardian Review,* October 2004, pp. 4–6. Burn argues that sport provides one of the great themes of the American novel.

2    Kenneth Millard, *Contemporary American Fiction* (Oxford: Oxford University Press, 2000), p. 200.

3    Ibid., pp. 200–03.

greatest living novelist, Philip Roth, is liberally referenced by allusions to sport. One of the most influential of American plays in the second-half of the twentieth century – Arthur Miller's *Death of a Salesman* – relies strongly on sport for its moral.[4] And through Scott Fitzgerald, Ring Lardner, Ernest Hemingway, Bernard Malamud, John Updike and Don DeLillo, sport has enjoyed a constant place in the most lauded reaches of American writing.

Of course, such easy assertions should not go unquestioned. The use of sport in fictional work is not necessarily an indication of anything other than that American literary culture, for any number of reasons, accepts the subject of sport more tolerantly than does the European.[5] In other words, it is perhaps a literary convention we are faced with here rather than any compelling social force. Until critics are prepared to explore a little further the cultural roots of sport in European societies, some of the contrasts drawn between America and Europe can only sustain provisional notions of the different role of sport in each place. A further consideration should also be noted, and this is the nature of the sport that is being registered through this literary activity. One of the effects of America's commitment to sport has been a strong sense of the country's sporting history.[6] As with all histories, what is deemed worthy of recording is a decision influenced by a range of essentially political judgements. Much of sport history, and not only in America, has been shaped by an assumption that the institutions that manage sport are the most important bodies in ensuring the continuity of the sports process; this in turn has produced histories which foreground some activities at the expense of others. Only relatively recently have some historians of sport fought free of these assumptions and adopted a view of sport 'from below', which in

4    See, for example, Frank Ardolino, 'Like Father, Like Sons: Miller's Negative Use of Sports Imagery in *Death of a Salesman*', *Journal of Evolutionary Psychology,* 25: 1–2 (March 2004), 32–39.
5    For a discussion of the place of sport in modern German literature see Allen Guttmann, 'Faustian Athletes? Sports as a Theme in Modern German Literature', *Modern Fiction Studies,* 33: 1 (Spring 1987), 21–34.
6    The world's oldest organisation devoted to the professional historical study of sport is the North American Society of Sport Historians (N.A.S.S.H.), founded in 1972.

its wake has brought new perspectives on the subject to include a greater emphasis on issues of gender, race, age and language.[7] There remains nonetheless a marked conservative force in the history of sport, evident for example in American male sport historians' devotion to the history of baseball.[8] One of the effects of such a trend is that sport itself becomes a symbol of a romanticized past in which certain things are remembered whilst others are written out of history. It was this aspect of history as public memory that Philip Roth in part challenged in *The Great American Novel* (1973), a surreal evocation of American baseball that features a sustained rant by the character Word Smith on how the official history of the game is constructed. In describing Smith's attempts to have the long-forgotten Patriot League and its players remembered Roth deliberately confounds fact and fiction (did the Patriot League ever actually exist, or is it a product of Roth's imagination?) to make a point about the processes of remembering.[9]

In the light of these precautionary observations, it is nonetheless significant that Don DeLillo, for example, begins his epic fictional appraisal of America in the second half of the twentieth century, *Underworld* (1997), with a baseball match. Nor is it just any baseball game, but the third of a three-game play-off between the Giants and the Dodgers for the championship pennant at New York's Polo Grounds. It is 3rd October 1951, the day of Bobby Thomson's famous home run off Ralph Branca's pitch to win the National League pennant for the Giants: 'the shot heard 'round the world'.[10] It is one of

7    See, for example, Douglas Booth's appraisal of the state of sport history in 'Escaping the Past? The Cultural Turn and Language in Sport History', *Rethinking History*, 8: 1 (March 2004), 103–25. It is worth noting, in terms of the emphasis given by historians to sport, that the sport most discussed by professional historians in Britain has been association football; virtually all the history written on this game in the past thirty years has been directed to *professional* football, a very small proportion of the whole, and scarcely any to amateur/recreational football.

8    The subject still occupies a leading (though possibly declining) position in the annual programme of NASSH.

9    See Richard Alan Schwarz, 'Postmodernist Baseball', *Modern Fiction Studies*, 33: 1 (Spring 1987), 135–49.

10   See Jules Tygel, *Past Time: Baseball as History* (New York: Oxford University Press, 2000), ch. 7.

the great baseball moments, and a portentous occasion in another sense, because it is the very day the Soviet Union exploded a nuclear bomb and a new era of international conflict began. From that day onwards hyperbole has been summoned up to memorialise the event. The distinguished anthropologist Marshall Sahlins, for example, has claimed that '[E]very red-blooded American baseball fan of a certain age remembers where he or she was when listening to the broadcast of Thomson's great feat – just as they remember the news of Pearl Harbor, the death of Franklin Roosevelt, the assassination of President Kennedy.'[11] The first hundred or so pages of DeLillo's novel are a marvellous evocation of the crowd at the Polo Grounds on the historic day; and the spectators around whom the narrative of the event is woven, and through whose eyes the match is seen, are of course male. Baseball is a focal point of their lives, capable of drawing together into one common interest a disparate range of souls, from Frank Sinatra to the urchin Cotter Martin, who makes off with the ball that Thomson has hit into the crowd.[12] Whatever their subsequent experience in life might be they have all shared in an event that has forged them into Americans through sport. 'Perhaps', adds Sahlins, 'we have underestimated sport the way we underestimate talk about the weather, as the integument of an otherwise divided and only imagined community.'[13]

Other American sports do not quite have baseball's capacity to unite. Athletics ('track and field' as the Americans refer to it), at which the nation has excelled, only periodically captures its collective gaze, usually at the time of the Olympic Games. Golf, in which the Americans also lead the world, is individualised; for most of the time its stars represent themselves as much as their country. American football, in spite of its extensive appeal, is split between its college and professional branches.[14] Only baseball, 'a boy's game' as Scott

---

11    Marshall Sahlins, *Apologies to Thucydides: Understanding History as Culture and Vice Versa* (Chicago: University of Chicago Press, 2004), p. 135.
12    Don DeLillo, *Underworld* (NY: Scribner, 1997).
13    Sahlins, *Apologies to Thucydides*, pp. 135–6.
14    See Allen Guttman, *From Ritual to Record: the Nature of Modern Sports* (New York: Columbia University Press, 1978), ch. 5.

Fitzgerald once described it, can claim to be the 'national' game, and it has held this position since the passion for it first became evident in the 1860s. Its mythic status in American society is accounted for by a number of factors. Its longevity as an organised professional game; its supposed proliferation in the great defining national moment of the Civil War, when it supplanted the 'English' game of cricket; its expansion into leagues which incorporated all the major urban centres and, by extension, many of the little leagues in the rural areas; its multi-racial appeal in spite of the fact that baseball was segregated until the late 1940s; and its ability to generate national heroes and moments – Ty Cobb, the Black Sox scandal of 1919, Babe Ruth in the 1920s and his successors – Lou Gehrig, Joe DiMaggio, Willie Mays, Mickey Mantle, Mark McGwire – as kings of the game. Above all, according to Allen Guttmann, it is baseball's capacity to evoke the pastoral in American society that explains its special fascination in the male psyche: the game's success as the 'national game' comes from its nostalgic association with small towns and the past. 'The Gestalt is a complex one', claims Guttmann, 'which includes open space, grass, warm weather, the bright sun.'[15] Like cricket in England, baseball has the power to recall a lost past.

How this game has been represented to its followers over the years is therefore a crucial process in the construction and perpetuation of the 'meaning' of baseball. The newspaper press, radio, and eventually television (the first national baseball broadcast was the Giants-Dodgers 1951 National League play-off, perhaps not the least significant feature of this contest in popular memory) have each played their part in the process of representation.[16] De Lillo's recurring

15    Guttmann, *Ritual to Record*, p. 101.
16    See David Q. Voigt, *America Through Baseball* (Chicago: Nelson-Hall, 1976); Cordelia Candelaria, *Seeking the Perfect Game: Baseball in American Literature* (Westport, Conn.: Greenwood Press, 1989). The model for studying the process of media representation in American (and indeed any other country's) sport is Michael Oriard, *King Football: Sport and Spectacle in the Golden Age of Radio and Newsreels, Movies and Magazines, the Weekly and the Daily Press* (Chapel Hill: University of North Carolina Press, 2001); *Reading Football: How the Popular Press Created an American Spectacle* (Chapel Hill: University of North Carolina Press, 1993). See also Ronald A.

use of radio commentator Russ Hodges's narrative in his reconstruction of the 1951 Pennant game underscores the communicative role of the media. However, equally important in understanding baseball's continuing appeal is its place in fictional accounts of American life. Beginning with Gilbert Patten's Frank Merriwell stories in the late-nineteenth century, through John R. Tunis's Kid from Tomkinsville (an appropriately small town) to the Claire Bee tales of Chip Hilton from Valley Falls (another small town) there has been a steady stream of fictions memorialising the game. Among the better known, because often immortalised on film, are Gary Cooper's portrayal of Lou Gehrig in *The Pride of the Yankees* (1942), an archetypal example of sporting idolatry; Bernard Malamud's *The Natural* (1952 – filmed by Barry Levinson in 1984); Philip Roth's spectacular baseball epic *The Great American Novel* (1973); W.P. Kinsella's *Shoeless Joe* (1982 – also filmed as *Field of Dreams* by Phil Alden Robinson in 1989); and Harry Stein's *Hoopla* (1983).[17] A constant point of reference in much of this literature has been the Black Sox scandal of 1919, following which eight members of the Chicago White Sox were banned from baseball in contentious circumstances for 'fixing' a World Series. The incident has provided an intriguing and enigmatic story, not to mention a fascinating source of study in cultural history and memory.[18] Out of these and other baseball stories has been created a rich fund of legends through which American masculine heroism with all its injustices, tragedies and triumphs has been nurtured.

It is especially noteworthy that the past quarter century has seen the fascination with the Black Sox case intensify.[19] Its associations

Smith, *Play-by-Play: Radio, Television and Big Time College Sport* (Baltimore, MD: Johns Hopkins University Press, 2001).

17  The late 1980s and early 1990s saw a rash of baseball films in America; *Field of Dreams* was accompanied by *Bull Durham* (1988 – also starring Kevin Costner), *Eight Men Out* (1988), *A League of Their Own* (1992) and *Cobb* (1994).

18  See Daniel A. Nathan, *Saying It's So: A Cultural History of the Black Sox Scandal* (Urbana, IL; University of Illinois Press, 2003).

19  See Steven A. Reiss, 'History, Memory and Baseball's Original Sin: the Telling and Retelling of the Black Sox Scandal', *Journal of Sport History*, 30: 1 (Spring 2003), 101–7.

with lost innocence and its representation in many accounts as a conflict between capital and labour, good and evil, might have possessed a particular resonance at a time when changing values brought a longing for past certainties. Kinsella's *Shoeless Joe*, for example, is a magical fiction which conjures a restoration of justice for the damned eight, as in a certain sense does John Sayles's film *Eight Men Out* (1988), a radical, independent film maker's sympathetic portrayal of the Black Sox as victims of political circumstances and mean-minded employers. In the 1980s Ronald Reagan presented an ambiguous figure who in some ways fed this nostalgia. Though right-wing in economic and foreign policy Reagan nonetheless maintained features of his past Democrat affiliations,[20] and as a former baseball radio commentator he embodied the history of the game in one of its a 'golden' periods. It was not so much Reagan's politics that brought unsettling reverberations to bear on what had once been regarded as settled norms; rather it was the effect of deeper cultural processes, the principal ones among many being the legacy of Vietnam, and the impact of the women's movement on gender relations.

1

In two novels, *The Sportswriter* (1986) and *Independence Day* (1995), Richard Ford has charted through the character Frank Bascombe the disorientations in American male territory provoked by these influences. In a scene towards the end of *The Sportswriter*[21] Bascombe encounters, in the offices of the magazine for which he writes, 'a face to save a drowning man. A big self-assured smile. A swag of honey hair with two plaited strips pulled back on each side in a complex private-school style. Skin the clarity of a tulip. Long fingers. Pale blond skim

20    Hugh Brogan, *The Penguin History of the United States of America* (London: Penguin Books, 2001 edn), describes parts of Reagan's inaugural speech of 1981 as 'Rooseveltian in its tribute to the forgotten man'. (p. 685).
21    All references are to the Vintage Books edition, 1995.

99

of hair on her arm, which at the moment she is rubbing lightly with her palm. Khaki culottes. A white cotton blouse concealing a pair of considerable grapefruits' (357–58). It is Catherine Flaherty, down from Dartmouth on an internship, deciding whether to try her hand at sportswriting or go to medical school, and caught here in a typically Bascombian male gaze. His advice to her is also typically Bascombian 'fuzzy': 'Medicine's a pretty damn good choice. You participate in people's lives in a pretty useful way … though my belief is you can do that as a sportswriter - pretty well, in fact' (360). The scene brings together many of the novel's themes – sport, writing, gender relations, careers (all of them matters in which Bascombe has had some dismal experiences) – with Bascombe's characteristic 'fuzziness'. But meeting Catherine offers him the prospect (subsequently briefly realised) of renewal, another of the novel's principal themes. Renewal both in Bascombe's life itself, as well as in the renewal of the sportswriter's craft, with the prospect of its being passed on (and in keeping with contemporary equalities, enlarged by inclusion of women) to the next generation in the form of Catherine.

For this is what Frank Bascombe does. As the novel's opening line announces: 'My name is Frank Bascombe. I am a sportswriter' (3). Over the course of an Easter weekend in the early 1980s he reflects on the direction of his life, which has thus far included a career change from novelist to sportswriter, marriage, the death of a son four years earlier, followed by a divorce, then a new relationship, current in the narrative but seemingly lacking in substance and purpose. It is the story of a man isolated, without bearings, and looking to sport to provide him with the compass to reorientate his life. Ford weaves together the story out of the small events and personal dramas that make up what Bascombe describes as 'the normal applauseless life of us all' (10). He is amiable but aimless, almost content to be lulled into the comfortable but soporific middle-class life of Haddam, New Jersey, a middling town of decent middling sorts. Bascombe's condition, which he describes as 'dreaminess', is one that he is attempting to come out of. The time is Easter, 'a time of resurrection and renewal' (185). Resurrection is also a mystery, and this appeals to Bascombe who though not a religious man nonetheless finds something consoling in lack of explanation, loose ends not all tied together. He had previously shied away from a brief teaching post at a college in the Berkshires where he found the professors too rational: 'the place was all anti-mystery types … all expert in the arts of explaining, explicating, and dissecting, and by these means promoting permanence' (222). Unlike his ex-wife ('X'), a no-nonsense Northerner whose certainties are too cut-and-dried for him, Bascombe is unsure of which direction in life to take, when all around him he sees attempts to establish and build – in family, relationships, acquaintances, even the life of a nine-year old son – become unstable and end. He is a detached wanderer through the byways of middle America, an amused and bemused observer of its mores. When his ex-wife claims that he has 'awfully odd relationships', he replies that he doesn't have any relationships at all. 'I know that', she says. 'But it's the way you like it' (328). Is this the condition of 'new' man in postmodern America?

Like all good novels *The Sportswriter* is not 'about' one particular thing so much as all the things that plausibly come together in the life of an individual. In the tradition of the novel since the eighteenth century it explores individual psychology, in this case the focus of exploration being the mentality of the male. Because Bascombe is an American male, born in the south (Biloxi), grown up in the post-Second World War years, college educated, briefly drafted into the marines, it is more than likely that one of the plausible aspects of his psychology will be sport. It is what men do; indeed, what they are expected to do if they are 'real' American men with a proper sense of tradition. The novel is not 'about' sport in the sense that its plot depends on a sports setting for its force, in the way, for example, that Glanville's soccer novel *The Rise of Gerry Logan* (1963) does. We learn nothing about sport as a lived practice from Ford's writing. But sport is a constant theme in the book, operating in various ways to illustrate Bascombe's predicament. His ex-wife, for example, is a golfer, who teaches the game at a local country club and who, after the divorce, plays 'the best golf of her life' on the mid-east club pro tour, 'challenging other groups of women in Pennsylvania and Delaware' (373). There is something that is simultaneously determined and yet dreadfully mundane in that idea; it expresses X's resourcefulness and energy, her ability to cope, even prosper, independently; and it contrasts with Bascombe's own inertia and uncertainty. But it also sums up X's satisfaction with the achievement of defined goals and a life of *local* certainties, moral and material, bounded by the lines on a map. His new girlfriend Vicki is, like Bascombe, a southerner-moved-North but unlike him in that she displays an honest determination to succeed in her career (nursing) and her relationships (she has ditched one ineffectual partner just as she will ditch the ineffectual Bascombe himself). There is in Vicki, as in 'X' (and in Catherine Flaherty), a direction and energy that Bascombe is unable to summon. He could never commit to anything with such devotion. He possesses few aims, has few illusions about what life might offer or amount to – sports writing, he is told by a colleague, teaches you that there are 'no transcendent themes in life' (16) – and he is sceptical of attempts to create meaning out of life. He has given up novel writing after a brief success because, he feels, it attempts to deal with transcendent themes, which are merely a 'lie of literature'. His philosophy, if such it can be called, is a stoical one-damned-thing-after-another perspective on life:

> It's exactly like when you were young and dreaming of your family's vacation; only when the trip was over, you were left faced with the empty husks of your dreams and the fear that that's what life will mostly be - the husks of your dreams lying around you. I suppose I will always fear that whatever this is, is it. (83)

It is not that he lacks interests, and sport is his chief one. He can settle down with relish to watch the most dreary basketball match on television. On the whole he admires athletes, people who live, as he claims, 'within themselves', focused on their craft and doing what they enjoy doing more than anything else. His job is to communicate that interest and admiration to others; he is a sports*writer*; he writes features on personalities or tactics, rather than simply reporting events. It places him at the centre of a certain kind of American masculinity, and makes him a supposed expert in the knowledge and opinion that circulates among men, brings them together, and defines their gender. 'If you're a man in this country', his editor tells him, 'you probably already know enough to be a good sportswriter' (41). Moreover, he is part of the whole ideological process of creating and communicating the *idea* of sport to the public, a privileged but dangerous influence especially for a man of Bascombe's scepticism. Bascombe recognises that his profession is a business dealing in moralities expected to enrich people's experience. It is a process of illusion-making, 'false dramas', as Bascombe calls them.

In the course of his Easter weekend Bascombe has three encounters with illusion. It is doubtful, however, whether he learns much from them. First, he travels to Walled Lake, Michigan, to write a story about Herb Wallagher, a famous former footballer now confined to a wheelchair after a water-skiing accident. Wallagher is supposed to be an inspiration to all, showing the kind of courage and determination in adversity that had made him renowned as a player; he has gone back to college, obtained a degree, married his physiotherapist, and become the honorary chaplain for his old team. Bascombe's angle is going to be 'make a contribution'. The meeting with Herb, however, on a grey day in a seedy suburb with a storm coming in, is a disaster from the outset.

> His legs have shrunk and his shoulders are bony. Only his head and arms are good-sized, giving him a gaping, storkish appearance behind his thick horn-rims. He has twice cut himself shaving and doctored it with toilet paper, and is wearing a T-shirt that says BIONIC on the front, and a pair of glen-plaid Bermudas below which a brand new pair of red tennis shoes peek out. It is hard to think of Herb as an athlete. (153)

And indeed Bascombe doesn't really try. To his eyes Herb is a charmless neurotic – 'as crazy as a betsy bug' (160) – disorientated by his new state and clearly incapable of adjusting to life in a wheelchair. He wants to talk about art, life and death, to communicate his despair. Bascombe's failure to understand is a mark of his own superficiality. There are no heroic qualities to be found in Wallagher, and the meeting serves only to bring Bascombe to the banal conclusion that his own life isn't so bad. For the rest of the novel he tries various 'angles' on Wallagher, in the end writing nothing. Bascombe's real problem with Herb, though, is his inability to see him as other than the former sports star, carrying on his star qualities and living 'within himself' in his new life. Bascombe simply cannot understand the depths of Herb's depression; there is no narrative available to describe this in his sportswriter's lexicon.

Then, on his way back from Michigan, heading for an Easter dinner in New Jersey with his girlfriend's family, Bascombe drops in for a drink at a bar in Bamber – 'a town that is no more than a post office and small lake across Route 530' (240). It is Sweet Lou Calcagno's place he has happened upon, where the photographs on the wall proclaim that Lou was a center on the '56 Giants, and a close friend of many old celebrities, including President Eisenhower. He enquires of Lou's whereabouts from the woman behind the bar. Bascombe is already framing a 'Where Are They Now?' piece, and as he poses the question an opening paragraph is forming in his mind. But Sweet Lou is not there. 'He's dead', says the woman. 'He's been dead maybe, thirty years? That's approximately where he is.' 'I'm sorry to know that' replies Bascombe. 'Right', she says. '"Lou was a nunce … And he was a big nunce. I was married to him … She pours herself a cup of coffee and stares at me. I didn't want to ruin your dreams. But. You know?"' The story of Lou's demise is told, and a brief post-Lou history sketched in. As he departs, feeling stupid, Bascombe says; 'I'm sorry I didn't know him', to which Mrs Lou retorts; 'Well, I'm sorry I did. So we're even.' (240–2) Here is another no-nonsense, plain-speaking woman.

Finally, having arrived at his girlfriend's and begun watching a televised Knicks-Cavaliers match Bascombe recognises on the screen the Clevelands' manager, Mutt Greene, and recalls an interview with him shortly after Bascombe had taken up sportswriting. Greene's line on sport and the reporting of it comes into Bascombe's mind:

> People surprise you Frank, with just how fuckin' stupid they are … I mean, do you actually realize how much adult conversation is spent on this fuckin' business? Facts treated like they were opinions just for the simple purpose of talking about it longer? Some people might think that's interesting, bub, but I'll tell you. It's romanticizing a goddamn rock by calling it a mountain range to me. People waste a helluva lot of time they could be putting to useful purposes. This is a game. See it and forget about it. (250)

The inference drawn by Bascome from this fusillade makes one doubt his common sense. Naively, he remembers that the lesson in life he took back to the Sheraton Commander that night after talking to

Greene was; 'Keep things in perspective and give an honest effort' (251). It is recalled without any hint of irony.

But then Bascombe, the ordinary Joe who lives in an ordinary town and believes that people are fundamentally decent, has no commonsense. He is a victim of his own illusions, one of a group of flawed men in a novel whose force comes from sensible, purposeful, steely-minded women who set clear goals and then determinedly pursue them, on the whole successfully. Sport provides for Bascombe a romanticized view of the world which he refuses to abandon even when the ideals of sport are undermined by its realities.

This is why, as the critic Kenneth Millard has said in a perceptive essay, the book is called *The Sportswriter* and not (for example) *The Postman.*[22] It is not, in other words, accidental on Ford's part that Bascombe has drifted out of novel writing to become a sportswriter. Nor is it by chance that in his constant attempt to re-invent himself and his world Bascombe re-appears in the follow-up novel *Independence Day* (1995) as a realtor (estate agent). Millard shows how the story develops an intertextual thread of meaning by reference and allusion to the works of American literary figures such as Ernest Hemingway, Scott Fitzgerald, and Raymond Carver. Bascombe, in fact, inhabits a world not of sport, but of *fictions about sport,* created in some cases by others but mostly by himself. Like Arthur Machin, the rugby player in David Storey's *This Sporting Life,* Bascombe's masculinity is framed by cultural traces of what and how men should be. Whereas Machin's ideal is the hard man of crime fiction and film noir, Bascombe's is an altogether woollier amalgam of romantic heroism (men living 'within themselves') and nostalgia for the past. Both, however, are positioned by the representations of sport and masculinity available to them, and are especially prone to seeing the world through the lens of fiction. For Ford, as for Storey, the analysis of the flawed hero offers an opportunity to expose the power of the sporting fiction, and to scrutinise contemporary conceptions of manhood and the function of sport in constructing them.

22   Millard, *Contemporary American Fiction*, p. 205.

Ford explores the contribution of sport to the postmodern American male psyche by showing how men inhabit a dreamy world of sport in no less a way than Ronald Reagan lived his thought through his films. Sport becomes a metaphor for late-twentieth century masculinity in America, with old paradigms of the gender order challenged by feminism and the concept of the 'new man'. And perhaps that is why Catherine Flaherty, with her female Dartmouth knowingness, rejected sports writing and opted instead for medicine.

2

Philip Roth is America's leading novelist of the late-twentieth and early-twenty first century. In recent novels he has explored some of the country's fundamental problems: 'Red' hysteria and incipient McCarthyism in *I Married a Communist* (1999), race in *The Human Stain* (2001), anti-Semitism in *The Plot Against America* (2004), and in *American Pastoral* (1998) the profound historical changes that overtook America in the quarter century after the end of the Second World War.[23] It is the disruption of what had previously appeared to be settled expectations and practices that forms a principal theme in Roth's work. As the critic Al Alvarez has noted Roth, born in 1933, is a product of 'the last generation of well-behaved, sternly educated children who believed in high culture and high principles and lived in the nuclear shadow of the cold war until their orderly world was blown apart by birth-control pills and psychedelic drugs.'[24] Throughout the works there is an emphasis on Roth's own Jewish family background in the Weequahic district of Newark, New Jersey. Here the Roths and others, whose families had migrated from eastern Europe in the late-nineteenth century, made up an intensely family-centred working-class community with little in common with the

---

23    All references are from the Vintage edition, London, 1998.
24    Al Alvarez, 'The Long Road Home', *Guardian Review*, 11 September 2004, 6.

highly assimilated wealthy Jews in the rich part of town.[25] The Roths lived a secular Jewish life that owed nothing to religious or even historical associations. 'I [...] never saw a skullcap', Roth has said, 'a beard, sidelocks – ever, ever, ever – because the mission was to live here, not there. There was no there.'[26] It is Jacobson's Manchester without even the memory of Bug and Dneister. 'These were Jews who needed no large terms of reference, no profession of faith or doctrinal creed, in order to be Jews [...] Their being Jews issued from their being themselves, as did their being American.'[27] In none of these novels does sport occupy a central place though it is never entirely absent, and on occasions it is an important part of what it means to be American. In *The Human Stain,* for example, boxing at the Newark Boys' Club consumes a considerable amount of time in the early life of Coleman Silk, coached by the Jewish dentist Doc Chizner. It helps to build Coleman's self-confidence, primarily by participating in something that springs from his own initiative and which, had he known about it, would have earned his father's serious disapproval. When the youthful Nathan Zuckerman (Roth's *alter ego* narrator) first meets the communist Ira Ringold in *I Married a Communist* they sit on the front steps of Ringold's house talking baseball and boxing. Talk quickly slips from sport to politics, from the considerable merits of boxer Tony Zale to the absence of any such qualities in Winston Churchill. Roth sees sport as part of the natural fabric of American male society, but it is a fabric that was beginning to unravel in the 1960s, 'the demythologizing decade', when a number of things that had previously appeared to be permanent, indestructible or beyond reproach were now in question. In Newark the race riots of 1966 brought to an end the town that Roth had known since his childhood, where the adolescent camaraderie of baseball was one of the chief means by which his Jewish friends deepened their American-ness. In

25 See Philip Roth, *The Facts: A Novelist's Autobiography* (New York: Farrar, Straus and Giraux, 1988). 'Family indivisibility [was] the first commandment.' (p. 14)
26 Ibid., p. 6.
27 Philip Roth, *The Plot Against America* (London: Jonathan Cape, 2004), p. 220.

addition, there was Vietnam.[28] Roth claims that he used baseball to dramatise some of these changes, in particular the contrast between the benign myth of America as a great power and the 'demonic reality' counterposed to it. In *The Great American Novel* (1973) Roth took a subject – baseball – about which he knew a great deal, but on which 'a certain snobbishness [...] held my imagination in check'[29], and created a humorously savage critique of a sport and a society that many, including Roth himself, held dear.

In much of the fiction of Philip Roth there is an inescapable sense of decline and disillusion. It comes through especially strongly in *American Pastoral* (1998) with its triptych-like structure - 'Paradise Remembered', 'The Fall', and 'Paradise Lost'. Where, for example, Brian Glanville's novel, in spite of its wider significances, is tightly circumscribed by the world of sport, Roth only *alludes* to sport in *American Pastoral*. Like Glanville he uses a realist mode of fictional representation, but his text is scarcely 'about sport' in the same sense as Glanville's; rather, sport is employed metaphorically by Roth, to make statements about things other than sport. Seymour Levov, the principal character in *American Pastoral*, is a *former* sportsman, whose sport stopped short of the highest level of achievement, though he is remembered by the novel's narrator Nathan Zuckerman as a celebrity, a high-school and neighbourhood star of the 1940s, whose all-round athletic skills had been a symbol for the hopes of a whole generation of immigrants who wanted to integrate, to be all-Americans, and to forget the perils of the Second World War. Seymour is always known as 'Swede' because, although of a Jewish immigrant family, he possesses what Zuckerman describes as an 'anomalous face':

> Of the few fair-complexioned Jewish students in our preponderantly Jewish public high school, [he says] none possessed anything remotely like the steep-jawed, insentient Viking mask of this blue-eyed blond born into our tribe as Seymour Irving Levov. (1)

---

28    George G. Searles ed., *Conversations with Philip Roth* (Jackson: University of Mississippi Press, 1992), pp. 63–76, 264.

29    Ibid., p. 71.

108

'...through the Swede', says Zuckerman, 'the neighbourhood entered into a fantasy about itself and about the world, the fantasy of sports fans everywhere: almost like Gentiles ... our families could forget the way things actually work and make an athletic performance *the repository of all their hopes* [my italics]' (3–4). It is a time, says Zuckerman/Roth, when 'the Swede, his neighbourhood, his city (Newark) and his country were in their exuberant heyday, at the peak of confidence, inflated with every illusion born of hope' (87). Swede marries the gentile Mary Dawn Dwyer, Miss New Jersey of 1949, daughter of an Irish immigrant family. They are a beautiful pair, almost perfect. Like the Kid from Tomkinsville in the novel of John R. Tunis (1940), Swede's credentials as the good man whom the gods destroy are grounded in duty and sport. But Swede's nemesis comes not (as with the Kid) from boisterous team mates, or from a running catch smack up against the center-field wall, but from within. His American dream is shattered by internal relationships allied to the external forces of 1960s counter-cultural radicalism and Vietnam. The Swede's fall comes as an essentially biological fissure in the form of his daughter, who in 1968 in protest against the war in Vietnam blows up the village post office and with it the local doctor out posting a letter in Old Rimrock, New Jersey. It is an act of defiance that simultaneously destroys Swede's life and the dream that accompanied it. Sport represents the world that has been lost.

*American Pastoral* is a novel about immigrants, aspirations, generational conflict, ideas of America, and particularly, as Roth puts it, 'what happened to his country in a mere twenty-five years, between the triumphant days at wartime Weequahic High and the explosion of his daughter's bomb in 1968, *of that mysterious, troubling, extraordinary historical transition*' (88). (My italics). For most of the novel there is no relationship to sport, and chronologically in the novel's narrative time Swede Levov is only a former sportsman who has become a glove manufacturer in Newark. It would have been perfectly possible for Roth to give Swede Levov a different fictional background, but had he not been the neighbourhood athletic star of fond memory the tragedy would have been less. It is important that his credentials as a person are grounded, not just in commerce, but also on the football field, the baseball park, and the basketball court. Few things could be more central to the life experience of American males.


# 4


Both of these texts are concerned with sport, though it figures more centrally in Ford. He examines some of the great myths about the value of sport that have exercised Americans in the past hundred years. At the same time, however, the eye he casts on them is for the most part a sceptical one. What is interestingly emphasized is the 'constructedness' of the myths. As Millard has pointed out, much of *The Sportswriter* deals with how notions of sport come into being and are perpetuated through the sport media. This, of course, is Frank Bascombe's job. He creates a world that he himself inhabits. The novel is an example of 'postmodern' writing – postmodern in the sense, that is, of thoughts being determined by language and texts. Ford is a southerner, searching for a place in American fiction conventionally held by north-easterners.[30] Searching is also Bascombe's mission; for values, and for a settled place in life which can confirm what life is about. This is another aspect of the novel's postmodernism – the traditional verities and certainties are not there, or have been found wanting, and there is no fixed star by which to guide one's moral development. Perhaps memories of baseball are the best that can be offered (which recalls Guttmann's explanation for the game's popularity). This is certainly what Roth seems to want from sport in *American Pastoral*; it is a link with a time when life was good, a memory of a golden age, of Roth's own adolescent development before the changes of the 1960s. There is a good deal of nostalgia in all Roth's writing, especially the autobiographical novels. In his most recent, *The Plot Against America*, he allows himself a text in which


30    Laura Barton, 'Other voices, other rooms', (profile of Richard Ford), *Guardian Review*, 8 February 2003, 20–3.

the settled past of Weequahic is disrupted by an imagined fascist takeover of the White House in the form of a successful presidency of the right-wing American hero-aviator Charles Lindbergh. It splits the nation, puts the Jews in peril, and also threatens to drive the Roth family apart. Significantly, however, the threat is contained; even in fiction the status quo cannot be upset, and the rupture is healed, though it requires some nimble footwork on Roth's part to remove the Lindberg junta and set the historical record straight. This accomplished, Philip Roth the author can send nine-years-old Philip Roth the character safely back to his room in the two-family house in Summit Avenue, Newark.

# Chapter Six
## 'The Relentless Pain and Responsibility of Club Football': Nick Hornby's *Fever Pitch*

Thirty years after Brian Glanville's story of Gerry Logan, football in Britain began to acquire an aura that Glanville had anticipated with some dread. It became, or at least *appeared* to have become, part of the entertainment business centred on the Premier League. The creation of this new plutocracy has, it is claimed, produced new social relations in soccer. The 'working man's game' has disappeared and soccer has become, in the sociologists' clumsy term, 'embourgeoisified'. By the 1990s there was much talk about a 'middle-class revolution' in soccer.[1] To be sure, there are various signs to suggest that this might be true. Admission prices for Premier League matches, which often vary according to the quality of the opposition, have soared. The introduction of foreign players brought a new cosmopolitanism to the game, reinforced by the dominance of clubs from the big conurbations, traditionally powerful but now threatening to erase altogether the localism that had always been a part of the game. Such is evident in what has happened to the F.A. Cup, once the pride of English football, now a competition for which some leading clubs appear to have little time.[2] More attention was now being given to international football, and this itself was a consequence of new deals struck between the

1  See A. King, *The End of the Terraces: The Transformation of English Football in the 1990s* (Leicester: Leicester University Press, 1998), part IV. For a recent statement of the 'embourgeoisement thesis' see Brian Glanville, *Football Memories* (London: Virgin Publishing, 1999), p. 269. On the development of the relationship between football and the (mainly electronic) media see Raymond Boyle and Richard Haynes, *Football in the New Media Age* (London: Routledge, 2004).
2  See J. Hill, 'Rite of Spring: Cup Finals and Community in the North of England', in J. Hill and J. Williams eds, Sport and Identity in the North of England (Keele: Keele University Press, 1996), pp. 85–111.

football clubs and television companies. The original Premier League-BSkyB contract of 1992 gave the League £304 million and the viewers more 'live' football on television in Britain. It was presented, moreover, in a new artistic (or at least 'arty') style.[3] The association between football and opera, for example, in the staging of the 1990 World Cup finals in Italy – 'Italia 90' – was a prime case in point. Increasingly, too, leading players were acquiring a cult status as nouveau riche icons whom the press lauded for their lifestyle and conspicuous spending. The trend, which began with the idolization of George Best in the 1960s, culminated with the beatification of David Beckham in the early 2000s.[4]

1

Much of this new wave happened in a changed political culture, which was itself inspired by a new brand of Conservatism. 'Thatcherism', as this new tendency was frequently described, purported to be reviving and modernizing British society around a set of values derived from the principles of the free market, sometimes traced historically to the Victorian bourgeoisie. They included a much-hailed reduction of the powers of the state in areas of welfare and spending though a less-noted increase in the state's authority in matters of law and order. Football had a curious part to play in this politics. Mainly because of the behaviour of some supporters – the 'hooligans' whose activities in the 1980s had become a blight on the game that threatened its commercial viability – football had come to be seen as a 'problem'. It

---

3    A good example was the BBC's opening sequences for its coverage of the 1998 World Cup final tie. Staged in Paris, the match gave the BBC the opportunity to fuse images of football, food, wine and 'civilised' living with 'classical' music to form a single framing collage.
4    See Chas Critcher, 'Football Since the War' in J. Clarke, C. Critcher and R. Johnson, *Working Class Culture: Studies in History and Theory* (London: Hutchinson, 1979), pp. 161–84.

was not just a problem of sport but a manifestation of assumed wider social ills which included a loss of respect for authority. This and other disturbing features of the cultural landscape were in turn seen as having been engendered in the 'dependency culture' of the welfare state. Coercive and containing measures were perceived as providing the required correctives to prevent the slide into chaos. Such a discourse was conducted mainly at a rhetorical level, and served as a means of generalizing views about 'what had gone wrong' in Britain.

The working class (and especially its organized trade union elements – 'the unions', a term uttered with evident distaste by many prominent Conservatives) was held in part responsible. Among the areas that needed attention to rectify problems was football. Margaret Thatcher's own particular preference was an idea with which few others agreed, namely an identity card scheme as a solution to crowd problems. Apart from this her governments of the 1980s had no particular policy on football to bring to the discussion. Their stance was that of middle-class people with the notion that the game could be improved through rational reforms but who possessed little feeling for football's traditions, and in many cases little knowledge of or interest in the game. A similar view was inscribed in the Taylor Report, sponsored by the Home Office to inquire into the causes of the disaster in 1989 when 96 soccer supporters lost their lives as a result of overcrowding and poor crowd management at the Hillsborough ground in Sheffield. [5] The report produced a series of practical recommendations to improve safety standards at football grounds, the chief one being the removal of the perimeter fences that had been installed at all leading grounds to prevent invasions of the pitch by unruly spectators. In other respects, however, Taylor's tone and assumptions were those of the modernizer who regarded the football stadium as a rational business enterprise that should be presented as such. In the matter of catering, for example:

5    Home Office, *The Hillsborough Stadium Disaster, 15 April 1989*; Inquiry By the Rt. Hon. Lord Justice Taylor, Final Report, Jan. 1990 (The Taylor Report) cm 962, (London: HMSO, 1990).

The refreshments available to supporters are often limited and of indifferent quality. They are sold in surrounding streets from mobile carts and inside many grounds from other carts or from shoddy sheds. Fans eat their hamburgers or chips standing outside in all weathers. There is a prevailing stench of stewed onions. Adequate numbers of bins for rubbish are often not available; so wrappings, containers and detritus are simply dropped. This inhospitable scene tends to breed bad manners and poor behaviour. The atmosphere does not encourage pride in the ground or consideration for others. I accept that many fans are quite content to eat on the hoof when visiting a match, but there is no reason why the fare available should not be wholesome, varied and decently served from clean and attractive outlets. Fast food establishments meeting these requirements are readily to be found at railway stations and on high streets; why not at football grounds?[6]

Attitudes of this kind were inclined to provoke derision from those fans who saw football grounds as being different from multiplex cinemas and supermarkets. They claimed actually to like the very ambience that Taylor was condemning. In resisting the sanitizing of football grounds with all-seating arrangements and wholesome food 'outlets' the opponents of Taylor were rejecting a vision in which the soccer club was to become a rational business and the fan a 'customer'. It was a vision that lacked sensitivity to the atmosphere of the crowd, especially its male sociability, and which did indeed appear to have as its principal aim the casting out of the troublesome working-class fan who was giving soccer its bad name: 'a slum sport played in slum stadiums' as the *Sunday Times* described it in 1985.[7] At this time the prospect of soccer as a game with the spectators left out was a not entirely fanciful one; the big Italian club Juventus was reported to be considering building a new stadium in Turin to hold only 32,000 spectators. The implication was clear: the 'real' audience was out there in television-land.

6  Taylor Report, p. 6.
7  Quoted in I. Taylor, 'Putting the Boot Into a Working-Class Sport: British Soccer After Bradford and Brussels', *Sociology of Sport Journal*, 4: 1 (1987) 182. See also A. King, 'New Directors, Customers, and Fans: The Transformation of English Football in the 1990s', *Sociology of Sport Journal*, 14 (1997), 224–40.

Whether all these new commercial and political pressures did effect a transformation of bourgeois proportions on the elite soccer clubs, let alone the lesser ones, is far from certain. One of the over-riding features of English football at this time was the conflicting pressures brought about by the different interests of clubs, spectators, players and governments. When, for example, Manchester United achieved its remarkable feat of winning the European Champions' League, the Premier League and the FA Cup in the same season of 1998–99, many of its supporters moderated their delight at the club's success with deep fears for its commercial future. United, because of success and the extensive international fan base it enjoyed, had become the subject of a takeover bid by Rupert Murdoch and Sky television. Campaigns by fans to prevent this from happening revealed a mixture of old and new attitudes. They were glad enough to embrace the Premier League and its new European associations, yet hesitant about committing 'their' club to the full force of the stock market.[8]

Even at this most commercial of British sports clubs there seemed to be plenty of people willing to retain some of the old traditions. These sentiments illustrated another trend that had become apparent in football during the 1980s: the wish on the part of football fans to have their voice heard. The traditional supporters' organisations, rather too closely associated with their clubs for the most part, had lost the ability to act as an independent voice[9] and their role was in many cases supplemented by the emergence of 'fanzines'. These fan-related magazines, often short-lived and usually produced on a voluntary and often fairly amateurish basis, purported to speak as the voice of the terraces, scrutinising the manoeuvrings of club directors, attacking

---

8    See *Guardian,* 10 April 1999, 35; Matthew Horsman, 'Sky Blues', *Media Guardian,* 12 April 1999, 2. These problems did not go away; in 2005 the club was still the object of takeover bids, causing Greg Dyke, a former Controller-General of the BBC, to say that football clubs were 'not suited to being public companies.' (*Guardian,* 14 April 2005, 36.) The club was soon afterwards taken over by the American businessman Malcolm Glazer. On the general business developments in football at this time see King, *End of the Terraces.*

9    See Rogan Taylor, *Football and Its Fans* (Leicester: Leicester University Press, 1992).

those responsible for hooliganism and racism, and defending football against the attacks launched on it by government.[10]


2


Nick Hornby's *Fever Pitch* (1992) is part of this independence of spirit and also ambivalence about recent developments in football. It is an autobiographical memoir of life as a football fan over the period from the end of the 1960s to the early 1990s.[11] It is well written, cleverly structured, and perceptively witty. It is often taken to be symptomatic of these new departures in football, a defining text which cast the game in a new 'bourgeois' light and signified the demise of what had, for a century, been regarded as the 'working man's game'. At first glance a number of things did appear to have been triggered by the success of *Fever Pitch*. One of them, perhaps the most evident, was a new literary interest in soccer, described by Steve Redhead in the awkward (though useful) term 'literaturisation'.[12] It was exemplified in a clutch of attractive magazines such as *When Saturday Comes* and the more glossy and fashionable *FourFourTwo*. They managed to balance a serious approach to discussions of the game with an interesting format which linked football with other branches of the entertainment industry, such as music and fashion. In their wake a succession of books and magazines, often written by celebrity fans or, in some cases, players themselves, combined to give soccer a fashionable, quasi-intellectual image as a subject for lively debate and

10   See R. Haynes, *The Football Imagination: The Rise of the Football Fanzine Culture* (Aldershot; Arena, 1995). Steve Redhead identified some 1,400 such magazines in the mid-1990s. (Steve Redhead, *Post-Fandom and the Millennial Blues: The Transformation of Soccer Culture* (London: Routledge, 1997), pp. 104–29.)
11   Nick Hornby, *Fever Pitch* (London: Victor Gollancz, 1992). All page references are taken from the Penguin Books edition (London, 2000).
12   Redhead, *Post-Fandom*, pp. 88–92. It is one of various 'isations' perceived by Redhead at this time.

118

comment among a readership of relatively prosperous, youngish males.[13] Where once football was the subject of pub talk among men it now, one sensed, was an acceptable topic at the middle-class dinner table.[14] It was all very new, and contrasted with the stale forms in which football had been represented in the past: the sensational tabloid reportage of football, for example, or the 'ghosted' player autobiographies that had been the stock-in-trade of football literature for many years. The fact that Hornby himself, on the strength of *Fever Pitch*, quickly rose to the status of serious novelist and critic [15] reinforced the feeling that football had suddenly acquired a new image. There is a sense of this in Julie Welch's review of *Fever Pitch* in the *Times Literary Supplement*.[16] Welch comments on the common perception of football as a game incapable of producing good literature, but notes Hornby's original approach to his subject and the feeling of 'wry heroism' he works into the text. It is, she feels, a good book – 'funny, poignant, knowing'. What she dislikes about it is not the quality of its writing so much as its male-centred-ness – 'a game for the boys'. In contrast to all this, however, it is interesting to note that in an interview with Hornby in 2005 Simon Hattenstone of the *Guardian* noted that Hornby 'hates the way the middle classes have colonised football – and he hates it even more that some people say *Fever Pitch* is partly to blame.'[17]

13    One of the first of the genre was Hunter Davies, *The Glory Game* (London: Sphere Books, 1973). The first, and still the best, of the 'realist' school of players' autobiographies is Eamonn Dunphy, *Only a Game?* (London: Peacock Books, 1977). Among the more interesting of the newer publications are Harry Pearson, *The Far Corner: A Mazy Dribble Through North-East Football* (London: Warner Books, 1995 ed.) and Colin Shindler, *Manchester United Ruined My Life* (London: Headline, 1998). Shelley Webb, *Footballers' Wives* (London: Yellow Jersey Press, 1998) is an illuminating study by a footballer's wife.

14    See Fiachra Gibbons, 'Lowry football painting comes home for £2 million', *Guardian*, 2 December 1999, 11.

15    Hornby published *High Fidelity* in 1995, and *About a Boy* in 1998. Both were quickly made into films.

16    Julie Welch, 'A Game for the Boys?', *Times Literary Supplement,* 18 September 1992, 32.

17    Simon Hattenstone, 'Laughing All the Way to the Cemetery', *Guardian Weekend*, 23 April 2005, 20.

This brings us to a second aspect of football's 'revolution' of the 1990s: its ambiguous relationship with new forms of masculinity. The emergence of 'women's liberation' in Britain in the 1960s and the subsequent consolidation in public life of many feminist tenets created a serious challenge to the established patriarchal order, resulting in what has been described by some commentators as a 'crisis of masculinity'.[18] Sport was implicated in this by virtue of its traditional position as a site where the physicality and difference of men is celebrated. David Storey understood this very well, and *This Sporting Life* is a superb analysis of the particular cultural experience. Boys, note American sociologists Messner and Sabo, are initiated into the world of sports by men and into the world of men through sports.[19] British football had been imbued with a strong sense of its being a 'man's game' – symbolised in the traditional virtue of the hard tackle – albeit that an over-emphasis on this quality might have worked to the detriment of the game's technical development. One aspect of the possible 'crisis' as it affected the world of sport is the change that has overcome the representation of sport and sports people in the stories that are told about them: how, in the term used by Garry Whannel, they are 'narrativized'.[20] The omnipresent David Beckham is probably the exemplar of this development, a new male sporting subject of the early twenty-first century whose masculinity is clearly stated but tempered by a 'female' side signified in his attitude to his children, his soft spoken demeanour, and his love of fashion.[21] It is an interesting development, and a world away from the vision of the football star of

---

18    See RW Connell, *Masculinities* (Cambridge: Polity Press, 1995); Jeffrey Hill, 'Sport Stripped Bare: Deconstructing Working-Class Masculinity in *This Sporting Life*', *Men and Masculinities,* 7: 4 (April 2005), 405–23; Fiona Dowling Ness, 'Narratives About Young Men and Masculinities in Organised Sport in Norway', *Sport, Education and Society*, 6: 2 (2001), 125–42.
19    Michael A Messner and Donald F Sabo, *Sex Violence and Power in Sports: Rethinking Masculinity* (Freedom, CA: The Crossing Press, 1994), p. 3.
20    Garry Whannel, 'Sport Stars, Narrativization and Masculinities', *Leisure Studies* (1999), 249–63, See also the same author's *Media Sport Stars: Masculinities and Moralities* (London: Routledge, 2002), esp. ch. 6.
21    See David Beckham, *My World* (London: Hodder and Stoughton, 2001).

fifty years earlier.[22] Another area in which football connected with this new discourse was in the genre of 'lad-lit', a fictional tradition which had its origins in Kingsley Amis in the early 1950s, and which might have reached its end with the writings of his son Martin in the 1990s.[23] Lad-lit, according to Elaine Showalter, was comic, romantic and confessional, and produced a range of different 'lads', latterly many of them football-obsessed and, behind an aura of bravado, insecure.[24] They might not have conformed to a feminist's idea of a 'new man' but lad-lit represents them as something other than 'old man'. Hornby's *Fever Pitch* falls into this category.

A third aspect of *Fever Pitch* is its concern for the spectator. After all the comments made about Hornby's gender and class associations, it is worth remembering that the book is about a football spectator. And perhaps above all else it was the subject of the spectator, especially the unruly one, on which discussion about football was centred in the 1990s. If the game was moving away from its traditional masculine image it was the perceived distasteful behaviour of some of its working-class fans that had much to do with the move. Taylor's attempt to reconstruct football as a consumer product was prompted to a large extent by it. The feeling was sustained by an extensive and long-running academic debate about unruly football fans that sought by rational analysis to dispel some of the myths that had been developed in the press about hooligans and their motives. Though the debate was ultimately somewhat inconclusive it nonetheless had the effect of keeping the topic in the public eye, insofar as academic discourse is capable of creating a public profile.[25]

22    See, eg, Nat Lofthouse, *Goals Galore* (London: Stanley Paul, 1954).

23    It was *not*, as Hattenstone claims in his interview, invented by Hornby. (Hattenstone, *Guardian Weekend*).

24    Elaine Showalter, 'Ladlit', in Zachary Leader ed., *On Modern British Fiction* (Oxford: Oxford University Press, 2002), pp. 60–76. See also the BBC television version of lad-lit *Men Behaving Badly,* which summed up many of these characteristics.

25    The literature is extensive. Among the more important contributions are: I. Taylor, 'Soccer Consciousness and Soccer Hooliganism', in S. Cohen ed., *Images of Deviance* (Harmondsworth: Penguin Books, 1971), pp. 134–64; 'On the Sports Violence Question: Soccer Hooliganism Revisited', in Jennifer

To a degree Hornby's portrayal of the spectator as ordinary, vulnerable, someone just like you and me (though inclined to be rather obsessive about his team) went some of the way towards rehabilitating the image of the spectator. For, in spite of the fact that the admission charges paid by spectators had been the main funding source of commercial football in Britain for a century, the individual spectator had been a remarkably neglected figure. As organised groups of supporters their views were often ignored by clubs,[26] their material comforts at the stadium did not, as the Taylor Report acidly noted, command high priority, and as objects of historical and sociological enquiry they scarcely existed. When sociologists did turn their attention to football crowds it was the hooligan element that claimed it.[27] *Fever Pitch* links with each of these issues: the embourgeoisement of football, the crisis of masculinity, and place of the spectator. But if we are to place it in the discourse we have also to recognise its ambivalence towards it; to pick out those aspects with which it

Hargreaves ed., *Sport, Culture and Ideology* (London: Routledge and Kegan Paul, 1982), pp. 152–96; 'Football Mad: A Speculative Sociology of Football Hooliganism', in E. Dunning ed., *The Sociology of Sport: A Collection of Readings* (London: Frank Cass, 1971), pp. 352-7; P. Marsh, E. Rosser and R. Harre, *The Rules of Disorder* (London: Routledge and Kegan Paul, 1978); J. Maguire, 'The Emergence of Football Spectating as a Social problem, 1880–1985: A Figurational and Developmental Perspective', *Sociology of Sport Journal*, 3 (1986), 217–44; E. Dunning, J. Williams and P. Murphy, *The Roots of Football Holliganism: An Historical and Sociological Study* (London: Routledge and Kegan Paul, 1988); J. Williams, E. Dunning and P. Murphy, *Hooligans Abroad: The Behaviour and Control of English fans in Continental Europe* (London: Routledge, 1989).

26    See Taylor, *Football and Its Fans.*

27    Brimson, *Everywhere We Go: Behind the Matchday Madness* (London: Headline, 1986); Bill Buford, *Among the Thugs* (London: Secker and Wraburg, 1991); Colin Ward, *Steaming In* (London: Simon and Schuster/Sportspages, 1989); Tom Watt, *The End* (Edinburgh: Mainstream, 1993); John King, *The Football Factory* (London: Jonathan Cape, 1996). Tony Mason, *Association Football and English Society, 1863–1915* (Brighton; Harvester, 1980), is something of an exception in football studies for its attempt to offer a serious analysis of the whole crowd (and not just the 'rough' elements) at football matches.

converges, and those against which it is in violent opposition; in short to identify, the text's mixed messages.

At first sight Hornby seems himself to be the product of the modern commercialism of the game. If fans are supposed to have some organic attachment to their club (geographical proximity, familial loyalties and traditions, sectarian associations, or shared community loyalties) there are none of these in Hornby's make-up. The object of his fan-ship is Arsenal F.C. in North London, a club which, as a 12-year old boy from Maidenhead in the Thames valley, some thirty miles distant, he chooses by accident. Arsenal is by no means the nearest football club to his home, and not even the nearest *famous* club. It just happens to have been a team he was taken to watch by his father as part of his afternoon-out duty during a painful parental separation and divorce. The loyalty grew from such inauspicious beginnings. In one scene he describes how, watching Arsenal at Reading (the club nearest to his home) he has to *pretend* to some kindly Reading supporters that he has come from North London to watch the match. But when he lets slip that he actually lives in Maidenhead the full irony of the situation is exposed: '*You shouldn't be supporting Arsenal this afternoon*' says the Reading fan with a fine sense of tradition. '*You should be supporting your local team.*' It was, therefore, a rootless and unconventional attachment initially, not dissimilar in some respects from that of youngsters thirty years later, who choose their football teams as they select their favourite rock stars; not by any organic process, but according to current fashion. It differs in one important respect, however; the choice was not governed by any obvious wish to be associated with winners. Arsenal was a famous club with a history of glittering success, largely in the 1930s and 1940s. It had undergone a long period of underachievement after winning the League Championship in 1953. In the 1960s the team was generally regarded as 'boring', and ironically only returned to the limelight in 1969 when they lost a League Cup final to Swindon Town of the Third Division: an ignominious outcome in a second-rate competition. It was not high glamour, therefore, that took Nick Hornby to Highbury. It was a random event which, as he grew to realise, was actually in keeping with the wholly irrational process of being a football fan.

# 3

*Fever Pitch* presents a 'view from the terraces' and tries to show what it is like being a football fan. It is the emphasis on *fan* that is important. It is more than simply spectatorism, and more than simply turning up on Saturdays at football grounds and being passionately involved in the action for ninety minutes. It attempts to deal with the way football takes over a life, infiltrates thoughts and shapes patterns of behaviour. In short, the *obsession* of the fan is what Hornby is dealing with in a quasi-psychological way. It is appropriate that he himself, as he grows into manhood, experiences depression and an abiding sense of both failure and *ennui.* Like a love affair, or perhaps like depression, football fan-ship is not easily subjected to rational analysis. Much of Hornby's account of his life as a fan assumes an existential tone, describing what being at a football match and experiencing winning or defeat is *like*, rather than seeking to explain what it means. When Arsenal won the League Championship for the first time since 1971 in the most dramatic fashion at Liverpool in the final minute of the final match of the 1989 season Hornby watched the game on television (he was not an assiduous 'away' supporter). In the closing seconds:

> I found that I was reining myself in, learning from recent lapses in hardened scepticism, thinking, well, at least we came close at the end there, instead of thinking, please Michael [Thomas -the Arsenal midfield player] please Michael, please put it in, please God let him score. And then he was turning a somersault, and I was flat out on the floor, and everybody in the living room jumped on top of me. Eighteen years, all forgotten in a second.' (221)

How to explain the feeling? He searches for analogies. Not like an orgasm – 'the feelings that [sex] engenders are simply not as intense as those brought about by a once-in-a-lifetime last-minute Championship winner' (222). Nor childbirth ('it doesn't really have the crucial surprise element') (222). Not the fulfilment of personal ambitions like promotion or an award. Nor a huge pools win. 'There is (...) literally nothing to describe it (...) I can recall nothing else that I have coveted for two decades (...), nor can I recall anything else that I have desired as both man and boy' (223). Being a football fan is not a rational, or even a moral, choice. It is, as Hornby claims, something you are stuck with 'like a wart or a hump' (227). His friend Pete is the same. 'He is gripped by the same stomach-fizzing fear before big games, and the same dreadful glooms after bad defeats' (144). Neither is this feeling something that can be mitigated by being shared, on the principle that a problem shared is a problem halved. One of Hornby's girlfriends tried this tactic only to meet his unequivocal disapproval: *'You don't understand'*, I shouted, 'as I had wanted to shout for months ... once I had uttered the words that most football fans carry around with them like a kidney card, it was all over' (165–6). Part of this psychology is a visceral fascination with the community of fans – the crowd. Hornby claims to be able, for example, to distinguish between the different categories of *noise* heard at football grounds; he loves the sights and smells: 'the overwhelming *maleness* of it all - cigar and pipe smoke, foul language (words I had heard before, but not from adults, not at that volume)' (11).

Along with this male camaraderie goes a fascination for the aggression on the terraces. Hornby makes it clear that he has no time for hooliganism, and the behaviour of the fans at the Heysel stadium in 1985 when 30 Italian supporters died because of the behaviour of unruly Liverpool fans crowd cannot be tolerated:

> In the end the surprise was that these deaths were caused by something as innocuous as running, the practice that half the juvenile fans in the country had indulged in, and which was intended to do nothing more than frighten the opposition and amuse the runners. The Juventus fans - many of them chic, middle-class men and women - weren't to know that, and why should they have done? They didn't have the intricate knowledge of English crowd behaviour that the rest of us had absorbed almost without noticing. When they saw a crowd of screaming English hooligans running towards them, they panicked, and ran to the edge of their compound. A wall collapsed and, in the chaos that ensued, people were crushed to death. (147)

And yet Hornby admits to a feeling of awe in an earlier stage of his life, as a teenager, by having been part of the *power* of the football crowd as it makes its way to the match – 'an organ in the hooligan body' (46). Later, when he takes his half-brother to Arsenal he sees that the lad is fascinated by the hooligans. 'It wasn't the football that captivated Jonathan. It was the violence. All around us people were fighting […] my little brother was beside himself with excitement; he kept turning round to look at me, his face shining with a disbelieving glee' (123). Hornby is not a hooligan, and his book does not attempt, as some memoirs of the period did, either to understand or to glorify the excessively aggressive version of masculinity that hooliganism represented. But it is part, though a regrettable part, of the game. Altogether, these sentiments about football and its sociability might be cast in new ways of describing the game and its experiences, in fact a new 'lad-lit' of the game, but the feelings are a century old. They go back to the origins of the game as a spectator sport in the late-nineteenth century. They have not been manufactured from the Taylor Report. They are part of what Hornby calls 'the relentless responsibility and pain' of being the true supporter of club football (23–4).

This is not to say that his memoir is entirely backward looking, a 'traditionalist' account. In his attitude towards the Taylor Report's proposals, for example, Horny has a progressive view, rejecting some of the conservative sentimentalism uttered by supporters who objected to all-seater stadiums and increases in ticket prices. Hornby accepts that many aspects of being a football supporter involve commercialism – 'I have stumped up thousands of pounds to watch Arsenal over the last twenty years; but each time money has changed hands, I have received something in return […] Why is football any different from the cinema, say, or a record shop?' (214). He opposes, however, certain kinds of capitalist enterprise in football that attempt both to transform the audience and to talk down to it. He sees the introduction of bond schemes, for example, at Arsenal and West Ham United, as a device both to increase income from spectators and to exclude the traditional core support of working-class males. It might, Hornby argues, prove counterproductive, since part of the attraction of football spectating is the atmosphere in the stadium – the noise particularly – largely produced by the very people the bond schemes will keep out. 'Who would buy an executive box if the stadium were filled with executives?' (69). Hornby's view of football spectating is that it is not a simple act of watching. He would need to answer his own question – 'why is football any different from cinema?' – by

126

asserting that, in some respects, it is very different, because the crowd is different from a cinema audience. The latter will go in the hope of seeing a good film. Some football spectators hope to see a good match with exciting play and plenty of goals. Such spectators were the ones Hornby encountered, and who treated him in a kindly way, at the 1978 Cup Final between Arsenal and Ipswich – 'Dad got me a ticket […] via work contacts' (99). He sat alongside some pleasant middle-aged men for whom the match involved no particular partisanship. 'To them it was an afternoon out, a fun thing to do on a Saturday afternoon'. (99) The match was only a game, something enjoyed while it lasted but quickly forgotten. It contained no greater significance. These men might have been at the cinema or, as Hornby suggests, watching rugby or golf or cricket. They were passive spectators, not in the sense that they did not understand or appreciate what was happening, but because they were not passionate about the experience. They would have drawn the ire of nineteenth-century proponents of amateurism who thought that sport was about active participation. Standing watching was for old men or young children, either too old or not yet old enough to be involved. But to modern commercial managers of football these men were ideal types, probably already being primed to subscribe to some club's the debenture scheme.

This is not what Hornby understands by being a fan. A fan is neither passive, nor is he interested in entertainment. '[T]hose who say they would rather do than watch are missing the point. Football is a context in which watching *becomes* doing' (178). By this he means not a physical activity but an emotional one, at its most evident in moments of high triumph or, conversely, deep despair.

> The joy we feel on occasions like this is not a celebration of others' good fortune, but a celebration of our own; and when there is a disastrous defeat the sorrow that engulfs us is, in effect, self-pity, and anyone who wishes to understand how football is consumed must realise this above all things. (179)

There is an organic connection between football clubs and their spectators. The players and managers come and go, developing new affiliations and loyalties. It is the spectators who, according to Hornby, provide the vitality of the organism. They are the continuing element.

Such fans are not tricked by the veneer of glamour glossed over the game to increase its attractiveness, and are therefore suspicious of the media hype generated around players of dubious worth (a trend that has if anything intensified since Hornby wrote the book). Moreover, the very idea of football as 'entertainment' is viewed with distaste. Hornby reminds us of a statement made in 1980 by the manager of embattled Stoke City after a gritty display against Arsenal: 'If you want entertainment go and watch clowns' (125). It was received with some dismay by those who felt that the game needed more glamour, enjoyment, and style. Hornby, however, appreciated its honest realism, its understanding of what spectators want. They go to see 'their' team win, and would far rather that objective were achieved in a grim 1-0 victory; an exciting 4-3 defeat might be full of breathtaking play, but in the last analysis it is a disappointment. Football is not like the cinema, where audiences have 'thrilled' across the years to Garbo, Monroe, Kirk Douglas and Al Pacino. As Hornby notes, football fans do not enjoy seeing the star names of the opposition; they might play well, and thereby bring about the defeat of 'our' team. 'I go to football for loads of reasons, but I don't go for entertainment, and when I look around me on a Saturday and see those panicky, glum faces, I see that others feel the same' (127–8).

*Fever Pitch* presents an ambiguous stance on developments in football in the early 1990s. It embraces new ventures, especially those concerned with the safety of spectators, and is critical of 'neurotic sentimental attachments' (213) that some fans wrongly see as part of the 'traditions' of the game. Yet it is itself suffused with neurotic attachments to the point of contradiction. Does he love Arsenal, or hate it? Does he love the art of football – as performed by his idol Liam Brady, the ultimate intelligent midfielder whose passing is a joy to behold – or does he want his team to grind out boring victories that accumulate points? 'Boring' Arsenal seems to be a badge he wears with some pride: 'no-one likes us, we don't care' as the terraces might sing. Perhaps, in both cases, it is both. These ambiguities are compounded by the book's form. It was first published in 1992, and presumably written during the late 1980s to early 1990s. Though the author acknowledges that he has never kept a football diary (73) *Fever Pitch* nonetheless assumes many of the features of a diary. The narrative is structured by three distinct periods of his life (1969-76, 1976-86, and 1986 onwards) each representing a stage in his development: childhood, adolescence, maturity. They also approximate to particular phases in the Arsenal story. Within these stages events are framed by match reports; or to be more precise particular matches are used as triggers to set off a discussion of personal or football thoughts. 'I have measured out my life in football fixtures' (73). The convergence of club and personal life is most clearly in evidence when Hornby looks back to the Littlewoods Cup semi-final replay of March 1987 between Arsenal and Spurs. He had been reluctantly seeing a psychiatrist for some months previously as a means of dealing with his depression: 'All I know is that I felt, inexplicably, *unlucky, cursed* in some way that would not be immediately apparent to any one without a job or a lover or a family. I knew myself to be doomed to a life of dissatisfactions' (169). Travelling down from the psychiatrist's he experienced, at some point on the tube line between Baker Street and King's Cross, a sudden transformation. 'I felt better, less isolated, more purposeful [...] I no longer had to explain where I was going or where I had been, and I was back in the mainstream' (170). The end of his 'decade-long downer' (173) was confirmed when Arsenal won the replay. His own explanation of this remarkable epiphany is that he stopped feeling unlucky, and that Arsenal's success (after a long period without it) was responsible for his transformation. The experience was also responsible for Hornby's seeing his football loyalty in a more mature light: 'That night, I stopped being an Arsenal lunatic and learnt how to be a fan, still cranky, and still dangerously obsessive, but only a fan nonetheless' (174).

The episodic formula beckons the reader on in easy stages. It appears, on the surface at least, to be a straightforward record of a life. As in the genre of documentary, attention to detail and accuracy is important in establishing the verisimilitude and 'realism' of the actions depicted. The overall narrative is not a simple linear progression; because of football's ups and downs and Hornby's own aimless history, the story is one of discontinuities. This itself has a kind of truthfulness; how many people's lives have a shape, meaning and direction? And Hornby's confessional relationship with his reader, in which he bares his soul and admits to his weaknesses, reinforces a feeling of realism at work. We are inclined to believe, just as we are expected have an implicit belief in autobiographies, in spite of their frequent embellishments of the truth.

We know, however, that autobiographies are deceptive, if not deceitful; they are in many senses 'subtle fictions', as Terence Hawkes described them in a review of Terry Eagleton's memoirs.[28] Perhaps some of the fascination with *Fever Pitch* lies in the suspicion it arouses about its realism. Hornby's story relies a great deal, as it must in the absence of a 'real' diary (and even that would have had its flaws), on imaginative reconstruction. This raises several questions. How much Hornby the child, whose relationship with his father seemed to exist only at football matches, is real, and how much an invented character? Indeed, is the Hornby who appears in the book the same Hornby as the author? Is his obsession plausible? Is football *that* important to *anyone?* Is supporting Arsenal such a bad deal? Perhaps the bigger the team the more there is to risk – an instance of Geertz's 'deep play'?[29] But as one of the biggest clubs in Britain, which has never remotely threatened to drop out of the top division since it first joined (not by normal promotion) in 1919, Arsenal could scarcely have taxed the resilience of its supporters in the same way that a Brentford or a Gillingham could. And what did Hornby do when he was not at football matches, or thinking about being at them? The questions raised by the book place it in a similar category to two autobiographical narratives which doubtless influenced Hornby – Tobias Wolffs's *This Boy's Life* and the yet more relevant and psychotic *A Fan's Notes* by Frederick Exley.[30] Both are books of memory, aware of the ways in which recollections merge into fiction. Indeed, the macabre Exley – a fan of the New York Giants football team – asks to be 'judged as a writer of fantasy' (7). In spite of

28    Terence Hawkes, 'Putting on Some English', *London Review of Books,* 7 February 2002, 25–6.
29    Clifford Geertz, *The Interpretation of Cultures: Selected Essays* (New York: Basic Books, 1972), ch. 15.
30    Tobias Wolff, *This Boy's Life: A Memoir* (London: Bloomsbury, 1989); Frederick Exley, *A Fan's Notes: A Fictional Memoir* (Harmondsworth: Penguin Books, 1970).

appearances then, *Fever Pitch* could well be Nick Hornby's first work of fiction: a classic bourgeois novel with its motive force coming from the psychological drive of the central character.

None of this is to doubt the book's importance. Of all the literature that relates to football's transformation at this time *Fever Pitch* is probably the most intelligent, capturing as it does the complex cross currents of tradition and modernity that swirl around the game.[31] Unlike some of the contributions to the subject of hooliganism, for example, it seeks neither to condemn nor to glorify. It treats its main subject – football supporting – with a ruthlessness that leaves the reader to ask whether the obsessive fan might not be the chief problem afflicting the game. How can so many people invest so much time, money and emotional capital in a game?

Matthew Engel, writing in the *Guardian* at the time of the book's publication sought, in the way of reviewers confronted by something artistically different, to scale down its sporting content and emphasise its essential truths. '[It] has everything to do with Arsenal, and nothing at all. It is a book passingly about sport, more profoundly about sport's role in our relationships and lives.'[32] To be sure, *Fever Pitch* attempts to relate sport to personal problems and relations, but to deny that it is quintessentially a study of football supporting seems wrongheaded. Hornby and his publishers timed their intervention in football discourse with fine judgement. It is a book of the early 1990s, offering a critical reflection on the mood of optimism that accompanied the founding of the Premiership, and on the new media-led glamour that had developed in the wake of the World Cup in Italy. It both reflects and constructs the ideological processes affecting the

31  *Fever Pitch* was voted top in a reader poll of sporting books by the *Observer Sport Monthly* in 2005; it was 'the overwhelming choice of readers […] no one has written better about the tragic-comedy of supporting a team than Hornby'. (*Observer Sport Monthly*, 63, May 2005, 38). Colin Shindler's *Manchester United Ruined My Life* (Headline Book Publishing: London, 1998) - written from the point of view of a Manchester City supporter - offers an entertaining account of a fan's life, and might have achieved what Hornby achieved had Hornby not come first.
32  Matthew Engel, 'Books: Arsenal Fan is Prized Above Lords', *Guardian*, 28 November 1992, 16.

game at this time, and not the least of its attributes comes from its being a part of the football milieu. It does not attempt to stand outside its subject, and its very passion for the game ensures that *Fever Pitch* is a vital primary source for historians working on the football culture of the late century. Engel was right, however, in one sense: the book also serves as a prototype for the novels that were to come.

# Chapter Seven
## 'I'll Kill 'Em All' - The Psychopath As Hero: Ring Lardner's *Midge Kelly*

From the earliest days of modern sport boxing (or 'pugilism' as it was originally called)[1] has occupied a special position. It was among the first sports in Britain to have a literature, preceding cricket in this respect.[2] Because of this some of the early heroes of sport were pugilists, such as the famous Nottinghamshire trio of John Shaw, William Thompson ('Bendigo') and Ben Caunt, all bare-knuckle prize-fighters.[3] They were held to be national champions, who combined the virtues of manliness and patriotism. Shaw, indeed, was killed at Waterloo.[4] In the early nineteenth century the Irishman Pierce Egan, author of the five-volume *Boxiana* (1813–28) did more than anyone to place pugilism, and himself, in the forefront of the sporting world, though it is the literary figure William Hazlitt (perhaps because he is a 'name' in the literary canon) whose work on boxing in this period is best remembered today. His essay on the Neat-Hickman contest of 1821 set down an early marker for sports writing. It contains most of the ingredients from which the ideal fight report was later to be concocted; it brought out not only the thrill of the brutal,

---

1   'Pugilism' and 'boxing' are, strictly speaking, different sports; there was no smooth transition from the one to the other. Moreover, 'prize fighting' was not necessarily only fist fighting; staffs and swords could also used. ('Pugilism' in R. Cox, G. Jarvie and W. Vamplew eds, *Encyclopedia of British Sport* (Oxford: ABC-Clio, 2000), pp. 307–10.

2   See Eric Midwinter, *Quill on Willow: Cricket in Literature* (Chichester: Aeneas Press, 2001); David Underdown, *Start of Play: Cricket and Culture in Eighteenth-Century England* (London: Penguin Books, 2001).

3   See Dennis Brailsford, *Bareknuckles: A Social History of Prize-Fighting* (Cambridge: Lutterworth Press, 1988).

4   See Richard Holt 'Heroes of the North: Sport and the Shaping of Regional Identity' in Jeff Hill and Jack Williams, *Sport and Identity in the North of England* (Keele: Keele University Press, 1996), pp. 137–64.

bare-knuckle physical contest between two men of immense strength and courage, but at the same time it created a place in the contest for the spectator. Hazlitt, who was observing a prize fight for the first time, spent a good deal of his essay describing the personal logistical problems and pleasures of making his way to Hungerford in the Berkshire countryside to witness the spectacle, and then returning home again afterwards.[5] But it is Hazlitt's visceral thrill in the physical confrontation that emerges most clearly from his account, never more than when Neat[6] lands a terrifying blow on Hickman, 'full in the face'.

> It was doubtful whether he would fall backwards or forwards; he hung suspended for a second or two, and then fell back, throwing his hands in the air, and with his face lifted up to the sky. I never saw any thing more terrific than his aspect just before he fell. All traces of life, of natural expression, were gone from him. His face was like a human skull, a death's head, spouting blood. The eyes were filled with blood, the nose streamed with blood, the mouth gaped blood. He was not like an actual man, but like a preternatural, spectral appearance, or like one of the figures in Dante's *Inferno*. (43)

In America, where prize-fighting (as in Britain earlier) was outlawed in many states in the nineteenth century, there has been a similarly continuing fascination for such events: 'surely its popularity since the days of John L. Sullivan', suggests novelist and boxing enthusiast Joyce Carol Oates, 'has a good deal to do with what Americans honor as the spirit of the individual – his "physical" spirit – in defiance of the state.'[7] Perhaps it is also boxing's pared-down nature compared with other sports, where everything is stripped away to isolate the basic human confrontation of skill and strength, that gives the sport its special attraction and enduring place as the 'noble' and 'manly' art, the ultimate masculine physical contest. It is, as Michael Oriard has

---

5    'The Fight' in Rosalind Vance and John Hampden eds, *William Hazlitt: Essays* (London: Folio Society, 1964), pp. 30–46. Norman Mailer's account of the Mohamed Ali-George Foreman fight is similar in a number of ways, and not just in the title. Norman Mailer, *The Fight* (London: Penguin Books, 2000). Page references are to this edition.
6    Incorrectly given as 'Neate' throughout the essay.
7    Joyce Carol Oates, *On Boxing* (London: Bloomsbury, 1987), p. 114.

said, 'the most constricted of all sports'.[8] It is this characteristic that has no doubt made the sport attractive to film-makers. Part of boxing's 'literaturisation'[9] is the way this has not been confined simply to the written word but has extended to other forms, notably the cinema, especially in America. The portrayal of boxing as a sport of physical pain, drawing upon the images inscribed in Hazlitt's early account, is perhaps most vividly brought to mind today in Martin Scorsese's film *Raging Bull* (1980), a much-praised biopic of the American middleweight fighter of the 1940s Jake LaMotta. Representations of this kind are responsible for the sport having a close and familiar relationship with its public, though one that is at the same time profoundly equivocal. People are both fascinated and repelled by the brutality of boxing.

1

In Ring Lardner's short story 'Champion', first published in 1916, Midge Kelly is an irredeemably bad character.[10] The story is a crude and melodramatic tale of cruelty, selfishness and sadism, all characteristics exhibited by Kelly on his way to becoming middleweight champion. In its basic form it is a conventional sport story of 'rags to riches' but Lardner gives the reader nothing to admire in either its star or the sport at which he succeeds. When Lardner refers to the 'manly art' it is with clear irony, a surprising fact considering Lardner's

8       Michael Oriard, *Dreaming of Heroes: American Sports Fiction, 1868–1980* (Chicago: Nelson-Hall, 1982), p. 98.
9       The idea of 'literaturisation' is used to interesting and rewarding effect in Anthony Bateman, 'The Politics of the Aesthetic: Cricket, Literature, and Culture 1850–1965', unpublished Ph.D. thesis, University of Salford, 2005. The term originates in Steve Redhead, *Post-Fandom and the Millennial Blues: the Transformation of Soccer Culture* (London: Routledge, 1997), pp. 88–92.
10      All references are to David Lodge ed., *The Best of Ring Lardner* (London: J.M. Dent and Sons Ltd, 1984).

background. He had achieved celebrity (which by the time this story was published was considerable) as a sportswriter, with boxing and baseball his principal subjects. As a young man he had edited the *Sporting News* in St Louis and from 1913 to 1916, in his late twenties, had a column in the *Chicago Tribune*. His sports reports were famous, and from 1914 until his death in 1933 his short stories, initially appearing in the immensely popular *Saturday Evening Post*, made him a leading name in America. David Lodge has described Lardner as 'a key figure in the development of modern American fiction'.[11] In the world of sport he was a close friend of the Welsh-American boxer Freddie Welsh, who held the world lightweight title just before the Great War, and was on close terms with many of the country's leading baseball players. But his involvement with the Chicago White Sox, the team involved in the 'fixing' scandal of the 1919 World's Series (referred to by F. Scott Fitzgerald, another close friend, in *The Great Gatsby*) is said to have turned him away from that sport.[12] His fame rested on his writing style, simple and expressive, depending to a great extent for its impact upon the use of popular idioms and speech rhythms:

'they's no use kiddin' ourself any more,' said Tommy Haley. 'He might get down to thirty-seven in a pinch, but if he done below that a mouse could stop him. He's a welter; that's what he is and he knows it as well as I do. He's growed like a weed in the last six mont's. I told him, I says "If you don't quit growin' they won't be nobody for you to box, only Willard[13] and them. "He says, "Well, I wouldn't run away from Willard if I weighed twenty pounds more."' (60)[14]

11   Ibid., p. vii.
12   Daniel A. Nathan, *Saying It's So: A Cultural History of the Black Sox Scandal* (Urbana: University of Illinois Press, 2003) claims that the affair 'scarred' Lardner (p. 57) though notes that his son John Lardner wrote an influential piece for the *Saturday Evening Post* in 1938 which revived interest in the scandal (pp. 78–9).
13   The world heavyweight champion from 1915 to 1919, when he was defeated by Jack Dempsey.
14   See Jonathan Yardley ed., *Selected Stories: Ring Lardner* (New York: Penguin Books, 1997). 'He is the man who taught us how to talk'. (p. xvii)

It is in this vein that Lardner presents Kelly's success in boxing as a triumph of brutality. The character is a natural bully, who uses his strength to achieve his ends against anyone who stands in his way, in the ring or out of it. Family members are not excluded from his sadistic treatment, and the opening of the story has Kelly beating his younger crippled brother in order to extract from him a half-dollar coin. In fact, most of the punches landed in the story fall on people outside the boxing ring: his brother, mother, wife, and former friend. Physical violence, or the threat of it, is a constant feature of Kelly's demeanour. When, for example, he announces to his girlfriend that he intends to ditch her in favour of another woman, her protests are cut short by Kelly's threat: '[…] if I see where you're going to make a fuss, I'll put you in a hospital where they'll keep you quiet.' (70). Similarly, he dismisses the entreaties of a former friend for financial help with a savage punch. 'It's lucky I didn't give him my left or I'd of croaked him. And if I'd hit him in the stomach, I'd of broke his spine.' (69) He solves his problems by resorting to, or threatening, violence. The family, presumably Irish immigrants in Chicago, possesses nothing, and for Kelly boxing becomes a way out of the ghetto. But instead of the sport and Kelly's success in it serving as a meal ticket for the whole family, in the manner of many boxing stories, Lardner turns the convention on its head and shows Midge profiting only for himself. He denies money to his family, even to his estranged wife; she writes:

> I have wrote to you so many times and got no anser and I don't know if you ever got them, so I am writeing again in the hopes you will get this letter and anser. I don't like to bother you with my trubles and I would not only for the baby and I am not asking you should write to me but only send a little money and I am not asking for myself but the baby has not been well a day since last Aug. and the dr. told me she cant live much longer unless I give her better food and that's impossible the way things are. (64)

Midge 'tore the letter into a hundred pieces and scattered them over the floor.' (64) His last contact with his wife was 'a crushing blow on the bride's pale cheek.' (60) It is a remorseless account of sadistic masculinity, partly bred of poverty, and which lends itself to the giving and taking of the brutal treatment that prize-fighting depended upon. 'I'll kill 'em all' is Kelly's refrain. In some ways Lardner's Kelly is a precursor of the cruel, amoral anti-hero typified in much of twentieth-century American pulp fiction.[15]

Lardner's purpose in 'The Champion' becomes clear in the story's conclusion. There is no retribution offered for the evil purposes committed in the story. The repulsive Kelly actually prevails in his designs, without a hint of poetic justice on hand to bring about a fall. On the contrary, his status as a champion ensures that a persona is created by the press to portray Midge as it is believed the reading public would like to see him. This fictional character is a polar opposite of the one elaborated in Lardner's narrative. A reporter from *The News* hears from Kelly's new manager that Midge is 'just a kid; that's all he is; a regular boy [...] Don't know the meanin' o' bad habits.' (71). There follows an inventory of homely virtues which depict a clean-living man committed to domesticity. 'The story in Sunday's *News* was read by thousands of lovers of the manly art.' (72). Lardner's acerbic final comment aims a blow at his own profession and the process of hero worship in which the press was implicated during the early years of the century. No impressions of Kelly from those he has betrayed, hurt and deserted had been gathered by the reporter. As Lardner notes, 'a story built on their evidence would never have passed the sporting editor.' 'It wouldn't get us anything but abuse to print it. The people don't want to see him knocked. He's champion.' (72)

## 2

Lardner's story indicates an ambivalence about boxing in American society. There were some groups of reformers, pursuing the ideal of

---

15    Some of the themes in this kind of writing are discussed by George Orwell, 'Raffles and Miss Blandish' in Sonia Orwell and Ian Angus eds, *The Collected Essays, Journalism and Letters of George Orwell, vol. 3, As I Please* (Harmondsworth: Penguin Books, 1970) pp. 246–59.

the 'virtuous Republic', who sought to abolish pugilism alongside other perceived evils such as alcohol. Opposition to the sport was driven not only by its physical violence but by its association with racketeering. However, the sport's popularity during the First World War, when it was used as physical training for soldiers and thus promoted as cultivating the attributes of skill and courage, deflected some of the criticism, as did the willingness of boxing promoters to accept a degree of state control over their operations. This no doubt ensured that the sport avoided the fate that befell drink with the introduction of Prohibition after the War.[16] Nonetheless, the world of boxing found it hard to establish a 'respectable' reputation, and by the late 1940s its esteem had hit a low point. As two of America's leading boxing historians have noted the fight game was seen as 'a low life sport populated by seedy characters.'[17] The vast majority of championship bouts were controlled by one syndicate, the International Boxing Club, which developed close associations with the *de facto* power in the sport, the gangster known as Frank Carbo.[18]

Mark Robson's film *Champion*, loosely based on the Lardner story, appeared in 1949 in the midst of these developments. It was also a time when the fear of communism was beginning to envelop Hollywood. Radical film-makers had already come under scrutiny in 1947 from the House Committee on Un-American Activities (HUAC), which under the direction of Judge Parnell Thomas sought to root out supposed communists and their influence in the American film industry. Many were identified and pilloried, including the Hollywood Ten, a group of mostly screenwriters who took the Fifth Amendment but were fined and jailed. They included Lardner's son, Ring Lardner Jnr., who wrote the screenplay for *Champion*. In the same year that the HUAC was formed the film director Robert Rossen had made

16  Jeffrey T. Sammons, *Beyond the Ring: the Role of Boxing in American Society* (Urbana: University of Illinois Press, 1988), pp. 60, 62.
17  Randy Roberts and James S. Olson, *Winning is the Only Thing: Sports in America Since 1945* (Baltimore: Johns Hopkins University Press, 1989), p. 79. They point out that in the 1950s 32 per cent of boxers and 12 per cent of managers had criminal records.
18  Ibid., pp. 78–9; Nick Tosches, *Night Train: the Sonny Liston Story* (London: Penguin Books, 2001), pp. 73–9.

what many critics regard as one of the finest films about boxing, *Body and Soul*. It starred the radical Jewish actor John Garfield as Charley Davis, a boxer whose successful career has been embarked upon for the worthy purpose of supporting his needy family, but which ends with the fighter owned 'body and soul' by a crime syndicate. The film is a bitter indictment of both the brutality of the sport and its criminal associations. However *Body and Soul* was made in a climate freer of the witch-hunt paranoia that was to prevail a couple of years later when Robson and his producer Stanley Kramer were making *Champion*, and this affected the way in which the latter film's social comment was construed and mediated.

*Champion* takes the Lardner text and works it into a far more complex and interesting story; it is both visually powerful and much less didactic in its relationship with the viewer. One of the most significant changes to the original is in the character of Midge Kelly himself, whose nastiness is moderated (though only moderated, not fundamentally changed) by the infusion of a certain rogue-ish charm. The alteration was undoubtedly occasioned by the fact that *Champion* was a mainstream Hollywood production whose promoters were seeking box-office appeal. The presence in the film of Kirk Douglas in the Kelly role was the principal means of achieving this, but it equally necessitated an adaptation of Lardner's character to fit the star's own screen persona. Douglas was not as famous in 1949 as he was later to be, when together with actors such as Burt Lancaster[19] he became the apotheosis of a certain kind of American masculinity: white, heterosexual, athletic. He had, however, already made a mark in Hollywood with his appearances in such films as *The Strange Love of Martha Ivers* (1946) and the quintessential film noir *Build My Gallows High* (1947), in which he played a gangster. The following year he was partnered with Burt Lancaster in *I Walk Alone*. At this time Douglas, a relative newcomer to film acting, was fashioning an individual style with distinctive mannerisms to accompany it; the

19  For an actor who specialised in 'athletic' performances, especially early in his career, Lancaster's only foray into sport came when he played the 'disgraced' American athlete Jim Thorpe in *Man of Bronze* (1952). Interestingly, the real-life Thorpe was not white, but indigenous American.

critic David Thomson has noted his speciality in portraying a 'smiling scoundrel',[20] a type Douglas first perfected in the Kelly role. Douglas's characteristic smile is much in evidence during the film, and this gives his character a charm that is completely absent from Lardner's psychopathic Kelly. Moreover, the film gains in emotional warmth by expanding the character of Kelly's crippled brother Connie into a main figure. He is Midge's constant companion and boxing trainer, his physical disability serving as a counterpoint to Kelly's sheer masculine power. He is also Kelly's conscience, a sensitive and considerate man who attempts to provide moral moderation to Midge's unscrupulous nature. In spite of their differences the relationship between them brings to the plot a reminder of family unity which Lardner deliberately negated in his story, so that between Midge and Connie there is something of the sense of companionate teamwork which was later to become familiar in a host of Hollywood 'buddy' films.[21] In *Champion* the device works effectively to emphasize the solidarity of male culture in the boxing gym, a theme that has been a perennial feature both of boxing fictions and the observed 'real' world of the sport.[22] At the same time, however, *Champion* pulls its audience in contrary ways. Alongside the behaviour that makes plausible Kelly/Douglas's attractiveness to other characters in the film, both male and female, and which therefore gives dramatic credibility to the plot, there are a series of loathsome traits. Kelly is manipulative, cruel, and all-too-ready to resort to physical violence to solve his personal problems. They gradually render the character the antithesis of the admired family man, and prepare the audience to accept his death at the end of

---

20  David Thomson, *The Whole Equation: A History of Hollywood* (New York: Little, Brown, 2004), p. 313. See also Stanley Kramer (with Thomas M. Coffey), *A Mad, Mad, Mad, Mad World: A Life in Hollywood* (New York: Harcourt, Brace and Company, 1997), pp. 23–30.

21  The most celebrated of these was probably *Butch Cassidy and the Sundance Kid* (1969).

22  See Laurence de Garis, '"Be a Buddy to Your Buddy": Male Identity, Aggression, and Intimacy in the Boxing Gym' in Jim Mackay, Michael A. Messner and Don Sabo eds, *Masculinities, Gender Relations and Sport* (Sage: London, 2000), pp. 87–107; Loic Waquant, *Body and Soul: Ethnographic Notebooks of an Apprentice Boxer* (Oxford: Oxford University Press, 2003).

the film with equanimity. Evil is punished, and the good man (Connie) walks away with the girl (Emma – Kelly's abused wife). The love that has been nurturing between these two characters is thus sealed and the world of normal family relations set to right.

Focusing thus on the character of Kelly and his rise from nothing to become world champion, Robson touches upon a number of themes that are to be found in other boxing films of the post-war period.[23] Indeed Aaron Baker, reading the film in the broader context of other such pictures, has placed *Champion* historically in a cycle of late 1940s/early 1950s boxing films dealing with the capitalist exploitation of working-class fighters, and which therefore provide a critique of capitalist culture in general.[24] In this respect, Baker argues, *Champion* has a different emphasis from both earlier and later films which foreground, at different times, issues of community, race and individual ambition. Baker further insists that the main theme of *Champion,* its critique of capitalism, is muted as a result of the combined influences of the political circumstances in which the film was made and the director's own career concerns.[25] Both, it is felt, had the effect of displacing the central political subject of the film through the use of a stylised visual montage.[26]

---

23  See, for example, the aforementioned *Body and Soul,* Robert Wise's *The Set-Up* (released at the same time as *Champion* in 1949), Robson's own *The Harder They Fall* (1956), and Martin Scorsese's *Raging Bull* (1980). The theme of corruption was most in evidence in Robson's 1956 film, based on a Budd Schulberg novel, which dealt with fight fixing. It was also the last appearance on the screen of Humphrey Bogart.

24  Aaron Baker, *Contesting Identities: Sports in American Films* (Urbana: University of Chicago Press, 2003), p. 104.

25  See Steven J. Ross ed., *Movies and American Society* (Blackwell Publishers: Oxford, 2002), ch. 7.

26  This was Robson's first directorial role; he had worked his way up through the studio system, learning his craft in particular through working in horror films with Val Lewton; Robson did not, Baker claims, wish to jeopardise his career by falling foul of the politicians. (Baker, *Contesting Identities*, p. 120). Criticism of *Champion's* visual style has come from the American film critic Manny Farber who felt that the depiction of the fights lacked reality, and that Robson's 'vaudevillish' technique produced over-staged and prepared 'strategizing

Baker's analysis brings out some important features of the film, though it might be suggested that his categorisation of it as a 'critique of capitalism' is a little over-rigid. *Champion* is a far more complex film than is allowed for by Baker's representation. The film incorporates a range of topics each of which, to be sure, may be included within the concept of capitalism, though to see them all as confined within it is unduly limiting. Gender issues, for example, come across particularly forcefully. Representations of particular types of masculinity and femininity are a striking feature of the narrative. These are linked to issues of power and the relationships engendered through it. They are both personal (between men, and men and women) and corporate (the power exercised by corrupt businesses over boxers). As is often the case in boxing films – with *Body and Soul* pointing the way – personal ambition ('making it') as a factor in taking up the sport and enduring its harshness is emphasized as a key motive. Last though by no means least, the representation of the sport itself and especially its aesthetic appeal, using the various visual and aural techniques at the disposal of the film-maker, is a major ideological effect of the film. Which of these elements came across to audiences of the day as the major one is difficult, if not impossible, to determine.

The overriding visual effect of *Champion* is a dark one. The film is a clear example of the psychological dramas popular in the late 1940s that have collectively come to be known as *film noir*.[27] The visual appearance of the film is important in establishing the audience's reaction to the sport portrayed. The boxing scenes are filmed in dark interiors, as if suggesting a subterranean world where menace lurks in the broad margins that lie outside the glare of the single bright light which habitually frames the characters. The montage presents a form reminiscent of the paintings of Edward Hopper, *Nighthawks* in particular.

scenes'. Manny Farber, *Negative Space: Manny Farber on the Movies* (London: Studio Vista, 1971), pp. 64–7.

27  See James Naremore, *More Than Night: Film Noir and Its Contexts* (London: University of California Press, 1998). The term was actually first used in France in 1946 to describe a series of American films – *The Maltese Falcon, Double Indemnity, Laura, Murder My Sweet,* and *The Lost Weekend* – which were felt to have been influenced by the work of certain French directors of the late 1930s.

When, for example, Kelly is given his first professional fight he leaves an outdoor scene, sharply shot in contrasting black and white to emphasise the glare of the sun in a mid-western town, and enters an altogether more crepuscular interior. The mood conjured by this cinematography supports the critic Manny Farber's contention that 'while the gangster, cowboy, ballplayer are lauded, the boxer is never presented as anything but a bad nickel.'[28] Nothing of value to ordinary decent people, it seems, can exist in such an environment. And yet it holds a visceral fascination for the viewer, all the more compelling because it is *distanced*, viewed from a position of security.

As may be imagined *Champion* is essentially to do with men operating in a hard, sinister world. Audiences are therefore predisposed to seeing notions of domesticity challenged. In this, the film would not have surprised its audiences. Those already familiar with the Lardner story might have expected domesticity to have an ephemeral place in the film, but the screenplay works the subject rather more subtly, constantly offering prospects of stable married relationships, only to have them dashed to the ground. Kelly has relationships with three women; they represent homeliness (Emma), sex and control (Grace), and sophistication (Mrs Harris). In none is the relationship anything more than an opportunistic one for Kelly, in the sense that the woman will either help further his business ambitions or, in the short term, satisfy his sexual hunger. The liaisons confirm his masculinity but mean nothing emotionally. Kelly's attitude towards women is exposed in a scene with his new manager, Jerome Harris, whom Kelly has appointed to remove Tommy Haley in order to further his own ambitions. Harris's wife, the sophisticate, quickly becomes the object of Kelly's lust, though to his alarm she appears to respond to him in a more emotional way. To end the affair and reclaim his wife Harris resorts to a form of manipulation to which Kelly readily succumbs. Unable to confront the boxer physically to reclaim his wife – Kelly rules in this form of masculinity – Harris simply buys him off. Faced with the choice between woman and money Kelly has no problem in making a decision. Money, and the power it bestows, is what really matters to Midge. By contrast women

---

28    Manny Farber, *Negative Space* (London: Studio Vista, 1971), p. 64.

represent 'trouble' and domesticity, which means a burdensome attachment that might hinder Midge's egotistical lifestyle; even women who have no designs on marriage seem to worry him. He ditches Grace, the sex object, at the point when her designs to control him as a boxer become apparent; and he does it with a chilling threat of violence: 'I'll put you in the hospital for a long, long time.' Is he afraid of women? In his final fight Kelly is taking a terrible beating, the consequence of having been complacent about his preparations. What galvanises him into a frenzy of action, turning the prospect of defeat into a victory, is the sight of Harris's wife in the crowd. It stirs a well of hatred, no doubt in part for the system that Harris himself represents as a fat-bellied businessman; but it is clearly a hatred also of women. It is with the image of Mrs Harris burned in his mind (raising, perhaps, a suggestion of homoerotic undercurrents in the story) that Kelly summons up the energy and violence needed to knock his opponent out and retain his title.

*Champion* is a story of ambition, of a desire to succeed in American society by applying the skill and resources at an individual's disposal, and of doing whatever is necessary to climb the ladder. To a degree it is a success story. Kelly rises to become champion, but as in many other fictional portrayals of sport the audience is left wondering whether success is worth achieving if the means necessary to achieve it are despicable ones. Do we really want to take people like Kelly as heroes and invest our admiration in them? The answer to a large extent, as in Lardner's short story, is of course 'no'. And the fact that the film offers an ending contrary to Lardner's only points up the similarity in theme of the two texts. Where Lardner leaves Kelly as a hero manufactured by the press, though with the reader having been privileged by the narrative to see behind the press image, the film exacts moral retribution for Kelly's behaviour. In the very aftermath of his retaining of his title after a brutal contest the champion suffers what is presumably a brain haemorrhage and dies in his dressing room.

The film therefore denounces not ambition but the means by which it has been pursued. Moreover, in an echo of the Lardner story, the sport itself is absolved of blame by a final statement from brother Connie, who tells a newspaperman that Midge was 'a credit to the fight game'. He and Emma (Midge's wife) then walk off in the film's final scene, which suggests not only a restoration of family values, but a return to social normality through the elimination of Midge and the triumph of good over evil. However, the couple leave the scene down one of the familiar dark corridors, framed only by the single light. A feeling of doubt and uncertainty lingers over the final shot.

Baker has argued that the film presents an easy and naive resolution to the social problems it has raised. 'By punishing Midge for his greed and violence, *Champion* exemplifies how even many social problem films made in Hollywood conclude with the naive assumption that America is a place where any injustice can be fixed with only minor reform'.[29] This may well be the message taken away by many viewers, and to that extent the film is a good deal less ambiguous than the story, where Lardner leaves moral questions unresolved, at least within the narrative if not within readers' minds. But might there not remain a certain residual sympathy for Kelly, not because of his personal demeanour but for the 'cause' he has struggled to advance during the film? This takes us to the heart of the film's political discourse about boxing as a sport and the men who perform it. For alongside the picture of a repulsive character there is also, we should recall, the attractive aspect of the Midge/Kirk Douglas figure. One of the film's recurring themes is his insistence on success through individual effort, to preserve the place in American society of the 'small man'. Midge typifies this figure throughout the film, far more than the character in the Lardner story. The film's first main scene (after the opening credits have established that Kelly has become the champion) takes the viewer in flashback to the beginning of Midge's story. He and Connie are travelling to California in the hope of claiming a share in a business venture that has been promised them, though it subsequently emerges that they have been the victims of a fraudster. On a railway train they are confronted by three desperate men who attempt to take by force what few savings Midge and Connie have. Midge's fighting skills get the two of them out of danger, and we are thus introduced to Midge the incipient boxer. The symbolic

29    Baker, *Contesting Identities,* p. 123.

power of the scene, however, derives from its taking place in a boxcar of a moving train; the two are taking an illegal ride, like thousands of hoboes before them, to seek a better deal elsewhere. The thugs, for all their menace, are fellow travellers, victims of an economic system that has ditched them; they are unwanted labour. While the film's narrative is placed within the post-war period these images provide instant connotations of the Depression and the despair of the 'forgotten man'. They remind filmgoers of a particular political intervention in American life that caused millions to place their trust in FDR and the New Deal in the 1930s. *Champion's* political theme of the struggling little man is thus established through the visual images of a fight in a boxcar in this early scene. The politics draw from a longstanding European and American tradition of the independent artisan seeking to preserve his autonomy against the power of both big business and, more especially, the parasitic financiers and rentiers who profit from the labour of others. For the most part, bearing in mind the political circumstances surrounding the making of the film, these ideas are focused upon Midge and often become confused with expressions of his personal greed. 'I'm not going to be a "hey you" all my life', he says, giving voice to a sentiment which could be read as either an individual aspiration or a clarion call on behalf of the downtrodden masses. Similarly, when Midge declares that 'no fat bellies with big cigars are going to make a monkey out of me' it is as much a broader and unseen economic context to which he is alluding as to his own personal enmities. Cinema audiences of the late 1940s would surely have been awake to such political references without the film needing to reinforce the point by including representative characters. There are, however, some such examples encountered by Midge and Connie. Their first fight, which comes about adventitiously, is set up by an unscrupulous promoter who scandalously fleeces Kelly of his rightful earnings. The man has a fat belly and a big cigar. But, as Baker has noted, there are relatively few such emblems of personal economic power in the film; Jerome Harris is clearly one of them, though a somewhat effete case.[30] What is more pertinent is the ever-present *suggested* threat of corruption and of the control exercised by forces

30    Ibid., p. 122.

outside Kelly's immediate world. In one of the film's key scenes this threat is indeed introduced, not by actual people but by their *shadows*, as Kelly, Connie and Tommy Haley are menaced by unseen hoodlums seeking revenge for gambling losses following Kelly's refusal to 'throw' a contest as instructed. This scene leads immediately into another, perhaps the most striking in the entire film, where the gangsters emerge from yet more dark corridors and corner Kelly in the boxing ring. The fight that ensues has, of course, nothing to do with sport. Its purpose is to bring Kelly to heel, to make him aware of who controls the sport. It is an ironic comment on the idea of the noble and manly art, all the more powerful for the scene's being set in the boxing ring itself. Kelly, bravely resisting, is outnumbered and overpowered, saved from possible maiming or even death only by the sound of approaching police sirens which cause the hoodlums to scatter. The threat they pose, however, does not go away and remains a brooding presence throughout the film.

Kelly's struggle is one of maintaining the place of the small man in sport, and by extension, in society at large. The boxing business of which Kelly is a part, and which he seeks to safeguard, is essentially a small-scale economy – himself, Connie, and Tommy Haley, supplemented by the sparring partners and gym staff employed in the training camp before a big fight. Kelly's relationship with Tommy Haley, also a more central figure in film than in story, is important to his development as a fighter. It is Haley who 'discovers' Kelly as a raw slugger, recognising in his strength and courage the potential for success. He schools him for the big time by instilling the ring craft and discipline necessary for success in the sport. If not precisely a father figure Haley is Kelly's mentor, and his presence alongside Connie serves as a reminder that there is good to be derived from the sport. When Kelly dismisses Haley in favour of Harris, a businessman rather than a boxing trainer, he soon realises his mistake and reverts to Haley, with whom he wins his title. The team's success is built upon each member fulfilling a specific productive function; there are no fat bellies with big cigars living off the profits. The team is the nearest Midge and Connie come, during the narrative time of the film, to a settled family. In general Midge himself is at his most settled in this milieu and in the wider context of boxing culture,

148

focused upon the gym. The scene in which Midge and Connie forge their relationship with Tommy takes place in Brady's Gym, Los Angeles. It is a man's world of good friendship and sociability; boxers are training; there is activity; everyone is busy; it is a *good* place to be. The scene is shot, significantly, in a stark brightness produced by sunlight through windows which contrasts with the film's predominantly *noir* tones. It is focused upon Haley. His ideas lead the discussion of the three men, which provides a statement of the film's stance on boxing. Haley first tries to dissuade Kelly from going into the sport; it is violent and brutal, it carries the danger of physical injury, and it is pervaded by the smell of corruption: 'take a deep breath – it stinks in here doesn't it, and it's not sweat.' But Kelly is unmoved by this indictment. The sport, for him, is a meal ticket, he has little alternative unless to turn to lowly and demeaning jobs that undersell his ambition. It is this – his ambition – that convinces Tommy of Kelly's determination, and we learn Tommy Haley's true feelings about the sport. He is addicted to boxing for the pleasure the sport brings. In this scene, as in others, his riposte when asked why he bothers with boxing at all is: 'Me, I like to watch a couple of good boys in action.' It is the stance of the pure sports lover. It is an existential statement, a confession of something that cannot rationally be accounted for but which is part of male psyche. In spite of the degradation to which boxing can sink there is still something at the heart of it for people like Tommy, an aesthetic to be admired and, therefore, to be encouraged. With Tommy around, there can be good in sport. For all of Midge's conceit and selfishness, something of Tommy's love for boxing rubs off on him. And after Midge, there is Connie to carry the banner of decency into the world at large.[31]

31   It could be argued that the Brady's Gym scene represents the homoerotic element in sport, as discussed, for example, in Brian Pronger, *The Arena of Masculinity: Sports, Homosexuality and the Meaning of Sex* (London: GMP Publishers, 1990), ch. vi. Pronger suggests that sport carries a basic paradox for masculinity in that on the one hand it promotes competitiveness and strength while on the other it sustains male affinity and the exclusion of women. 'The orthodox world of sports is a covert world of homoeroticism.' (p. 178). I prefer to interpret the scene simply as placing sport in a conventional world of male

3

These two versions of the Midge Kelly story are difficult to pin down in any categorical way because each takes a contradictory stance on sport. Herein lies their chief interest. Lardner made his living as a sportswriter, at which he was very successful. He was responsible in much of his writing for creating sporting heroes of a populist kind, who behaved and spoke like ordinary folk, and who took their place in the first great blossoming of the mass media in the twentieth century. He might even have been responsible for transforming, through his writing, the 'low' sport of baseball into some kind of respectability.[32] To do this, however, required that his readers reacted to his stories with a degree of sympathy. His story about Midge Kelly therefore goes against the grain of his own project. It is not so much 'anti-sport' as 'anti' the people in sport, including those like himself who represented the spectacle and its heroes to the public. His treatment of the fight milieu in 'Champion' seems therefore less affectionate than that to be found in his other sports writing of this period. Whilst his characters, notably in 'Alibi Ike' and 'A Bushman's Letters Home', are painted warts and all they nevertheless retain a mark of humanity; none is quite as unremittingly dreadful as Kelly. Lardner's story therefore leaves open the possibility that boxing might contain worthwhile endeavours, whilst at the same time cautioning readers about the emotional commitment they place in heroes who are represented to them disingenuously. In the last analysis it is sporting hero-worship, rather than sport, that is the object of Lardner's criticism.

Some thirty years later, the film of *Champion* makes Kelly less of a loathsome bully though without by any means transforming the character into someone fundamentally different. It also attempts to disconnect boxing itself, as an athletic practice, from some of its

exclusiveness, although the ambiguous attitude towards women in the film might lend some support to Pronger's ideas.

32    See Gordon Burn, 'The Games Writers Play', *Guardian Review*, 9 October 2004, pp. 4–6.

criminal attachments. Although there remains in the film-noir montage a residual sense of the sport lying outside the pale of respectable society, Tommy Haley's addiction to watching 'two good boys in action' suggests something pure and innocent at the core of the sport. We are inclined to believe this because the film portrays Haley (in contrast to the story, where he is a marginal figure) as a 'good' man, honest, forthright and untainted by any double-dealing. His threat, made in the key scene where he takes Midge under his wing, to leave the sport behind because of its corrupt associations, reinforced his position as the film's moral centre alongside the equally pure Connie. Haley's addiction to the boxing aesthetic might also be interpreted as a plea for individual freedom to indulge in a physical contest that calls not only for skill but for courage, and which therefore makes demands beyond the call of 'normal' life. Yet, in the final analysis, the film challenges a narrative about boxing that was both popular and persistent in American society in the twentieth century. There are countless stories, biographies and films in which the socially disadvantaged no-hoper is plucked from the gutter and set on the road to fame and fortune in the boxing ring. To emphasize the quasi-sacred nature of the redemption it is often a priest who sees the potential of a poor boy (frequently a prison inmate), and in the gym harnesses for sport the energies that had previously been applied to crime or some other form of moral aberration. In the case of Sonny Liston, world heavyweight champion in the early 1960s, life apparently imitated art in this respect.[33] It is a narrative of sport's power to redeem and which therefore worked to give boxing a social value as well as being a route to success. In this way boxing was made to exemplify, perhaps as effectively as any sport, the American Dream.

Both texts of the *Champion* story skirt around these issues but offer no unequivocal position, either on the sport of boxing or on the role of sport in society. Their equivocation indicates a continuing ambivalence about boxing. From its earliest days the sport has provoked both support and hostility in almost equal measure. It can undoubtedly be brutal, though rarely in the ways portrayed in cinematic representations of fight scenes. Manny Farber was right to

33    Tosches, *Night Train*, 50–2.

condemn *Champion* for its exaggerated depiction of savagery – real boxing matches simply do not have so much direct hitting.[34] The sport is, as its advocates will always maintain, the noble art of *self defence*, and professional fighters are, for the most part, just too skilful to allow their defence to be breached so often by a slugger like Midge Kelly. Nevertheless, in recent years demands for the banning of the sport have been revived following death and serious injury in the ring. The case of Michael Watson, who suffered brain damage in a contest with Chris Eubank in 1991, has ensured that the ethical implications of the versions of masculinity on display in the boxing ring will continue to be scrutinized. Kelly's death at the end of the film of *Champion* is not only a case of the plot's logical poetic justice; it also stands as a symbol for a terminal decline that the sport of boxing itself might have invited.

34    Farber, *Negative Space*, p. 65.

# Chapter Eight
## 'A Perfected Model of an Imperfect World': Thomas Keneally's *A Family Madness*[1]

Thomas Keneally is famous for a book – *Schindler's Ark* (1982)[2] – that became a major film. In *A Family Madness* (1985) he follows up the same theme: the terrible history of eastern Europe during the Second World War. Much of the novel is concerned with Belorussian politics and the attempts of nationalist groups, through collaboration with the Germans, to achieve an independent state. Strangely, though, this story is juxtaposed with one that is literally and figuratively thousands of miles apart from it. This other story concerns working-class Australians in the 1980s and one in particular, Terry Delaney, a semi-professional rugby league player for Penrith, near Sydney.[3] It is his involvement, following a first accidental meeting that grows into a deep relationship, with an Australian-Belorussian family – the Kabbels – which provides the link between the two contrasted settings. The narrative shifts between different locations and the events are narrated in different voices. Much of the story comes in the form of journals, diaries and histories composed by the characters, while some is from the standpoint of a conventional third-person narrator. The disjointed narrative is a familiar technique of Keneally's, used in his more recent *Bettany's Book*.[4] In this sense *A Family Madness* poses problems familiar to historians – dealing with 'sources', deciding on their reliability, composing a plausible chain of events, and also taking different perspectives, from the top-down and the bottom-up. There seems no doubt that Keneally is bridging the 'big' political issue of

1 All references are to the Sceptre edition, London 1986.
2 Subsequently re-titled *Schindler's List* following the success of the film.
3 An iconic town in Australian sporting history, being also the birthplace of Richie Benaud, the former Australian cricket captain.
4 London: Sceptre, 2001.

genocide with its immense moral problems – an issue which had not disappeared from the international arena with the defeat of the Nazis – with an 'ordinary' life in the western-Sydney suburbs. In this setting there are many personal domestic dramas, mostly about marriage and money, but nothing occurs that has the same momentous effects as life in Belorussia in the early 1940s. The mundane entries in Terry Delaney's match diaries, for example, provide an extraordinary contrast with the events related in the journals of Stanislaw Kabbelski, Chief of Police in Staroviche, Belorussia, and Nazi-collaborator.

# 1

The Kabbels are 'a family marred by history' (294). Their Australian story is in a certain sense a sequel to the story of Oskar Schindler. It is about adapting to life after war, and in particular living with the memories of the atrocities and compromises with which the family has been implicated through its involvement with the Nazi state. Stanislaw's son, Radislaw (Rudi) Kabbel, cannot recreate a fulfilling life, even in distant Australia where, in the late 1940s, he was taken by his father. He carries a guilt learnt through his own personal memories of the war and through the influence of his father. It is a guilt also passed to Rudi's three children, though all are Australian-born and were it not for the family's terrible legacy might have grown up, like many other immigrants, into an 'Australian way of life'. Though successful materially, ironically as a 'security' firm, the Kabbels cannot find any spiritual solace. In the desolate urban landscape of New South Wales where they live, a vengeful sense of history bears down on them.

Their story interweaves with that of Delaney. He is also of immigrant stock (Irish) married to the daughter of an immigrant (Italian). Religion, matrimony, and social class bind them. Although their Australian lineage is longer than that of the Kabbels, the Delaneys are 'outsiders', set somewhat apart by their working-class origins and by their religion. One of the great Australian legends is that of Ned Kelly – Irish, Catholic, marginal, criminalised, unjustly treated.[5] Delaney, however, is making some kind of mark in Australia and has certainly attained what traditionally has been expected of immigrants by the country's governors – 'the Australian the way of life'. His father is well respected in his work as a lorry driver turned despatch clerk at a local transport firm, and Terry, though lacking in educational qualifications, has a steady job with a security firm. He and his wife, Gina, have a nice home, with prospects of a family. By contrast, his workmate Brian Stanton is beset by money troubles, the demands of a young family, and the consequences of his own wayward temperament. The Delaneys, therefore, seem comparatively well set. What gives Delaney the edge is his own solid demeanour - he is a typical Aussie 'battler' – and, crucially, the extra money he earns from match fees as a rugby player. He is not a leading player, but clearly has expectations of improvement, though in his dour way he does not imagine that there is any easy route to success. During the course of the novel, however, he does succeed in making the upward move to the first-grade team of his club. Delaney's life has been shaped by such prospects. His job in security, doing night shifts, was chosen at an early stage of his career because it allowed him time for daylight rugby training. 'His football was to be his career. It would lead him to jobs in Public Relations or writing for the tabloids' (45). Sport, then, forms one of the central pillars in the construction of Delaney's life; a path to material rewards as well as a consuming passion.

The rugby provides a number of reference points for Delaney. He is, of course, a more than average player with ambition and a sharp sporting brain. This is revealed in the match diaries he composes. They show him to be an astute analyst of matches, a player who (with the good fortune to remain free of injury in a punishing sport) might well become a local star. His sporting pedigree, as a man who has played in high-level rugby competitions, accords him status: 'If you belonged to a Jersey Flegg team you had honour in your neighbourhood and your future was limitless' (110). However, he harbours a

5    Peter Cary, *True History of the Kelly Gang* (Queensland: Queensland University Press, 2000).

grievance that his talents might not be allowed to flourish because of the preference in the League for imported players. When a friend anticipates Delaney's promotion to the first grade, he replies: 'If they don't bring in a Banana-bender or a Pom. They probably will you know. They only pay lip service to the local blokes' (197). He has a particular dislike for an English player who occupies Delaney's position in the first-grade team; Delaney holds no respect for this man (Deecock), nor for another one (Tancred) brought over from England to strengthen the forwards:

> 'Deecock had it [...] looks like he'll be the weak link again this season like last [...] Tancred's the sort of thickhead who wouldn't work in an iron lung. That's the trouble with Pommy forwards - always knew it was, average bloke watching the game knows it is - they look sort of fast on muddy Yorkshire grounds, but when they get out here on a hard and fast Australian ground they're just as slow as they were back in the quagmire.' (75)

There is a feeling that Australian talent and common sense ('average bloke watching the game knows it is') is somehow being subordinated to international influences. Delaney's absence from the first-grade team, therefore, is not simply a matter of individual skill. Though Delaney is a sensible and honourable man, not fooled by simplistic answers to problems, he has an Australian's residual suspicion of foreign influences. Moreover, the locating of the story in the Penrith district is significant; not only is it a focal point of rugby league but an old British township. Just along the road towards Sydney is Parramatta, the 'cradle city' of Australia, as the town's history describes it, founded in 1788 and the second oldest settlement.[6] This is 'deep' Australia.

Rugby serves as an important social focus in Delaney's life. The Leagues club, the home of the rugby team, also has a key institutional role as a cornerstone of the community. The revenue drawn from the popular pastime of gambling on its poker machines provides the source of Delaney's and the other professionals' earnings from the game. It also finances the overseas imports. The club is equally important as a place of identity and stability in life. The Leagues club

---

6    James Jervis, *The Cradle City of Australia: a History of Parramatta 1788–1961* (Sydney: City Council of Parramatta, 1961), p. xiii.

represents 'us', where 'us' might be the local club in competition against other clubs, or the working class as a social group.[7] The camaraderie of the rugby team, with its sometimes exuberant displays of male bonding, is moderated into a Saturday evening neighbourhood 'mateship' at the Leagues club when wives, girlfriends and family gather together to celebrate their community in drinking, gambling, and socialising. Delaney describes rugby league at one point as the 'workers' game (110), a description which reminds us that this sport has a particular place in a society where sport generally is held in high esteem. Like its counterpart in Britain, where rugby league was devised in the 1890s, it was restricted geographically to certain areas - chiefly New South Wales and Queensland. Its origins in the inner-Sydney working-class districts of Balmain and Surry Hills meant that many clubs forged strong links with Labor and Catholic organisations in the years immediately before the 1914–18 War. There are several instances of labour leaders acting as patrons and officials of rugby league clubs.[8] The game's emergence and consolidation in the decade or so before the First World War reflected a growing labour consciousness and self-confidence after the reverses of workers' organisations in the labour disputes of the 1890s.[9] Unlike rugby union, however, league did not achieve a position in the sporting establishment. At school level it was generally confined to Catholic institutions, and this cachet held it back socially.[10] At the same time,

7    See Andrew Moore, *The Mighty Bears! A Social History of North Sydney Rugby League* (New South Wales: Macmillan, 1996), ch. 6.
8    See Chris Cunneen, 'The Rugby War: the Early History of Rugby League in New South Wales 1907–1915' in R. Cashman and M. McKernan eds, *Sport in History: the Making of Modern Sporting History* (Queensland: Queensland University Press, 1979), pp. 293–306; Moore, *Mighty Bears*, p. 118.
9    See Stephen Alomes, *A Nation At Last? The Changing Character of Australian Nationalism 1880–1988* (New South Wales: Angus and Robertson, 1988).
10   D. Adair and W. Vamplew, *Sport in Australian History* (Melbourne: Oxford University Press, 1997), pp. 74–5. It is worth noting that the greatest Australian sporting hero of the inter-war period, the cricketer Don Bradman, made public his attachment to the *Protestant* cause and allegedly did not get on well with some of the Catholic members of the national team. Moreover, soon after his arrival in Sydney in 1928 Bradman volunteered as a private in the new militia being formed in the face of economic depression and social unrest - he 'showed

however, and somewhat contradictorily in view of its Catholic-Irish connections, rugby league was an imperial game and preserved close ties with Britain through regular international competition. Though it has been claimed that Australians used their sport to develop a national identity with a strong anti-British feeling,[11] this does not appear to have been so much the case with Australian rugby league. At least until the 1970s relations with British teams and their officials were cordial, and the sport contributed to a sense of belonging to a 'British race', connecting its solidarities of social class to feelings of 'whiteness'.[12] Moreover, rugby is a moral code to those who play it. In fact, sport generally is seen to offer a space for sense and reasonableness. During the summer, in a jobless state, 'Delaney played cricket on Saturdays for the sake of his sanity' (272). His mate Stanton recounts how, when a policeman, he had dealt with a volatile wife-beating Serbian: 'Stanton would [...] remove the kitchen knife from the husband's hand, wave a truncheon at him, and tell him that in countries where cricket was played they had family law courts for dealing with the matters which in more primitive non-cricket and non-Rugby nations were dealt with by marital disembowelment' (33). When Delaney himself commits foul play in rugby, breaking the jaw of an opposing player, the full power of the game's rules is brought to bear on him. He feels the shame deeply. In these ways Delaney the rugby player can share in traditions and identities which, while keeping him out of the 'establishment' reaches of society, nevertheless give him a place in the white and essentially British Australian mainstream.

his hand as a supporter of the conservative Protestant supporters of Empire and ensured protection from the right-wing - legitimate and paramilitary - organisations should trouble arise.' (Charles Williams, *Bradman: An Australian Hero*, London: Abacus, 1997), pp. 32–3.

11    See W.F. Mandle, *Going It Alone: Australia's National Identity in the Twentieth Century* (Harmondsworth: Penguin Books, 1980), ch. 2.

12    Stuart Ward, *Australia and the British Embrace: the Demise of the Imperial Ideal* (Victoria: Melbourne University Press, 2001); Tony Collins, 'Australian Nationalism and Working-Class Britishness: the Case of Rugby League Football', *History Compass*, 3 (2005), AU 142, 1–19.

The importance of this is seen when the question of immigration is considered. It has been the area on which the issue of Australia's identity has been chiefly focused. Throughout the history of the country in the twentieth century there has been a clear line of thinking which has represented the country as 'white' and separate. 'The Australian nation', says one of its recent historians, 'was shaped by the fear of invasion and concern for the purity of the race.'[13] It is a fear that has been countered by the institution of Anzac Day with its symbol of the resilient 'Digger' battling gamely against the odds – which included incompetent *British* commanders in the case of the original Anzacs – while at the same time being part of an organic race community of British people. The continuing appeal of the song *Waltzing Matilda*, which laments the plight of the dispossessed and which has threatened on occasions to become Australia's national anthem, further underlines this notion of the country's 'soul'.[14] The threat of the Asian – the 'yellow peril' – has had a continuous presence since the nineteenth century, and frequently resulted in the exclusion of immigrants from Asia. During the Second World War, of course, the 'yellow peril' became very proximate: the combined fear of invasion and the threat to the purity of the race were physically close. Australian forces fought in New Guinea to hold the line against Japanese expansion, while the country's political opinion regarded Britain's capitulation at Singapore in 1942 as a strategic betrayal of Australia's place as a white dominion in the southern seas. After 1949 the spectre of communism in Asia reinforced the old sense of the yellow peril. Disenchantment with the 'mother country', and a simultaneous attraction towards the USA, can probably be dated from these momentous events of the 1940s. In the twenty or so years following the end of the war Australia experienced the immigration of some two million people, mostly from non-English-speaking

---

13    Stuart Macintyre, *A Concise History of Australia* (Cambridge: Cambridge University Press, 2004), p. 148.
14    Therese Radic, 'The Song Lines of *Waltzing Matilda*' in Richard Nile ed., *The Australian Legend and its Discontents* (Queensland: University of Queensland Press, 2000), ch. 6.

countries, though this influx was moderated by a determination to 'Australianise' the newcomers through the creation of a monoculture. Up to the mid-1980s Australia had received some two million British immigrants, alongside a further one million from the European continent. It was not, however, until the Labor government of Gough Whitlam in the early 1970s that a more accommodating stance towards non-white immigrants was adopted, with the introduction of a much more multi-cultural concept of Australian society which extended to immigrants an acknowledgement of their own cultural traditions.[15] It is in this context of changing cultural norms that Delaney's contact with the Kabbels takes place, bringing with it disturbing new experiences that threaten the certainties of the worlds of church, class, and sport.

*A Family Madness* brings the process of change that was taking place in Australia in the 1970s and 80s to a personal level. Delaney is assailed by change. His story, the narrative time of which is 1983 and 1984, is framed by a declining Australian economy in the hands of the neo-liberal Malcolm Fraser. Delaney's own security firm feels the effects, among which is the denial of a promotion to an administrative job for Delaney himself. A general despair appears to pervade the moral climate of the western suburbs, where welfare agencies have sprung up to provide assistance and counselling for the unfortunate.

---

15    Macintyre, *Concise History,* p. 225; Alomes, *Nation At Last?*, p. 236 ff; Tom Millar, 'Australia, Europe and Asia', *Australian Studies,* 1 (1988), 42–52. The recent case of the refugees, mostly Afghan, rescued from a sinking Indonesian boat by the Norwegian vessel the *Tampa* illustrates enduring Australian attitudes towards immigration. The Australian authorities refused to allow the *Tampa* to land the refugees on Australian territory, directing the captain to take them to internment camps on the island of Nauru and in Papua New Guinea. This so-called 'Pacific Solution' of off-loading refugees away from the mainland drew criticism from liberal circles in Australia but nevertheless brought popular support for the ruling Liberal-National Party. Thomas Keneally has denounced both the government's response to this incident and Australia's overall policy on the detention of refugees: 'The truth is that there exist in our plain outer suburbs [...] double-walled gulags for would-be refugees.' (Thomas Keneally, 'Gulags in the Sun', *Guardian*, 21 February 2004, 46; Macintyre, *Concise History*, pp. 270–2.)

160

At any of them you could meet the same tousled and bruised wives, and men who had once worked at the abattoirs at Homebush or Riverstone or at the forklift factory at Flemington or the heavy engineering at Clyde. As workers they had been loudly discontented and whimsically bought Lotto tickets each week, prepared to wait a lifetime for the gods of the numbers to do them a favour. Now they were reflective and awesomely docile, half-shaven, a sort of fluff of ennui caught in the crevices of their faces. (11)

The vision of Australia presented by Keneally is grimly counterposed to the notion of a rural idyll. It is typified by Stanton's house, a nineteenth-century timber building shaded by a large cypress tree, also a remnant of the previous century. It stands as a reminder of the country's history. Stanton has removed the tree because it causes damp in the house, but without it 'the lawn looked parched [...] and the little house, surrounded by hard-lined brick bungalows, looked naked and bereaved. The tree and the old house had been planted together. Delaney was aware of that, and he wondered why Stanton wasn't and had cut up the pine so willingly' (27). A further reminder of Australia's origins as a penal colony is the nearby prison, which is the cause of Stanton's eventual degradation on a charge of murder.

In these circumstances the financial rewards and the moral disciplines imposed by sport offer safeguards against disaster. Delaney sees in Stanton a warning against recklessness. Stanton had lost his secure job in the police as a result of his own sexual indiscretions, was forced to leave without a pension, and now scrapes by on the margins. At a later point in the story, without a job after the collapse of the Kabbels' security business, he resorts to robbing petrol stations to provide for his kids' Christmas presents. Delaney had resolved never to become the victim of what he called 'unlucky passions', chance events that have the power to change people's lives for the worse. 'Delaney intended to suffer no such unlucky passions in his own life' (32). Security is not only his job (perhaps a route to greater security) but also his watchword. The alternative is to be dragged down, like Stanton.

Such depressing material and psychological circumstances are accompanied by a worrying absence of bearings in Delaney's spiritual life. This comes to the surface when he becomes disturbed by a brief sexual unfaithfulness to his wife, brought about directly from sport. During a holiday to Hawaii for the players of his team as a reward for reaching the grand final at the Sydney Cricket Ground, Delaney finds himself with a girl who has come to a party at the team's hotel. It is all very transitory and accidental, Delaney joining in the party for the sake of tradition – 'A Rugby League team on a celebratory journey had to create a store of outrageous events to take home' (23). He remembers the girl as 'un-ethnic', and that she was a waitress. He did not even know her name. But the incident troubles him – it is an 'unlucky passion' – and he seeks solace from his priest, Father Doig, known to all as 'Andrew'. Doig is a Catholic modernist who has abandoned the confession and the pronouncing of absolution; he offers counsel, or 'the rite of reconciliation' as he prefers to call it; Delaney's father sees him as 'like some social worker on talkback radio' (39). Where Delaney seeks moral absolutes in his relationship with his wife, Doig offers pragmatism. He offers to negotiate a settlement, and is prepared to ditch traditional rules for the sake of reaching a compromise, a 'rational arrangement' (263). All credibility in Doig's brand of religion is lost when Delaney finally encounters him in a gay bar. Delaney is there against his will with mates who are out for a laugh. For Doig, however, it is a natural environment, 'part of my rational arrangement.' '"Are you going to tell your flock about this?" asked Delaney. "Are you going to explain it away for my old man the way you explain every other bloody thing?"' (323).

Meeting the Kabbels is also the start of Delaney's fall. They bring the awful legacy of Old World ethnic hatred to Australia. The result is the self-destruction of the Kabbel family and, connected to it, the disintegration of Delaney's life. What he has most feared – becoming a victim of an 'unlucky passion' – happens. In telling the story of the Kabbels, which takes up more than half the novel, Keneally adopts a literary technique similar to the one he employed in *Schindler's Ark*: 'To use the texture and devices of a novel to tell a true story'.[16] Of course, the character of Oskar Schindler was based on an actual person, whereas the Kabbels are fictional creations, but their story concerns historical events of an all-too-real nature. They relate to the struggle of a group of Belorussian nationalists to establish independence for their country under the leadership of the patriot

16    Thomas Keneally, *Schindler's Ark* (London: Sceptre, 1983 ed.), p. 13.

Radislaw Ostrowsky.[17] Stanislaw Kabbelski and his wife Danielle are an educated and cultivated couple who have experienced the transfer of their native country between Russians and Germans in the first half of the twentieth century. 'Both families were clans of lawyers, always political' (64). They are strongly anti-communist, a hatred of the Bolshevik revolution and its consequences being the driving force of their single-minded obsession. In other respects they have the appearance of latter-day 1848 revolutionaries, concerned with constitutions and national liberation. Following the Bolshevik revolution and the incorporation of Belorussia into the Soviet regime, they lived in Poland, where Stanislaw became a member of the Polish parliament representing Western Belorussia. The Kabbelskis have two children, Genia and Radislaw ('Radek' or 'Rudi'), the latter born in 1933, the former a little earlier. In September 1939, after a brief sojourn with Ostrowski's patriots at a Baltic hotel where a provisional government is formed, the family return to Warsaw. In the summer of 1941, in the wake of the German assault on the Soviet Union that ends the Nazi-Soviet pact, the Kabbelskis triumphantly make their return to their native land where Stansilaw is appointed Chief of Police for the city of Staroviche.

The family's experiences are narrated in two voices. One is that of Stanislaw himself, in the form of journals found by his daughter Genia, living in Paris, on a visit to Berlin in the early 1980s. There she meets an old friend with whom Stanislaw had left 'a dozen or so leather-covered notebooks' (57) which are passed to Genia, who in turn sends them to Radislaw. Since 1949 he has lived in Australia, taken there as an immigrant by his father. The other 'source' is Radislaw's own history of his family during the period from 1939 to 1945, which he has compiled from his own memories and his father's journals. Thus Keneally presents the events of Eastern Europe during the Second World War from the point of view of a man deeply

17    See Nicholas P. Vakar, *Belorussia: the Making of a Nation. A Case Study* (Cambridge, Mass.: Harvard University Press, 1956), esp. pp. 170–90, 204–6, 220. V. Kalush, *In the Service of the People for a Free Belorussia: Biographical Notes on Professor Radislaw Ostrowski* (London: Abjednannie, 1964). The two accounts contrast sharply; the former is critical of Ostrowski's feeble leadership and toadying to the Nazis, whilst the latter is pure hagiography.

implicated in the high politics of Belorussian nationalism and the complex relations this produces with both the Nazis and the various factions of the national movement. Stanislaw Kabbelski's overriding concern, the ultimate objective that justifies almost any action considered likely to advance it, is Belorussian independence. 'We have to come out of this war with a national integrity' he says at an early stage (71). This involves his collaboration with the German occupying force and the acceptance, indeed the joint responsibility for, its appalling measures of mass extermination. One of Stanislaw's first operations as police chief is to co-ordinate the execution of Staroviche's Jewish population. He justifies this to himself and his family by love of country. 'I loved my country well enough to supervise the Gomel road liquidations. I saw children squirming in the pit and pregnant girls singing the *"Shema Y'israel"*. I skirted insanity and dishonour for the sake of my nation!' (106). As the prospects for independence under German tutelage recede after Stalingrad the Belorussina nationalist movement begins to fragment. Kabbelski, loyal to Ostrowski, loses influence as rival factions seek to extricate themselves from the Nazi alliance and curry favour with the Allies. The flight to Australia is an indication that, although Kabbelski has been sufficiently well placed politically to have secured safe passage from Belorussia in the face of the Red Army advance, his influence is not great enough to have claimed for him a comfortable berth in CIA-funded anti-Soviet bodies in the USA or Paris.

Parallel with his father's account is Rudi's history. Though supposedly the reminiscences of a mature man, who is psychologically traumatised by the events he has lived through as a boy, Keneally makes Rudi's story a child-centred view of the family's life. It is as if his father's record of events, revealing as they do shameful instances of casuistry and selfishness, has made little impact upon him; or if they have, he prefers to overlook them. His history is therefore reconstructed with little of the perspective provided by hindsight, and the result is a romantic and heroic view of the family, seen from the point of view of the child enjoying 'good days' and wishing they could have continued. The relationship between the two accounts is revealed clearly in the treatment of the character of Oberfuhrer Ganz, the German commissar of the district of Staroviche. Ganz is a regular visitor to the Kabbelski household, where he forms a close attachment

164

to Danielle, and is known to the Kabbelski children as 'Onkel Willi'. The Onkel/Uncle motif recurs in the story. It becomes a fixture in Rudi's mind – a mythical saviour and father figure who intervenes to provide guidance in troubled times. The adult Rudi calls his business 'Uncle Security'. Ganz shares with the family the same cultivated tastes in the arts and cuisine that are common to all educated Europeans. He represents that frequently-noted duality in German society and culture where a high civilisation is juxtaposed with barbarity. In Ganz, however, the good outweighs the bad. He is the 'good German', in contrast to the barbaric SS officers with whom Stanislaw also has to work. Ganz, moreover, is given a Schindler-like quality in his approach to Jews; he employs a Jewish driver whom he shields from Nazi persecution, and he prevaricates in his dealing with the bureaucracy of extermination, either ignoring requests for action on genocide, or turning them into matters for philosophical discussion. This of course isolates Ganz from the local Nazi leadership and singles him out for elimination. Stanislaw Kabbelski realises that his family's association with Ganz compromises his own objectives, and he is therefore receptive to the entreaties of Ganz's enemies in the SS to collaborate in his removal. Kabbelski is complicit first in the death of Ganz's Jewish driver, and then in the channelling of information to Soviet partisans which is used to plot the assassination of Ganz. In this way Keneally pointedly portrays the moral bankruptcy of Rudi's father. Rudi's own account, however, carefully skirts around his father's role in the murder, which is narrated in a surreal form from the perspective of the ten-year old boy hiding under a table as the partisans burst into the room where he has been treated to lunch by Ganz. Then, what Rudi describes as 'an unspeakable experience' occurs in which he 'suffered the experience of being lifted on a fountain of light high in the corner of the dining room. I could see the ruined meal [...] and Onkel Willi staggering' (182). He utters the word 'Uncle' and hears a voice saying 'After the wave breaks, you'll still be in place (182); he sees the partisans discover the boy under the table and spare him with the words 'It's the Kabbelski kid' (183). Through this strange episode Keneally plants the explanation for Rudi's subsequent behaviour in Australia; he has been spared death, has witnessed the awfulness of humanity, and been invested with an apocalyptic vision. The innocence of childhood has vanished and all his future life is framed by a powerful sense of last things.

Keneally constructs a specific event as the climacteric of Rudi's trauma. The general circumstances of war and collaboration are refined to a final act of betrayal at the very heart of all that Rudi holds dear, namely his family. In a Displaced Persons camp in southern Germany in the spring of 1946 the complex rivalries that exist between the Belorussian factions and their Allied and Soviet patrons[18] conspire to produce allegations of an informer passing details to the Russians about Belorussian collaboration with the Nazis. Rudi is taken hostage in order to spur Stanislaw to expose the traitor who it is claimed operates in his own faction. From fragments of information pieced together for his history of the family, the last piece of evidence being gained early in 1984 from his sister (who in turn has gleaned it from her husband), Rudi learns that the traitor was his own mother. She had apparently been passing information to Soviet partisans in exchange for protection for her children. This explains Rudi's miraculous escape during the assassination of Ganz. Stanislaw was therefore presented with the awful moral choice of sacrificing either his wife or his hostage son to satisfy the demands of his political rivals. The evidence is unclear as to whether he denounced Danielle or whether she sacrificed herself that her son might live. The family's rendering of events had been that Danielle had committed suicide in the camp. Either way it represents an awful nemesis for the Kabbelskis, and it precipitates the final destruction of the family, by its own hand, in an ordinary Sydney suburb in the summer of 1984.

Other characters in the story are not privy to this narrative, which is communicated only to the reader as an insight into Rudi's psyche. To Delaney and Stanton Rudi is an enigma. He is charismatic, a skilled landscape painter, and successful in business to a degree they cannot fail to admire. To working-class Aussies on their beam-ends he looks prosperous, which is a cause of some resentment against immigrants. Stanton notes: 'My people've been in this country four generations and never worked for themselves. Beats me how the bastards are able to do it. Straight from Below Russia [Belorussia] into

18    See Vakar, *Belorussia*, pp. 70–2, 220.

166

a business of their own' (28). Stanton and Delaney come across Rudi by chance, as employees of a rival security firm doing their rounds in the same district. When Rudi offers them a job Delaney and Stanton are sceptical of the foreigner: 'I hope to Christ this doesn't turn out to be a Dad and Dave operation, with a two-way radio stuck in the corner of a garage or a laundry' (50). It is quite the opposite. Rudi and his two sons, Warwick and Scott, are well resourced and organised, established in a 'double-brick, Federation-style' house which 'looked like a permanent seat of business' (50). They have impressive weaponry, and a ruthless streak that worries both Aussies. Revenge on a meddlesome rival takes the form of a booby trap which blows the man's fingers off. Above all Rudi's obsession with waves strikes them as sinister. He is building up a remote redoubt in the outback against the day when civilisation will end in the natural cataclysm of a tidal wave. 'This is all for the sake of that wave you crowd talk about', says Delaney. 'Everyone knows it's on its way, Delaney', replies Rudi. 'Every cretin restocking the shelves in supermarkets from Tasmania to Finland. Everyone knows it's on its way' (203). Rudi, though, remains genial. He is not a straightforward crackpot. His charm and influence is most in evidence with his own family. He exercises a dominance over the men in particular, to whom he has passed on his vision: '"My father's a genius" Warwick said, with a faint smile. "That's good enough for me"' (44). His daughter Danielle seems more of an independent spirit. It is Delaney's desperate attraction for her – an 'unlucky passion' that is 'more than mateship, blood and bride' (130) – that leads him to leave his wife, become embroiled with the Kabbels, and have his ordered, circumscribed sporting life torn apart.

The Kabbels live by no rules that Delaney understands. Not only does the family have no interest in sport, its members reject the moral code that pronounces (in Delaney's case) a high tackle resulting in injury to be wrong, and therefore punishable. The incident is more than simply a spur-of-the-moment accident on the field. It is the result of Delaney's playing with a new-found 'tiger' which his team-mates think is a tactical choice but which in fact arises from his dealings with the Kabbels. Delaney's transgression of the norm, his 'infamy' (309), is the subject of a careful and considered legal hearing which delivers a judgement of a six-month suspension from the game. It might have been a stiffer sentence had not Delaney's demeanour during the proceedings been a restrained and dignified one. Although the matter is not clear-cut - there are arguments in mitigation for Delaney - the decision of the court is accepted. There is no alternative but to respect it. It is a part of the rules that govern his life. 'When people say that to someone like Delaney a sport is a religion they are uttering something more than a metaphor. A sport could be to people like Delaney not merely a sect but a cosmology, a perfected model of an imperfect world' (31). Rudi knows nothing of this. Danielle pinpoints the essential difference in the two backgrounds when she tells Delaney 'We grew up in a different sort of place, a place where there was no politics [...] I mean the sort of politics that kills people in the street' (189). Stanislaw's cruel subordinating of means to ends has been inherited by Rudi. '[...] the Kabbel family seemed to exist outside the hemisphere of sport' (110). Delaney is prepared to enter into this other world because of his love for Danielle. He too betrays, in his case his wife, because he believes he has found his true love. He describes himself as the 'happiest man in Australia' and even dreams of taking Danielle, and the child she has with him, to a haven in Queensland where he will be the local rugby star and they can live a secure and contented life. But the consummation of domestic bliss that he envisages is impossible with a Kabbel. They know too much about life and the unimaginable terrors it contains. '[...] there can't be any Aussie cosiness in life for her' (203). At the point when he is about to take to the hills Rudi delivers a warning to Delaney which both subverts the rugby player's designs for his daughter and presents a grim warning for Australia:

> Sometimes, Mr Delaney, history does make its claim on people. In places like Los Angeles and Sydney people try to live in an eternal and very base *now*, without any memory of the dead. The barbecue and the sun are *all*. Games are *all* - a game is *all* to you. But you have to face it: sometimes - I restate it so that you will know - sometimes even here history can't be avoided, history comes up and grabs people. Outside coffee bars in Auburn where Armenians wait with knives for the Turks to come out - there it can kill people. What I say is, don't try to marry Danielle. It will never work. She belongs to forces you can't negotiate with, Terry. (203)

There is no escape from those forces, which are Europe's legacy to mankind.

*A Family Madness* tackles two big themes: genocide and Australian identity. The two appear to have nothing in common. Popular images of Australia have seen the country as far removed from the sins of old Europe, a land of sunshine and opportunity where migrants of all kinds can forget their past and build a future. It is, of course, a false picture of innocence, but an image which no doubt attracted British migrants who took assisted passages to Australia in the 1950s, just as the tourist board representations of the outback draw young backpackers to Australia as a 'gap' year destination in the early twenty-first century. Australia's official stance on the outside world, especially its policy on immigration, has often reproduced such notions through the idea of isolation serving to immunise the country against the infections of others. But it is a scarcely credible notion. In its politics, economy and culture Australia is no less part of international influences than anywhere else. It has been progressively a product of Britain, Europe and (latterly) Asia. Delaney's family carries its Irish Catholic traditions just as much in the 1980s as it would have done a hundred years earlier. And superimposed on these are newer influences of a yet profounder nature brought by the Kabbels. They carry an infection in the form of a knowledge about mankind's inherent evil. There is no prophylactic against infection by this virus, as Delaney finds. The Kabbels had come in the 1940s; Rudi would have come to maturity during the so-called 'golden age'.[19] If the myth of 'Australia fair' was to have worked for anyone it should have worked for Rudi. But he was unable to find solace there. Even his children, Australian-born, shared the same inevitable sense of doom. And it does not end there, for Australia is a destination for many more immigrants whose traditions and memories are steeped in equally terrible ethnic conflicts.

Just as it is important in Richard Ford's *The Sportswriter* that his main character pursues that particular occupation, so it is significant that Keneally's Terry Delaney plays rugby league. It might have been

---

19  Macintyre, *Concise History,* ch. 8.

cricket were it not for the fact that rugby is one of Keneally's passions. Like most Australians he loves sport, which is a central part of the country's idea of itself as outdoor, active, and assertive. Australians are proud of their sporting achievements and have been elevated by others as a model to emulate.[20] If, as Keneally appears to believe, Australians have a basic sense of insecurity – an 'edginess' derived from their penal colony past[21] – then perhaps they are understandably proud of what they have achieved on the sports field. In which case, they should all read *A Family Madness* to be reminded that there are some things in life bigger than sport.

20    The British government recently set Australia's achievements in elite sport as a
      standard to reach for its own country's athletes. (Cabinet Office, *Game Plan*,
      London: Stationery Office, 2002.)
21    Emma Brockes, 'A Wizard from Oz', *Guardian*, 30 October 2000, p. 11
      (interview with Keneally).

# Chapter Nine
## 'You Don't Upset the Shaygets': Howard Jacobson's *The Mighty Walzer*

Manchester can scarcely be called a neglected city. On the contrary, it has been much-observed. Since its emergence in the nineteenth century as the place synonymous with industrialism it has been attended with close scrutiny by historians, sociologists, urban commentators and creative writers. Asa Briggs's comment has been frequently invoked: '[…] all roads led to Manchester in the 1840s […] it was the shock city of the age'.[1] It was the site and hub of some of the most celebrated, and lamented, events and movements of nineteenth-century Britain, including the Peterloo massacre, Chartism, and the Anti Corn Law League. Free Trade as an ideal was in effect invented there, and the city gave its name to a business philosophy – the Manchester School – which reverberated around the world. Germans knew it as 'Manchestertum'. It is perhaps not surprising that, being so much in the forefront of 'history', Manchester became the focus, one might say the 'embodiment', of a discourse on modernity, and its citizens and their publicists quickly developed from this a sense that their city was unique. 'What Manchester does today, the rest of the world does tomorrow' was a popular maxim that summed up very well Manchester's idea of itself. The historian A.J.P. Taylor, in a memorable essay, noted that in its heyday the city's renowned newspaper the *Manchester Guardian* led with *local* news on its first page, before moving on to other domestic and international issues inside.[2] As if to underline its special position Manchester was one of

1    Asa Briggs, *Victorian Cities* (Harmondsworth: Pelican Books, 1968 edn), p. 96. Briggs comments on the range of observers of Manchester in the nineteenth century (see ch. 3).
2    A.J.P. Taylor, 'Manchester', in *Essays in English History* (Harmondsworth: Penguin Books, 1976), pp. 307–25. This essay originally appeared in *Encounter*, 42, 1957.

only two provincial British cities (the other was Warrington) to erect a statue in honour of Oliver Cromwell.[3]


# 1


Manchester, an old Lancashire town, became an industrial city in the early nineteenth century. Then, as its mill economy declined in the third quarter of the century, it re-developed as a business centre dealing in the buying and selling of cotton and cotton goods. It had introduced to the world a new form of production and the new social relationships that went with it. That is why Frederick Engels, coming from western Germany in the late 1830s to manage Ermen and Engels's cotton-spinning factory in Manchester, was so fascinated by the place. Immigrants of all social classes were, like Engels, important to Manchester, though most were not fortunate enough to enjoy Engels's wealth, which enabled him in time to leave the city behind and live the life of a country squire in Cheshire. By the beginning of the twentieth century large parts of Manchester were given over to communities of people recently arrived from other parts of the world, many of them refugees from both poverty and persecution in Europe, taking advantage of Britain's economically-buoyant and tolerant society.[4] The most familiar and largest of these groups was, however, from nearer to England. With some 30,000 Irish-*born* inhabitants (and a possible further 50,000 by extraction) Manchester was the third largest English host of the Irish diaspora after London and Liverpool.[5] The great majority of the Irish were Catholics, concentrated in some of the poorest parts of the city. By the later part of the nineteenth

---

3   Terry Wykes, *Public Sculpture of Greater Manchester* (Liverpool: Liverpool University Press, 2004).

4   N.J. Frangopulo, 'Foreign Communities in Victorian Manchester', *Manchester Review,* 10: 1965, 189–206.

5   See John Denvir, *The Irish in Britain* (London: Kegan, Trench, Trubner and Co., 1892), pp. 429–33.

century these were mainly in the St Michael's ward to the north of the city centre.[6] The Irish possessed a distinctive cultural life evident in their occupations, trade unions, politics and, of course, their religious organisation.[7] The strong presence of Irish Catholics, not only in Manchester but in many of the western parts of Lancashire, had a profound impact on the region's political and social life until well into the twentieth century. It was arguably the cause of the social and cultural cleavages that characterised the north-west of England and which produced its distinctive political allegiances – notably an enduring form of working-class toryism. Because of this the emphasis given to the Irish presence by historians and others has tended to divert attention away from other, smaller immigrant groups in the region.[8]

Among these, and for many years a source of consensus rather than conflict, was an important Jewish community which had become established in the Cheetham Hill district of Manchester, also just to the north of the city centre. Manchester's Jewish community was not only the largest in provincial England but had its origins well before the familiar mass migration of Jews from Polish and Russian lands following the pogroms of the early 1880s.[9] It dated back to the eighteenth century.[10] As its historian Bill Williams has noted: 'Manchester Jewry grew with Manchester'.[11] In fact, Williams shows that immigration from eastern Europe had also begun in Manchester before the 1880s, so much so that by 1875 some half of the Manchester Jewish population was made up of migrants from Poland and Russia; 'in no sense', he says, 'can the Jewish community be regarded as "alien" to Manchester. It was not a late addition to an

6    *Manchester Guardian*, 16 November 1885, 16.
7    See Steven Fielding, *Class and Ethnicity: Irish Catholics in England, 1880–1939* (Buckingham: Open University Press, 1993), pp. 27–31.
8    See Panikos Panayi, *Immigration, Ethnicity and Racism in Britain 1815–1945* (Manchester: Manchester University Press, 1994).
9    Neville Laski, 'The Manchester and Salford Jewish Community 1912–1962', *Manchester Review*, 10, Spring 1964, pp. 97–108.
10   Frangopulo, 'Foreign Communities'.
11   Bill Williams, *The Making of Manchester Jewry 1740–1875* (Manchester: Manchester University Press, 1976), vii.

established pattern of urban life, but an integral part of the pattern itself.'[12] This state of affairs had given prominence to the middle-class Jewish community – initially some twenty families – which sought to take on the social leadership of Manchester Jewry and to impose on its poorer immigrant members the liberal values of the host community. In return it was favoured by a tolerant regard for Jewry on the part of the gentile middle class, notably illustrated in the pages of the *Manchester Guardian*. By the 1880s, however, this situation of pervasive consensus had started to fragment as a result of the rapid growth through increased immigration of a Jewish working class. Some of the Jewish immigrants from Iberia settled in the south of the city in Withington, and there was a pocket also in Salford, but many found employment in the garment trade, which in Manchester was based in small workshops rather than the larger factories to be found across the Pennines in Leeds. By the early 1890s there were over 250 such workshops, employing close on 2,000 Jewish workers mainly in the Strangeways, Red Bank and Lower Broughton districts, the core area of the Jewish working class. Their arrival prompted the removal of better-off Jews further up Cheetham Hill Road towards Prestwich, Whitefield and Bury. By 1910 a total Jewish population of around 30,000 was displaying signs of internal tensions that had not been evident earlier.[13]

Some elements of this new Jewish working class were not only less disposed to accept middle-class leadership, but were treated with more hostility by indigenous residents than was the established Jewish

---

12    *Idem.*

13    Lloyd P. Gartner, *The Jewish Immigrants in England* (London: Allen and Unwin: 1960), pp. 40, 43, 90–1, 145, 160; V.D. Lipman, *Social History of the Jews in England, 1850–1950* (London: Watts and Co., 1954), p. 67; Bill Williams, 'Heritage and Community: the Rescue of Manchester's Jewish Past', in Tony Kushner ed., *The Jewish Heritage in British History: Englishness and Jewishness* (London: Frank Cass: 1992), pp. 128–46; Rickie Burman, 'Jewish Women and the Household Economy in Manchester, c. 1890-1920' in David Cesarani ed., *The Making of Modern Anglo-Jewry* (Oxford: Basil Blackwell, 1990), pp. 55–75; Laski, 'The Manchester and Salford Jewish Community'.

middle class.[14] Anti-semitic propaganda was in circulation by the 1880s in newspapers such as the *Manchester City News*. Williams notes that the social tension between established Anglo-Jewish families and the east Europeans proletarians had its roots in religious and political differences – particularly socialism and Zionism – brought by the newer immigrants. These features caused elite Jews to attempt to 'anglicise' the immigrants through measures of social control, a strategy designed to ensure continuing tolerance for their own social position.[15] By the twentieth century, then, the Jewish community was far from homogeneous, divided by ethnic, religious, political, and class differences, and manifesting a complex set of attitudes towards the question of assimilation.[16]

2

Howard Jacobson's novel *The Mighty Walzer* (1999) is a celebration of the east European Manchester Jewish community.[17] It offers a particular fictional representation of ethnic life and culture. The community is remembered from an end-of-century perspective by the middle-aged narrator (the novel's hero, Oliver Walzer) as it was in the 1950s. It is a memory that merges with the author's own reminiscences of his life as a teenager at the same time and in the same place. The novel therefore has a distinct historical and autobiographical perspective focused on the gradual coming of age of the character Oliver and the writer Howard. It is a story of changes –

14 Bill Williams, 'The Anti-Semitism of Tolerance: Middle-Class Manchester and the Jews 1870–1900', in AJ Kidd and KW Roberts, *City, Class and Culture: Studies of Social Policy and Cultural Production in Victorian Manchester* (Manchester: Manchester University Press, 1985), pp. 74–102.

15 Williams, *Making of Manchester Jewry*, pp. 331–3. See also Alan Kidd, *Manchester* (Keele: Keele University Press, 1993), p. 124.

16 Bill Williams, '"East and West": Class and Community in Manchester Jewry, 1859–1915' in Cesarani ed., *Making of Modern Anglo-Jewry*, pp. 15–33.

17 All references are to the Vintage edition, London, 2000.

changes in a life, in a family, and of a sport. It has been described, not surprisingly, as a 'rite of passage' novel.[18] Its story time spans a period starting with the fictional Walzer family's life before Oliver's birth, when his parents were growing up in Cheetham Hill; it proceeds through Oliver's own middle age, when he has left Manchester behind for a rootless single existence as a lecturer in vaguely artistic matters in Venice; and it ends, appropriately, with Oliver's return to Manchester for his father's funeral. As in almost all Jacobson's work he interrogates his own experiences of Manchester life in the 1950s to reflect on the questions of Jewishness and Jewish identity which have been the chief subjects both of his novels and of his non-fictional work in the past decade or more.[19]

Jacobson approaches Oliver Walzer's history in a warmly nostalgic and affectionate mood, as well he might for it is his own history to a large extent. The past is recreated with fondness, and the memories are good ones. Jacobson's perception of the Jewish place in Manchester life is of a community finely poised in a social spectrum. He positions it as semi-respectable, not fully assimilated and accepted, and creates an immigrant assimilation of an in-between, apologetic kind: not too little integrated, but neither too much, just enough, treading a delicate line between Anglicisation and Jewish orthodoxy. Walzer's family and the many other families in Cheetham Hill had in a very Jacobsonian sense *got by*. They were not part of the established Jewish middle class whose achievements in the world of commerce had allowed them to be absorbed into the society of the English middle class and celebrated in the annals of Manchester's economic and artistic achievements.[20] The branch of immigration from which Walzer's family came had achieved nothing of great import – in the arts, business, the learned professions or even sport – to receive acclaim and acceptance by the host society. They had, to a degree, raised themselves up by the self-help means that the city's nineteenth-century philosophy had so lauded. Walzer's father Joel, a market

---

18    See Jonathan Bate, 'Ping Pong Boy', *Times Literary Supplement,* 20 August 1999, 19.

19    See Howard Jacobson, *Roots Schmoots* (London: Penguin Books, 1993); 'Being Jewish …', *Guardian(G2)* , 11 June 2004, 2–3.

20    See Williams, *Making of Manchester Jewry,* p. 336.

trader, is a wonderfully humorous example of this process. Equally, though, there are indications of a resistance to elite *mores* which resulted in Jewish support for socialism; Walzer's mother, for example, as a young woman in the 1930s had associations with free-thinking left-ish elements: 'She knew communists [...] she corresponded with men who were fighting with the International Brigade in Spain' (39–40) – reminding us that east European immigrants did not always accept the lead of the conservative Anglo-Jewish middle class in politics. But neither, in Jacobson's eyes, were the Walzers and their neighbours the victims of any vigorous discrimination. Of the Mosleyite presence in the 1930s (Manchester was something of a stamping ground for fascists) there is little indication, and none relating to the serious anti-Jewish rioting that occurred in Manchester and other major cities in the 1940s when Jewish resistance movements were campaigning to end the British Mandate in Palestine.[21] The Walzers' neutrality in itself is regarded as something of an achievement, an ambivalence they strove hard to preserve, and it accounts for the contradictory attitude towards Jewishness expressed by both Jacobson and his fictional characters. It allowed them just enough space to be English and at the same time afforded them a mark of Jewishness. They were Jewish English, rather than English Jews, careful not to invite attention from non-Jews. 'Stay shtoom. Don't draw attention, that was what we grew up with' Jacobson has said. 'If we saw a Jew driving a big car around Manchester, it was, "Don't do that, there'll be a pogrom."'[22] It is the main concern of Oliver Walzer's father: accommodate, live and let live, don't rock the boat. '*You don't upset the shaygets*' is his persistent refrain (104). The one outstanding signifier of Jewishness – religion – is rejected. Jacobson's family was

21    Geoffrey Alderman, *Modern British Jewry* (Oxford: Clarendon Press, 1992), p. 319; Tony Kushner, *The Persistence of Prejudice: Antisemitism in British Society During the Second World War* (Manchester: Manchester University Press, 1989), pp. 200–01.The contrast with Morris Beckman's account of anti-fascist campaigns in the Ridley Road area of Dalston, east London, in the late 1940s is very marked. Beckman's group was involved in some violent clashes with resurgent Mosleyites who sought to whip up opinion over the Palestine issue against local Jews. Morris Beckman, *The 43 Group* (London: Centerprise, 1992).

22    Allison Pearson, 'Howard Jacobson' 27 April 2004, www.telegraph.co.uk/arts

not outwardly religious. They did not observe the Sabbath, though at the same time retained a slight feeling of guilt about it.[23] For Jacobson himself, when visiting orthodox relatives in Llandudno, the observance of religious rituals is regarded with some scepticism, if not incredulity.[24] Towards the end of the novel the middle-aged Oliver explodes at the thought of his daughter marrying an orthodox Jew in a ceremony from which his sisters, for having married gentiles, are excluded:

> Yes, you are right, your father is a Godless bastard. But answer me this: if the Creator whom you and that wet-mouth Shmuelly worship holds it as a matter of urgency that the feelings of Aunty Hetty and Aunty Sandra are to be considered of no account because their husbands are defiled by the prepuces which were His fucking invention in the first place, what the Christ are you doing giving credence to a word He says ? Honouring God isn't compulsory, you know, even if He exists. You may choose not to. (348)

Equally, they were not ashamed of their origins, but at the same time wanted to 'move on'.[25] Before the Walzers' male child was born, in the early 1940s (the same time as Jacobson's own birth) the family had moved from Cheetham Hill to Heaton Park, a small step on the petty-bourgeois ladder. Oliver's father Joel never made much money, certainly not enough to take the family to Southport, the epitome of Lancastrian Jewish respectability. He was, and remained, a market trader, a dealer in tsatske – 'a toy or plaything, a shmondrie, a bauble, a whifflery, a nothing' (14). He works the markets in the Manchester area selling his nothings, a life dedicated to communicating trivialities – cheap trays, plastic poppet necklaces, travellers' refreshment packs, lamps, bags of chocolate truffles (misshapen). With these the Walzer house is stocked and decorated; tsatske, for Joel Walzer, is both merchandise and an aesthetic. Looking back Oliver wonders whether

---

23 See Todd M. Endelman, *Radical Assimilation in English Jewish History 1656–1945* (Bloomington: Indiana University Press, 1990), ch. 6.
24 Jacobson, *Roots Schmoots*, pp. 12–17.
25 Howard Jacobson, interview with Joan Bakewell for 'Belief', BBC Radio 3, 30 December 2004.

this accounts for his own failure to be serious and dignified. He ends up himself being a dealer in academic tsatske.[26]

Like his mother and father Oliver, though Mancunian to the marrow, is simultaneously only too aware of distant origins, of a life before Manchester. This sense of heritage, however, is more ethnic than religious. Eastern Europe exercises a mysterious hold on his psyche. 'Bug country, that was where we came from, the fields and marshes of the rock-choked River Bug, Letichev, Vinnitsa, Kamenets Podolski - around there. All we'd been doing since the Middle Ages was growing beetroot and running away from Cossacks' (5). Carrying this influence with them, Oliver's and his father's generation of Mancunians adapt it into a distinctive local vernacular, separate but not too separate from that of non-Jewish people. They have a patois. None of them speaks Yiddish, yet they incorporate into their speech a lexicon of Yiddish terms just as non-Jewish Mancunians perfect their own colloquialisms as a means of bonding together with whatever group they feel they belong to. It can lead to ambiguities, as when, after a table tennis match against Allied Jam and Marmalade, Selwyn Marks claims to have detected anti-semitism on the part of their opponents:

> 'Are you telling me that's why you lost now,' Twink said, 'because they were anti-Semites? I suppose the net was anti-Semitic.'
> 'I'm not saying it's why I lost. I'm just saying it's what they are.'
> 'You're messhugge,' Aishky said. 'They were nice people'.
> 'Then why did they call Oliver Mordechai?'
> 'Mordechai? Who called him Mordechai'
> The one with the shmatte bat.'
> Aishky and Twink wanted to hear it from the horse's mouth. 'Oliver, did he call you Mordechai?'
> 'Not that I remember. Why would he have called me Mordechai, anyway?'
> 'Because he's an anti-Semite. Mordechai the Jew.' […]
> 'No', I said. 'He said, "Better luck next time, me duck." Me duck, not Mordechai.' (74)

---

26   See Howard Jacobson, *Roots Schmoots:Journeys Among Jews* (London: Penguin Books, 1993), p.4. This autobiographical passage is almost identical to Jacobson's description of the Walzer household's production of goods for market sale (*Mighty Walzer*, 105–6).

Sport occupies a central place in Oliver's early life (just as the memory of it figures prominently in his middle age); to a large extent it also holds the novel together by exposing the fundamental dilemmas of the poor immigrant position. In this *The Mighty Walzer* is groundbreaking. For one thing, the place of sport in immigrant culture – Jewish culture in particular – has been generally ignored by scholars of immigration and minorities.[27] Ironically, since virtually all historians of immigration are themselves immigrants, Jewish historians appear almost to have imbibed the old myth that Jewish men were not physical; that they exhibited certain 'effeminate' characteristics.[28] Few historians, immigrant or otherwise, have turned their attention to this area, and those who have seem unable to decide whether the relative absence of Jews from organised sports in Britain is a reflection of lack of interest or of social exclusion. There is some evidence of the latter in golf, for example, with the black-balling from exclusive golf clubs of applicants from Jewish families. The apparent lack of a Jewish presence in cricket, on the other hand, may simply be explained by a lack of interest in the sport.[29] Considering the importance of sport to immigrant communities, as a means both of gaining acceptance from majority cultures and also of seeking to retain an element of ethnic distinctiveness, it seems a topic that is worthy of fuller investigation. Oliver Walzer's chosen sport is not connected to any such establishment activities as golf or

27    In the now well-developed historical literature of immigration, especially Jewish, there is much attention to economic, religious and political matters but scarcely any reference to the place of sport in Jewish life. See Alderman, Kushner, Cesarani, Endelman - among the more recent generation of scholars.

28    See Bryan Cheyette, *Constructions of 'the Jew' in English Literature and Society: Racial Representations, 1875–1945* (Cambridge: Cambridge University Press, 1993) ch. 1; *Between 'Race' and Culture: Representations of 'the Jew' in English and American Literature* (Stanford CA: Stanford University Press, 1996), ch. 1. The idea of the 'effeminate Jew' acquired some support in the early-twentieth century from the writing of the young German Otto Weininger, whose *Sex and Character* (London: William Heinemann, 1906) advanced some massive generalisations about women and Jews (and the British) and seemed to confirm existing conservative views on women and anti-semitism.

29    See Richard Holt, *Sport and the British* (Oxford: Oxford University Press, 1990), pp. 133, 351; on golf see John Lowerson, *Sport and the English Middle Classes 1870–1914* (Manchester: Manchester University Press, 1993), pp. 22–3; on cricket see Jack Williams, *Cricket and Race,* (Oxford: Berg, 2001), pp. 41–3.

cricket. His story is about table tennis, a sport of recent origins and humble neighbourhood proportions. It is a sport that has received scant attention in the growing literature of sport history in this country over the past twenty-five years.[30] It should not surprise us to learn that Jacobson was himself a fine player in his youth, and like David Storey in *This Sporting Life* he brings deep personal knowledge and understanding to his descriptions of the game. The novel not only alludes to sport in metaphorical terms, as a way of illuminating aspects of social behaviour; it also contains detailed *real* information about the game and its origins, development, and international context. Jacobson has also claimed (perhaps with an intentional irony) a certain Jewishness about the game as he knew it. 'Table-tennis was a very Jewish activity [...] It was an intellectual game; you almost played it in a suit [...] it was like athletic chess.'[31] And Oliver Walzer comes to see in the Jewish table tennis clubs of Manchester a unique style of play which contrasts with that of other ping-pong traditions: the southern style, exemplified in Oliver's partner and adversary Lorna Peachley – an 'all-round game of exaggerated loops and non-stop jigging' (153); or the game he encounters as played by boys from north-east Lancashire at the Ribble and District Table Tennis Academy in Burnley, who are 'greedier in their play, more pinched and avid, colourless, without flourish or bravura' (151). In later years, as a student in Cambridge, Oliver partners a man from Sri Lanka, 'a class act' as he describes him, whose style of play reminds him of the Jewish game in Manchester: 'the only non-Bug and Dniester ping-pong player I'd ever come across who had *wit* in his game' (319) [my italics]. For Oliver, table tennis embodied fun and sociability. It was not, in the last analysis, a game to be taken too seriously.

This mentality had its place in table tennis history. The game contrasted markedly with the 'betting sports' – football, boxing, horse-racing, greyhounds – for the virtual absence of any serious commercialism, media exposure, or stars. In the 1950s, to be sure, the names of Victor Barna, Johnny Leach and the Rowe twins gave the

30    See Richard William Cox, *British Sport: A Bibliography to 2000* (London: Frank Cass, 2003).
31    Francis Gilbert, 'Family Influence: Howard Jacobson', *e magazine*, 11 February 2001, 30.

sport some national recognition, but it was essentially a game played by local people in local clubs. It had originated in a country-house context as a domestic, social game for both sexes, played for pleasure. In the interwar years it began to develop an organisational structure of leagues which brought together players from a variety of occupations and associations – churches, pubs, businesses, public services, leisure centres, schools, families. In the absence of attention from academic historians one has to talk to former participants or dig down to locally-produced commemorative volumes of clubs in an attempt to re-create the game's story.[32]

Table tennis is the making of Oliver. He comes upon it by accident, finding a ball in Heaton Park lake (it is, he later learns, a ball of some distinction – a Halex***), and discovers that he is a 'natural'. Before ever setting foot inside a ping-pong hall he is an expert, honing his skills at home by playing, Bradman-style[33], against the plaster whorls on the living-room wall. The Halex*** comes back at unpredictable angles, sharpening the boy's reflexes. His bat is pure improvisation – a copy of Stevenson's *Dr Jekyll and Mr Hyde* 'in the soft green pitted-leatherette Collins Classic series' (15). With such home-based resources Oliver nurtures his talent. This introverted, domestic introduction to sport is typical of the boy, who is shy and withdrawn, pampered by the many women members of the family and given to secret pleasures in the lavatory. He also dreams of becoming a great table tennis player who will beat the new far-eastern champion Ogimura. Oliver the quiet daydreamer is, according to his father, a 'kuni-lemele': 'a rustic simpleton. Not quite the village idiot, more the shtetl schlemiel' (26). It is an aim of the male members of his family

---

32    See John Bromhead, 'Win or Lose: A Sample of Table Tennis History', paper presented to the British Society of Sport History, Leicester, April 2004. Bromhead argues that the competitive side of the game developed eventually to a point where the purely social aspects declined, to the particular detriment of women's participation.

33    The Australian batsman Don Bradman, who dominated world cricket in the 1930s, claimed to have developed his technique and co-ordination by throwing a golf ball against a corrugated iron water tank and playing the rebound with a cricket stump. See Charles Williams, *Bradman: An Australian Hero* (London: Abacus, 1997), p. 17.

to bring him out of his shell, and table tennis provides the means of doing so. Specifically, it happens when his father takes him to the Akiva Social Club, and the world of the table tennis leagues of Manchester and district opens to him[34].

Akiva is a club for Jewish players but, in keeping with the Walzers' equivocal philosophy, it competes in a mixed league. It is a world in which, for the first time, he relates on equal terms with adults, or at least 'sort of' grown men as (with their curiosities and foibles) Oliver regards them. ('They've all got something wrong with them' he exclaims to his family on arriving home after the first night at the club). The members take the twelve-year old in with much warmth and good spirit, and he acknowledges that he might, at other clubs and among other people, have been given a much tougher initiation into the sporting life. Compared with the eccentric domestic life of his family and the curious onanistic culture of his grammar school, the Akiva is a rational and orderly real world of competition rules (extracts from which introduce many of the chapters) drawn up to ensure fair, orderly play. Jewish clubs, the implication runs, are no strangers to the English concept of 'fair play'. Clubs have secretaries, matches are organised events, there are travel schedules, and there is a kind of dress code to which most members adhere. Oliver has a tracksuit with 'a wildly rhetorical "A" for Akiva' (65) embroidered by his aunt, modelled on the perfect outfit favoured by his mentor Twink Starr.[35] It is life with a purpose, and gives Oliver the chance to achieve something, to live up to the expectations his father has of him.

It is, moreover, another way of reinforcing his Jewishness while simultaneously integrating into English society. The Akiva team players are all Jewish working-class men and lads with a rich

---

34 Jacobson has presumably taken the name 'Akiva' from Rabbi Akiva, a great scholar of Judaism who was involved in the rebellion against Rome (132–35 C.E.) and subsequently executed. Akiva is associated with an optimistic world view – 'he could look at utter devastation and see future glory.' (See www.ou.org). The twin themes of rebelliousness and optimism chime well with the narrative.

35 Though his other mentor, Aishky Mitofsky, 'played in the clothes he came home from work in' (61) confirming Jacobson's assertion that ping-pong could almost be played 'in a suit'.

Mancunian-Jewish outlook, but Oliver's introduction to the league is in the most un-Jewish surroundings of the Allied Jam and Marmalade factory club. Here, with a new bat to replace *Dr Jekyll and Mr Hyde*, he is beaten by stolid gentiles; not good players, but 'canny' ones. Oliver is taught his first lesson in table craft. He is also made aware of the austerity and imperfections of playing the game in this local, make-do milieu, where resources are limited and the conditions far from perfect. The rooms always seem cold, there is furniture to lose balls behind and trip over, and floors are often unnecessarily polished and slippy. But the caretaker, a shayget, takes pride in polished floors, so nobody complains. You don't upset the shaygets. 'This was my first lesson in the ergonomics of ping-pong: every feature and dimension of the playing area must contribute to your discomfort [...] Tribulation, that should have been ping-pong's *nom de jeu*. No wonder the game came naturally to sun-starved Slavs and Magyars' (70). Oliver begins to believe that the game is in the blood, an ethnic characteristic. Why have east Europeans dominated it for so long? But equally, perhaps, it suits an indigenous Lancashire tradition in which the art of cotton spinning and weaving over two hundred years linked with the craze for Yo-Yo that had taken his father as a youth to the World Yo-Yo Championships in the Higher Broughton Assembly Rooms in August 1933, and from there to his son's passion for ping-pong. 'Wristiness', he imagines, 'was in their blood' (4). And so all players, Jews or gentiles, perform their natural art in the quintessentially British form of voluntary association, through which so much of the country's amateur sport has been fostered. Manchester table tennis, moreover, was open; for although Oliver plays for a Jewish club there is no separate Jewish *league*. [36] The races are thus conjoined in association, and for Oliver table tennis is his route into manhood.

36    See Laski, 'Manchester and Salford Jewish Community', *Manchester Review*, 1964. The attempt to extend the Manchester Maccabi tennis club into a 'base of culture and sport for all the youth activities of Manchester' was not successful, chiefly because of the separate interests of the small Jewish clubs (presumably those like Akiva). (p. 107). A Jewish Table Tennis League was formed in Manchester in the 1970s, mainly from north Manchester synagogues. It waned in the 1990s, when a rump of players joined with the Manchester Maccabi and

Oliver, Twink, Aishky, Sheeny, Selwyn and their team-mates at the Akiva bring an eccentric style to their playing of the game. They play a very Jewish game. All, in their different ways, are tragic ping-pong players. The despicable Gershom Finkel, who breaks the heart of one of Oliver's aunties by running away with another one, has played for England; he has been that good. But he is banned forever from international competition for betting against himself in a match against Sweden. 'He lost every match. Not by much, but by enough' (166). Aishky, who loves to win matches with dramatic smashes (and therefore often loses them by striving for that final flourish) loses fingers on his right hand in an accident; he then amazingly learns to play just as brilliantly left-handed (the Manchester League struck a special medal for him), only to lose left fingers in another accident. He devotes the rest of his life to studying the Holocaust. When Twink is called up for national service the Akiva 'as a fighting ping-pong force' (180) comes to an end. It has been a phase in Oliver's life, and he has learnt from sport something about both life and himself. Table tennis has brought him into contact with questions of winning and losing, and of the values to be cultivated, and the values to be despised, in a life. For all that sport has done for his personal rite of passage Oliver comes to see it with a deep scepticism.

In contrast to views that developed in the nineteenth century about immigrant Jews being provident, goal orientated, and individualistic, rising from the ghetto through a need to achieve[37], Jacobson provides us with a different narrative. The Mighty Walzer dreams, to be sure; he lacks nothing in imaginary 'grandiosity'. But in practice he cares little for the thrill of winning, and nothing for any conventional material enrichment ('swag') that victory might bring. This mentality is not confined to the world of sport. He is like his father in this respect. Joel's financial management is so chaotically careless that he eventually goes bankrupt. It is the 'buzz' of the 'gaffs', the excitement

formed a team in the Manchester District Table Tennis League. (See www.manchestermaccabi.org.uk)

37    See David Feldman, 'There was an Englishman, an Irishman and a Jew ...Immigrants and Minorities in Britain', *Historical Journal*, 26, 1 (1983), 185–199.

of market life that entrances him. Oliver is the same with table tennis. Winning in itself, especially against clearly inferior opponents, offers neither pleasure nor sense of achievement. He is good enough to win the Manchester Closed Junior championship but nearly 'blows it' because he knows he can beat his opponent easily, and so shrinks from securing what he sees as a hollow victory. What is winning all about, why is it so important? There is a kind of pleasure in losing, and Oliver takes a self-pitying delight in it. Above all he despises the strutting postures of the winners.

> Grandiose in my ambitions I may have been, but in the final analysis I was never comfortable winning. I didn't like the way it made me feel. And I never liked the way it made other people look. I remain a devoted student of the subject to this day – the illness of winning. I watch it day in and day out on television […] Nastase, McEnroe, Navratilova, Coe, Christie, Lewis, Budd, Klinsmann, Cantona, every member of every Australian cricket team, Tyson, Eubank, Ballesteros, Norman, Hill, Schumacher, Curry, Cousins, Torvill, Dean. A roll call of the psychotic […] The ultimate B-movie. *The Horror of the Human Will.* Forget the Creature from the Black Lagoon. Forget the Fly. This one's really sticky. This one's come out of soup too disgusting to describe. And the telly commentators call it character. (256)

With the end of Akiva Oliver graduates to the much tougher competition of Hagganah, where the players look like 'veterans of the Israeli independence wars' (209); they refuse on principle to play for England, even though they do not keep Shabbes, because the international team plays on Saturdays: 'If they want to pick Jewish players they have to respect how Jews live. Let them play on a Sunday' (209–10). These are hard men, who are not afraid to upset the shaygets. Oliver is not happy in this unambivalent environment, from which he withdraws after a life-changing match against the egregious aspiring winner Stanley 'Royboy' Rylance of Railways. Royboy is so anxious – over-anxious – to win that Oliver decides to give him the game: 'If he wanted it that badly he could have it […] I gave it to him as a gift. I had neither the character to win nor the character to consent graciously to his winning. So I gave it to him' (264–5). Oliver never played table tennis in Manchester after that.

He does play, however, when he reaches Cambridge as a student and makes the transition from semi-isolation in Manchester to the heart of the gentile Establishment. Indeed, it is Oliver's prowess at the table that secures him a place at the notable sporting institution, Golem College. Here again, playing for the most part against ludicrously poor opposition, he encounters his old distaste for winning. But he also comes to reflect on what, in his eyes, are seen as the true values of sport. In believing that winning is less important than the existential pleasure of playing a game Jacobson articulates through Oliver a sentiment that comes very close to that of the ethos of the Victorian amateur: the 'lover' of the game.[38] What else explains Oliver's concerns about the changing 'technology' of ping-pong that so affected the game in the 1950s? It was all to do with the bat, and sponge rubber. It is another rite of passage for Oliver – 'to sponge or not to sponge' (208) – which coincides with his joining Hagganah. 'Every match was hard these days. Harder to win and harder in the sense of less sociable and easeful' (209). It marks the passing of the game of the vellum bat, even the sound of which brought its own pleasure: 'plock plock, plock plock' was sweeter than sponge's anonymous 'oof plock, oof plock'.[39] 'The game', says Gershom Finkel, 'isn't worth a candle any more. The new rubbers have killed it. I wouldn't go to the bottom of the street to watch a match' (197). But watching was not what it was

---

38    See Lincoln Allison, *Amateurism in Sport: an Analysis and a Defence* (London: Frank Cass, 2001).

39    Oliver's reaction is connected with the changing 'technology' of the game. His heroes – Bergmann, Barna, Leach – would have used a bat with a plywood middle covered on each side with dimpled synthetic rubber. It encouraged the artistry of spin, with the chop as the standard defensive stroke. Long rallies were a characteristic feature of this form of table tennis. In the early 1950s this style began to change as a result of new technology (sponge bats) and tactics introduced in Japan. The bat became standardised in the form of the 'sandwich' bat, i.e. the traditional layer of wood in the middle, covered with a thin layer of sponge, and an outer cover of dimpled rubber. Oliver's game had been essentially a defensive one; the new technology made it a speedier, more attacking game analogous to the 'serve and volley' approach introduced into lawn tennis around this time. See Chester Barnes, *Advanced Table Tennis Techniques: How the World's Top Players Win* (London: Angus and Robertson), pp. 10–12.

about. The table tennis that Oliver remembers was a game that held his community together, and helped him fashion a sense of identity. When the Akiva comes to an end, with Aisky minus several fingers on both hands, Twink conscripted into the army, Sheeny Waxman gone over to Hagganah and Oliver thinking of following him, Selwyn Marks taking up swimming, and his brother Louis emigrating to Israel, Oliver asks Aishky what he will do now 'for sport'. 'Sport? Who's been doing sport?' asks Aishky. 'We both laughed. Of course ping-pong wasn't sport. Football was sport. Cricket was sport. Ping-pong was – But we both knew, without saying, what ping-pong was' (181).

3

David Nathan, reviewing *The Mighty Walzer* in the *Jewish Chronicle,* found that it recreated and celebrated a world of northern Jewish communities of the 1950s.[40] But is that fictionialised also world not a very fanciful one, an ultimately misleading, perhaps stereotypicalised, representation of times past and present? Do people *deliberately* lose? Was being a Jew in Heaton Park quite so untroubled an existence as Jacobson makes it appear? Perhaps the paranoia of the unfortunate Selwyn Marks, who believed that the gentiles were always out to get him, is a truer expression of the community's persona. Throughout the novel Jacobson gives us a sense of the tenuous nature of Jewish relationships with Manchester gentiles: 'you don't upset the shaygets'. It is a defensive approach to social relations. Jewishness is not *celebrated* so much as preserved in attenuated form *within* the community. Jacobson actually says little about the shaygets. They are opponents at ping-pong, often people, as with 'Royboy' and the players of Allied Jam and Marmalade, not to be admired. The novel's world is an introverted one, equipped with a number of self-sealing

40    David Nathan, 'North-West Passages', *Jewish Chronicle*, 20 August 1999, p. 24.

devices that prevent its engaging with the world outside. There is nothing that Oliver does before going to Cambridge that takes him away from his tightly-circumscribed community. This is not assimilation of the kind sought and experienced by middle-class Jews in the nineteenth century. It is self-imposed semi-exclusion, as is his eventual exile as a lecturer for tourists in Venice. Could it be that Oliver's seeing winning as a more troubling state than losing is part of this defensive psychology? In the novel's splendid finale, Oliver re-visits a Manchester which (predictably) fails to live up to his memories of the city; it has been 'Torn apart to make room for tsatske precincts for the post-industrial poor' (332). In the artlessly-named G-Mex (formerly Central Station) he finds taking place the Ninth World Veterans Ping-Pong Championships where, in the international company of veterans of all ages and various states of renown, he loses some of his grandiosity, acknowledging that he had never been exceptional as a player, only 'so-so' (357). He is made aware, however, of people's enduring fascination for sport:

> Why, there were men here, playing in the over-eighties' competition, wearing knee-supports and elastic hose and bandages round every joint, so arthritic that they required the assistance of a third party to retrieve any ball for them that didn't finish up in the net. They had to hold on to the table between strokes, some of them, so that their own momentum wouldn't knock them over. Could *their* imaginations still be rioting in futurity, looking forward to the day when they'd be world beaters? (361)

When his old adversary and girlfriend Lorna Peachley, whom he has not seen for 35 years, gives a brief show of affectionate recognition he surmises what it might mean: love, forgiveness? Neither. 'Just that she remembered who I was. Which is all any of us Walzers has ever asked' (387). It is an appropriately self-deprecating note on which to end. Life, like politics, is the art of the possible, especially for expatriots of the Bug and Dniester. In the last analysis 'grandiosity' is not their style.

'[...] We both knew, without saying, what ping-pong was.' Oliver's remark about his beloved game represents a Jacobsonian paradox. Of course ping-pong is in one sense a classic example of Britishness. The nation that Marx noted for its capacity to 'join' – to form clubs – which had a continuous tradition of voluntary associational life stretching well back into the eighteenth century[41], also produced the Akiva. By taking the kuni-lemele Oliver there and leaving him inside until he was accepted Joel was *forcing* his son into assimilation. What he imbibes there, however, is a peculiarly bastardised, Walzerian sporting ethos. It contains some of the principles nurtured in the British amateur tradition – in which playing for the *love* of the game is crucial – while rejecting other aspects: in particular, the desire to win. If sport is, as we are frequently told these days, a zero-sum game 'about winning', it is clearly not so for Oliver. It can also be about losing. It depends on mood, but mood depends to a large extent on the opponent. When the opponent is so clearly fixated with winning, when as with 'Royboy' sport has become a culture in which the need to achieve surpasses all other considerations, making it a ridiculous obsession, then Oliver is happy to lose; happy to reject a conventional masculinity, and to revert in some sense to being the 'feminised' Jew; to lose, indeed, to his girlfriend. Sport is not 'about winning' – at least it is not *all* about winning. It is also about being yourself, growing up, and enjoying the company of eccentric friends. Somehow it is not an activity for fully-grown men.

In *The Mighty Walzer* Jacobson gives us subversion on a grand scale on a number of fronts. In his view of Jewish life, which is not competitive and not obsessed with success; in his view of assimilation, in a neighbourhood that was Jewish, but not embattled; and in a family whose memories are mercifully happy ones, with no horrific experiences to recount. It was a family that was also stable, or at least as stable as a household could be where financial management was conducted according to Joel's surreal accountancy. And in his view of sport Jacobson questions much of the received wisdom about its potency in society. Would those arch framers of public-school games in the nineteenth century, on which the entire edifice of sport has been constructed, have recognised their vision of moral manliness in the world of the Akiva?

---

41    See Peter Clark, *British Clubs and Societies, 1580–1800: the Origins of an Associational World* (Oxford: Oxford University Press, 2000).

190

# Chapter Ten
# Conclusion

The importance of sport in contemporary society is undeniable. Whether in its commercial and professional forms, which are the ones that generally receive most attention from academics and the general public, or in its recreational forms, it both commands economic attention and exercises powerful cultural influences.[1] The changes that have taken place in sport and society over the course of the last century are numerous and complex, and have had the effect of placing sport at the centre of an international network of economic, political and cultural linkages that would have been unimaginable a hundred, or even fifty, years ago. At the beginning of the last century, in Britain as in most other countries, sport of whatever variety was considered to be a matter about which private individuals and organisations made their own arrangements. The voluntary principle was paramount, and government (except in states given to 'totalitarian' ambitions) had only minor responsibilities in this sphere of life. In addition, certain philosophical assumptions about the nature and purpose of sport were promoted, even if they did not attain universal acceptance. The assumptions can loosely be grouped together in the term 'amateurism'. But at the same time sport was a paradoxical entity in that, ideologically, it was both forward- and backward-looking. The organisation, practice and philosophy of sport were felt, on the one

---

1    See Richard Holt and Tony Mason, *Sport in Britain 1945–2000* (Oxford: Blackwell, 2000), p. 168 ff; Kathryn Jay, *More Than Just a Game: Sports in American Life Since 1945* (New York: Columbia University Press, 2004). An interesting example of the perceived influence and extent of sport, and of its importance to government in the contemporary world, is provided in a report by the Strategy Unit of the U.K. Cabinet Office, *Game Plan: A Strategy for Delivering Government's Sport and Physical Activity Objectives* (London: Cabinet Office, 2002). On the 'symbolic power' of sport see John M. Hoberman, *Sport and Political Ideology* (London: Heinemann, 1984), pp. 7–12.

hand, to typify much of what had come to be seen as 'modernity'. Association football, for instance, was taken up in several areas of continental Europe for the very reason that many people (especially young men) saw it as the epitome of progress and change; it was the game invented in the thrusting urbanised society of industrial Britain, and it seemed an obvious leisure activity for all those who wished to move out of the shadow of a stultifying past in which custom and tradition were lauded and change opposed.[2] For them football *was* modernity. Sometimes, however, other sports better fulfilled this objective. In the newly democratic society of Weimar Germany it was boxing rather than football that seemed to seize the avant-garde imagination, especially among intellectuals. They welcomed the honest vulgarity of the sport, with its naked aggression and commerce-minded promoters, which they saw as an antidote to the cultural norms of a despised old regime, and a means therefore of embracing the future.[3] When later academic observers came to scrutinise (often from a Weberian perspective) the organisation and ethos of sport, the perceived universal insistence on rules, bureaucracy and statistics was offered as a defining essence of modernity.[4] On the other hand, however, sport had by the early twentieth century absorbed a good deal of the culture of classicism which so saturated the English public school system in the nineteenth century. The public schools were, of course, one of the chief agents (perhaps *the* chief agent) of the games ethic at this time.[5] The successful revival in the late nineteenth century of the Olympic ideal of ancient Greece, a movement in which the French nobleman Pierre de Coubertin was prominent, owed much to

---

2    See Pierre Lanfranchi and Matthew Taylor, *Moving With the Ball: The Migration of Professional Footballers* (Oxford: Berg, 2001), ch. 1.

3    David Bathrick, 'Max Schmeling on the Canvas: Boxing as an Icon of Weimar Culture', *New German Critique,* 51 (Autumn, 1990), 113–36. I am grateful to my colleague Professor Mike Cronin of Boston College for drawing my attention to this interesting article.

4    Allen Guttmann, *From Ritual to Record: The Nature of Modern Sports* (New York: Columbia University Press, 1979), ch. 2.

5    See J.A. Mangan, *Athleticism in the Victorian and Edwardian Public School: The Emergence and Consolidation of an Educational Ideology* (London: Frank Cass, 2000).

the general inspiration found in the world of antiquity, especially as mediated through the English public schools.[6] The capacity of sport to accommodate these ambivalent mythologies of the new and the old has meant that the ideological effects of sport are equally contradictory. For all those who saw in sport the properties that improved mind and body there were as many who regarded it as a corrupting force which could too easily fall prey to mediocrity, especially when exposed to the exported popular culture of America. For the Dutch academic Johan Huizinga, who sought in the 1930s to argue that the idea of play had been at the heart of European culture, modern organised sports were seen as a sterile influence responsible for causing the old play element in society to become atrophied.[7] In a similar vein, though from a different political perspective, some recent sociological interpretations of the role of sport in society have assigned to it an alienating and dehumanising function, transforming the individual into a machine.[8] However, the two traditions – ancient and modern – have not always been in opposition; on occasions they have proved susceptible of harmonisation. The opening sequences of Leni Riefensthal's controversial film of the 1936 Olympic Games, *Olympia,* provide an example of how they might be fused into a single vision, unfortunately in this case a fascist one.

As may be imagined from these conflicting perspectives one of the attendant features of the development of sport in the twentieth century has been a spirit of critique. 'During the past two hundred years', says John Bale, 'there have been a number of oppositional

6    His admiration for Rugby School has frequently been commented upon, and still figures in the present-day public tour of the school premises, though de Coubertin's understanding of the internal workings of the school, and of the ideas of its distinguished headmaster Thomas Arnold, seems to have been distorted. It was the *moral* education of the boys, rather than games, that fired Arnold's educational purpose. See Mangan, *Athleticism*, pp. 16, 130; also Allen Guttmann, *The Olympics: A History of the Modern Games* (Urbana: University of Illinois Press, 2002), pp. 8–9.

7    Johan Huizinga, *Homo Ludens: A Study of the Play Element in Culture* (London: Routledge and Kegan Paul, 1949), pp. 46, 198, 206.

8    The clearest example is J-M Brohm, *Sport: A Prison of Measured Time* (London: Ink Links, 1978).

voices that have read sport against the grain.'[9] Such voices have been especially audible in literature. Many of the novels discussed in the present volume, in spite of their evident differences, are similar in this particular respect, that whilst they display obvious affection for sport they are nevertheless troubled by aspects of the circumstances in which it exists. In some cases – notably those of Roth, Jacobson and Hornby – the critical element might seem to be less in evidence because of the deep personal associations sport holds for each writer. Each one recognises the part sport has performed in the development of his own life history. It occupies a central role in Roth's memories of the Weequahic district of Newark, New Jersey where baseball, as it has done for many other American males, offers the retrieval (in the mind at least) of a lost past. It was similarly an essential part of Jacobson's upbringing in Manchester, where table tennis provided an ordered universe which contrasted with his own anarchic family background. For the lonely Hornby, experiencing the break-up of the parental home, the Arsenal football team offered all the assurances and tensions of a substitute family. In some senses, though, the personal value of sport in these cases is limited to a particular time of life, as a rite of passage in the period of youth and to growing up. Whether it has a continuing function in life is left open to question. Only in Hornby is the idea of sport as a fundamental part of living given credibility; 'the relentless pain and responsibility of club football' is a burden carried as part of the individual's obsession with sport, something to be accepted and coped with as best that individual might. In Jacobson's novel, however, a barb is directed at the fundamental principle of sport – winning; the zero-sum nature of much modern sport is clearly derided, and then subverted as the will to win becomes something to be opted out of, rejected in an act of personal choice and defiance. In spite of Jacobson's eagerness to balance his Jewish traditions with an anglicised working-class Mancunian heritage, there is still room to contest some of the enduring tenets of modern British sport philosophy; by resurrecting, perhaps, a

9    John Bale, 'Sport and Literary Oppositions: Lewis Carroll, John Betjeman and Alan Sillitoe', *Ludus,* 3 (2005), 6.

peculiarly Jacobsonian form of amateurism. For the characters in Jenkins's novel, however, winning at football is the only thing left to them, but for Jenkins himself this is not enough; although the game is a beautiful one capable of arousing high passions, it is not the only focus of life. Something is missing when only football holds the community together. Similarly for Ford's Frank Bascombe, the empty aspirations of sport cannot provide an unerring guide by which to steer a passage through life for a disorientated, late-twentieth-century American male. In Ford, however, as with Keneally, there is nonetheless a residual feeling that there are worse things than sport, and that as a moral compass it is not wholly inappropriate to the business of living. Their attachment to sport does not deprive Frank Bascombe or Terry Delaney of a degree of admiration or sympathy from the reader. Only for Storey and the authors of the *Champion* texts is there no (or very little) comfort in sport. Both come close to what John Bale in his discussion of the writings of Lewis Carroll, John Betjeman and Alan Sillitoe, has described as 'anti-sport'.[10] To a degree, therefore, the texts discussed here connect with a wider body of twentieth-century writing, most of it American. In his panoptic sweep of the development of sport novels written during the five decades before the 1970s Melvin Palmer found a persistent criticism of sport, inspired by sentiments similar to those expressed by Huizinga in his work of the 1930s; 'the sports novelist', says Palmer, 'finds that sports have squeezed out play, just as civilization has squeezed out the natural man.'[11]

The problem with Palmer's verdict is not simply that all the novels examined here do not exactly fit the statement. More significantly it is the attempt to extrapolate from a succession of novels grand universal themes such as 'civilization' and 'natural man'. It suggests the notion of a changeless, essential human nature that transcends historical periods, and it has much in common with the critical strategies of those schooled in the Leavisite tradition. This is not, as the reader may

---

10  Ibid., p. 23.
11  Melvin D. Palmer, 'The Sports Novel: Mythic Heroes and Natural Men', *Quest,* 19 (1973), 58.

imagine, an approach that has been found to be congenial in the present study. Instead, the intention has not been to isolate the 'essential' meaning of a particular text in relation to what it says about the human condition and universal 'truths', but to see the text as part of a specific historical conjuncture. In this sense the *critical* purpose of the novel becomes a matter of its engagement with the society in which it was produced by means of its ideological (literary) contribution to a particular discourse or set of discourses. To grapple with this project requires an emphasis on the *historical* circumstances in which the text exists. Often it involves a reflection upon the problems posed by changing social and cultural conditions, such as in Keneally's coming to terms with a 'new' Australia of the 1980s, or in Glanville's bringing to bear a European lens on the modernisation of Britain in the early 1960s. It might be felt by some literary specialists of a more traditional persuasion that such issues are minor ones; that not only are these novels not simply 'about sport' but that they are not (if they are any good as literature) about merely transient political and social issues. What, such critics might claim, distinguishes the good novel from the not-so-good novel is the ability of the former imaginatively to expose fundamental concerns and tensions in human society; they are fundamental because they are *constant*. Good literature, therefore, deals with timeless truths about ourselves as human beings.

However, novels are also part of a cultural process that produces, among other things, social constructions of identity such as social class, race, ethnicity and gender. Moreover they construct such notions in a process of contestation with established norms. The measure of the 'good' novel (in a historian's evaluation of 'good') is therefore less its artistic sensibility than its capacity for engagement, critique, and subversion.[12] Each of the novels considered here displays this capacity, deploying it in relation to some of the big questions of a troubled period: historical change, the idea of the nation, relations between the sexes, and the sense of 'crisis' that has often appeared to

---

12    There is, of course, a point at which its critical purpose is enhanced by the
      work's aesthetic finesse; without the latter it descends into mere polemic.

torment the observer of the latter part of the twentieth century. The novel therefore comes to exercise an ideological power. In the case of the sport novel it contributes to what is understood by the idea of 'sport' through a fluid, shifting, and complex process of negotiated meaning, what Stephen Greenblatt has called 'the unsettling circulation of materials and discourses that is [...] the heart of modern aesthetic practice'. [13] What then should a historian be doing with these imaginative representations of sport and society?

My answer to this question would take us into questions of evidence and texts, and I would place the sport novel as a historian's source in a range of sources that tell us something about the principal subject of our activity, namely sport. The novel is clearly not a source having the same function as that to be found in a heavily empirical book like, for example, Charles Korr's *The End of Baseball As We Knew It*, [14] in which is deployed an impressive array of primary evidence to substantiate its examination of the emergence of industrial organisation among Major League baseball players in the 1960s. But this is not to suggest that a novel has *less* value than sources of this kind, only a *different* value. It is certainly not, as a postgraduate student at a British university once told me after I had delivered a paper on Storey's *This Sporting Life,* 'worth only a footnote' in the history he was studying. Historians of sport mostly recognise (as this student I think did *not*) that the meaning of sport is constructed in a variety of forms, and that 'sport' exists as much on the page as it does on the field or in the committee room.

A number of these issues come to the fore in a recent discussion by Mike Cronin of the place of sport in Irish studies. It provides an excellent model of the historian's imaginative use of fiction, and converges at many points with issues raised in the present study. Cronin's aim is to enlarge the study of Irish sport from its previous narrow association with sectarianism and, at the same time, to link

---

13 Stephen Greenblatt, 'Towards a Poetics of Culture' in *Learning to Curse: Essays in Early Modern Culture* (London: Routledge, 1992), p. 159.
14 Charles P. Korr, *The End of Baseball As We Knew It: The Players' Union, 1960–81* (Urbana: University of Illinois Press, 2002).

sport with other aspects of popular culture as a way of understanding questions about identity, in particular masculinity. One element in this, which forms the core of Cronin's discussion, is the recent outpouring of artistic activity concerned with Irish sport. He focuses upon the literary representations of Irish soccer in the work of three younger Dublin writers – Roddy Doyle, Dermot Bolger, and Joseph O'Connor. All, in their novels and plays, have reflected upon the cultural impact on individuals and communities of the Republic of Ireland's soccer team in the peculiarly successful period it enjoyed in the late 1980s and early 1990s. Cronin also goes beyond literature by considering the place of popular music in presenting ideas of sport and community to the fans of bands such as the Folk Footballers and the Saw Doctors. He interestingly places these texts in a very precise historical context, noting how the experience of sport is given artistically as an ephemeral one, something 'of the moment' – a 'temporary excitement' – rather than the all-consuming obsession characterised most famously in the work of Nick Hornby.[15] Cronin demonstrates how novel, play and song can each illuminate aspects of the sporting experience; in the case of Roddy Doyle, for example, his depiction of an intensely emotional male response to Ireland's match in the 1990 World Cup against Romania shows that feelings 'normally submerged and unexpressed' allow men to reveal 'their true selves'. The point here, of course, is that Doyle is creating a *fictionalised* version of masculinity, using his position as a writer to challenge conventional notions of how men should behave. There is nonetheless a hint in Cronin's treatment of the text as reflective of Irish society – a mirror of what happens – rather than of fictions working to bring together inter-relating elements of both perceived 'reality' and the imagination. His chosen texts, like those selected in the present study, are essentially 'realist' fictions, offering a context for their narratives that readers will find reassuringly 'truthful', not too distanced from what might be recognised as being 'real life'. Such texts are perhaps

---

15  Mike Cronin, 'Beyond Sectarianism: Sport and Irish Culture', in Liam Harte and Yvonne Whelan eds, *Ireland Beyond Boundaries: Mapping Irish Studies in the Twenty-First Century* (London: Pluto, forthcoming 2006).

always going to have a conservative effect simply because, while pursuing their purpose of subversion, as Doyle does, they also rely upon traditional techniques of story-telling to bring their readers into a suspension of disbelief. A more surreal approach, which rejects realist modes in favour of something that subverts through its very form, would run the risk of alienating the reader and therefore of the point being lost altogether. What is offered in realist texts, then, is not a window onto the reality of society but versions of reality which stand a chance of being assimilated as a reasonable representation of 'the truth'. If this happens, if the reader takes the text to be a plausible explanation of life as s/he understands it, then a process of linguistic construction has occurred. A subject, as Joan Scott suggests in a powerful essay, has been 'constituted'.[16]

This process of knowledge formation through texts is what I describe as *ideology*. It is part of what happens in that rather complex art of reading a novel. It is why historians should take fictions seriously as sources in the process of writing history.

16    Joan Scott, 'The Evidence of Experience', in Gabrielle M. Spiegel, *Practicing History: New Directions in Historical Writing After the Linguistic Turn* (New York: Routledge, 2005), pp. 199–216.

# Bibliography

Adair, D. and Vamplew, W., *Sport in Australian History* (Melbourne: Oxford University Press, 1997)

Alderman, Geoffrey, *Modern British Jewry* (Oxford: Clarendon Press, 1992)

Allison, Lincoln, *Amateurism in Sport: An Analysis and Defence* (London: Frank Cass, 2001)

Alomes, Stephen, *A Nation At Last? The Changing Character of Australian Nationalism 1880–1988* (New South Wales: Angus and Robertson, 1988)

Alvarez, A., 'The Long Road Home', *Guardian Review*, 11 September 2004, 6

Anderson, Lindsay, *Never Apologise: The Collected Writings*, ed. Paul Ryan (London: Plexus, 2004)

Ardolino, Frank, 'Like Father, Like Sons: Miller's Negative Use of Sports Imagery in *Death of a Salesman*', *Journal of Evolutionary Psychology*, 25:1 (March 2004), 32–9

Baker, Aaron, *Contesting Identities: Sports in American Film* (Urbana: University of Illinois Press, 2003)

Bale, John, *Roger Bannister and the Four-Minute Mile* (London: Routledge, 2004)

Bale, J., Christensen, M.K., and Pfister, G. eds, *Writing Lives in Sport: Biographies, Life Histories and Methods* (Aarhus: University of Aarhus Press, 2004)

Barnes, Chester, *Advanced Table Tennis Techniques: How the World's Top Players Win* (London: Angus and Robertson, 1977)

Barthes, Roland, *Oeuvres complètes* (Paris: Editions du Seuil, 1994)

Barton, Laura, 'Other Voices, Other Rooms', *Guardian Review*, 8 February 2003, 20–3

Bateman, Anthony, 'The Politics of the Aesthetic: Cricket, Literature and Culture 1850-1965', Ph.D. thesis, University of Salford, 2005

Bathrick, David, 'Max Schmeling on the Canvas: Boxing as an Icon of Weimar Culture', *New German Critique*, 51 (Autumn, 1990), 113–36

Beckles, H. McD. and Stoddart, B., *Liberation Cricket: West Indies Cricket Culture* (Manchester: Manchester University Press, 1995)

Beckman, Morris, *The 43 Group* (London: Centreprise, 1992)

Black, Jeremy, 'Past Lives of the Pomos, Proto-Pomos and Pomophobics', *Times Higher Educational Supplement*, 27 August 2004, 24

Blackledge, Paul, 'Rational Capitalist Concerns: William Cail and the Great Rugby Split of 1895', *International Journal of the History of Sport*, 18:2 (2001), 35–53

Booth, Douglas, 'Escaping the Past? The Cultural Turn and Language in Sport History', *Rethinking History*, 8:1 (March 2004), 103–25

Blake, George, *Barrie and the Kailyard School* (London: Arthur Barker, 1951)

Brailsford, Dennis, *Bareknuckles: A Social History of Prize-Fighting* (Cambridge: Lutterworth Press, 1988)

Brannigan, John, *New Historicism and Cultural Materialism* (Basingstoke: Macmillan, 1998)

Briggs, Asa, *Victorian Cities* (Harmondsworth: Penguin Books, 1968)

Brockes, Emma, 'A Wizard from Oz', *Guardian Review*, 20 October 2000, 11

Brogan, Hugh, *The Penguin History of the United States of America* (London: Penguin Books, 2001)

Brohm, J.-M., *Sport: A Prison of Measured Time* (London: Ink Links, 1978)

Burgess, Moira, 'Robin Jenkins: A Novelist of Scotland', *Library Review*, 22:8 (1970), 409–12

Burn, Gordon, 'The Games Writers Play', *Guardian Review*, 9 October 2004, 4–6

Cabinet Office (U.K.), *Game Plan: A Strategy for Delivering Government's Physical Activity Objectives* (London: Cabinet Office, 2002)

Callan, Michael Feeny, *Richard Harris: A Sporting Life* (London: Sidgwick and Jackson, 1990)

Candelaria, Cordelia, *Seeking the Perfect Game: Baseball in American Literature* (Westport, Conn.: Greenwood Press, 1989)

Carter, Ian, 'Lewis Grassic Gibbon, *A Scots Quair,* and the Peasantry', *History Workshop Journal: A Journal of Socialist Historians*, 6 (1978), 169–85

Cheyette, Brian, *Constructions of 'the Jew' in English Literature and Society: Racial Representations 1875–1945* (Cambridge: Cambridge University Press, 1993)

—— *Between 'Race' and Culture: Representations of 'the Jew' in English and American Literature* (Stanford, CA: Stanford University Press, 1996)

Central Council of Physical Recreation, *Sport and the Community* (London: Central Council of Physical Recreation, 1960)

Charles, John (with Bob Harris), *King John: The Autobiography* (London: Headline Books, 2003)

Clark, Peter, *British Clubs and Societies, 1580-1800: The Origins of an Associational World* (Oxford: Oxford University Press, 2000)

Clarke, Elizabeth A., *History, Theory and Text: Historians and the Linguistic Turn* (Cambridge, Mass.: Harvard University Press, 2004)

Collins, Tony, *Rugby's Great Split: Class, Culture and the Origins of Rugby League Football* (London: Frank Cass, 1998)

—— '"Noa Mutton, Noa Laking": The Origins of Payment for Players in Rugby League', International Journal of the History of Sport, 12:1 (1995), 33–50

—— 'Australian Nationalism and Working-Class Britishness: The Case of Rugby League Football', *History Compass*, 3 (2005) AV 142, 1–19

Connell, R.W., *Masculinities* (Cambridge: Polity Press, 1995)

Cottrell, John, *A Century of Soccer Drama* (Newton Abbot: Sportsman's Books, 1972)

Cox, Richard William, *British Sport: A Bibliography to 2000* (4 vols; London: Frank Cass, 2003)

Cox, R., Russell, D. and Vamplew, W., eds, *Encyclopedia of British Football* (London: Frank Cass, 2002)

Cox, R., Jarvie, G. and Vamplew, W. eds, *Encyclopedia of British Sport (Oxford: ABC-Clio, 2000)*

Craig, Cairns, *The Modern Scottish Novel* (Edinburgh: Edinburgh University Press, 1999)

—— 'Robin Jenkins: A Would-Be Realist', *Edinburgh Review,* 106, 12

—— *Out of History: Narrative Paradigms in Scottish and English Literature* (Edinburgh: Polygon, 1996)

Critcher, Chas., 'Football Since the War', in J. Clarke, C. Critcher and R. Johnson eds, *Working Class Culture: Studies in History and Theory* (London: Hutchinson, 1979), pp. 161–84

Cronin, Mike, 'Beyond Sectarianism: Sport and Irish Culture', in L. Harte and Y. Whelan eds, *Ireland Beyond Boundaries: Mapping Irish Studies in the Twenty-First Century* (London: Pluto, forthcoming 2006)

Cronin, M. and Mayall, D., *Sporting Nationalisms: Identity, Ethnicity, Immigration and Assimilation* (London: Frank Cass, 1998)

Cuneen, Chris., 'The Rugby War: The Early History of Rugby League in New South Wales 1907–15', in R. Cashman and M. McKernan eds, Sport in History: The Making of Modern Sporting History (Queensland: Queensland University Press, 1979), pp. 293–306

Daiches, David ed., *A Companion to Scottish Culture* (London: Edward Arnold, 1981)

D'Cruze, Shani, '"Dad's Back": Mapping Masculinities, Moralities and the Law in the Novels of Margery Allingham', *Cultural and Social History*, 1:3 (2004), 256–79

Denison, Jim, 'Sport narratives', *Enquiry*, 2:3 (1996), 351–62

Dennis, N., Henriques, F. and Slaughter, C., *Coal Is Our Life: An Analysis of a Yorkshire Mining Community* (London: Eyre and Spottiswoode, 1956)

Denvir, John, *The Irish in Britain* (London: Kegan, Trench, Trubner and Co., 1892)

Dowling, Fiona, 'Narratives About Young Men and Masculinities in Organised Sport in Norway', *Sport Education and Society*, 6:2 (2001), 125–42

Eagleton, Terry, *Literary Theory: An Introduction* (Oxford: Blackwell, 1996)

Eastham, George, *Determined to Win* (London: Sportsman's Book Club, 1966)

Endelmann, Todd M., *Racial Assimilation in English Jewish History 1856–1945* (Bloomington: Indiana University Press, 1990)

Farber, Manny, *Negative Space: Manny Farber on the Movies* (London: Studio Vista, 1971)

Feldman, David, 'There was an Englishman, an Irishman, and a Jew: Immigrants and Minorities in Britain', *Historical Journal*, 26:1 (1983), 185–99

Fielding, Steven, *Class and Ethnicity: Irish Catholics in England, 1880–1939* (Buckingham: Open University Press, 1993)

Frangopulo, N.J., 'Foreign Communities in Victorian Manchester', *Manchester Review*, 10 (1965), 189–206

Gallagher, Catherine, and Greenblatt, Stephen, *Practicing New Historicism* (Chicago: University of Chicago Press, 2000)

Gartner, Lloyd P., *The Jewish Immigrants in England* (London: Allen and Unwin, 1960)

Geertz, Clifford, *The Interpretation of Cultures* (New York: Basic Books, 1973)

Gilbert, Francis, 'Family Influence: Howard Jacobson', *e magazine*, 11 February 2001, 30

Glanville, Brian, *Football Memories* (London: Virgin Publishing, 1999)

—— *People in Sport* (London: Secker and Warburg, 1967)

Greaves, Jimmy, and Gutteridge, Reg., *Let's Be Honest* (Newton Abbot: Sportsman's Book Club, 1973)

Green, Anna, and Troup, Kathleen, *The Houses of History: A Critical Reader in Twentieth-Century History and Theory* (Manchester: Manchester University Press, 1999)

Greenblatt, Stephen J., *Learning to Curse: Essays in Early Modern Culture* (London: Routledge, 1992)

Greenhalgh, Paul, 'The Work and Play Principle: The Professional Regulations of the Northern Rugby Football Union 1898–1905', *International Journal of the History of Sport,* 9:3 (1992), 356–77

Griffin, Colin, 'The Means-Test Man Re-visited: Proletarian Writers and the Social Psychology of Unemployment in the Nottinghamshire and Derbyshire Coalfield in the 1930s', *Transactions of the Thoroton Society of Nottinghamshire,* XCIX (1995), 113–20

Guttmann, Allen, *From Ritual to Record: The Nature of Modern Sports* (New York: Columbia University Press, 1979)

—— The Olympics: *A History of the Modern Games* (Urbana: University of Illinois Press, 2002)

—— 'Faustian Athletes? Sports as a Theme in Modern German Literature', *Modern Fiction Studies,* 33:1 (Spring 1987), 21–34

Hardaker, Alan, *Hardaker of the League* (London: Pelham Books, 1977)

Hattenstone, Simon, 'Laughing All the Way to the Cemetery', *Guardian Weekend,* 23 April 2005, 20

Haynes, Richard, *The Football Imagination: The Rise of the Football Fanzine Culture* (Aldershot: Arena, 1995)

Hedling, Erik, *Lindsay Anderson: Maverick Film-Maker* (London: Cassell, 1998)

Hill, J. and Williams, J. eds, *Sport and Identity in the North of England* (Keele: Keele University Press, 1996)

Hill, Jeffrey, 'Rite of Spring: Cup Finals and Community in the North of England', in J. Hill and J. Williams eds, *Sport and Identity in the North of England*

Hill, Jeffrey, *Sport, Leisure and Culture in the Twentieth Century* (Basingstoke: Palgrave, 2002)

Hill, Jeffrey, 'Sport Stripped Bare: Deconstructing Working-Class Masculinity in *This Sporting Life*', *Men and Masculinities,* 7:4 (April 2005), 405–23

Hill, Jimmy, *Striking for Soccer* (London: Sportsman's Book Club, 1963)

Hill, John, *Sex, Class and Realism: British Cinema 1957–1963* (London: British Film Institute, 1986)

Hoberman, John M., *Sport and Political Ideology* (London: Heinemann, 1984)

Hoggart, Richard, *The Uses of Literacy: Aspects of Working-Class Life with Special Reference to Publications and Entertainments* (London: Chatto and Windus, 1957)

Holt, Richard, *Sport and the British* (Oxford: Oxford University Press, 1990)

—— 'Heroes of the North: Sport and the Shaping of Regional Identity' in J. Hill and J. Williams eds, *Sport and Identity in the North of England*

—— 'Men and Rugby in the North: David Storey's *The Changing Room* and *This Sporting Life*, *Northern Review*, 4 (1996), 115–23

—— and Mason, Tony, *Sport in Britain 1945–2000 (Oxford: Blackwell, 2000)*

Home Office, *The Hillsborough Stadium Disaster, 15th April 1989: Inquiry by the Rt. Hon. Lord Justice Taylor* (London: HMSO, 1990)

Houlihan, Barrie, *The Government and Politics of Sport* (London: Routledge, 1991)

Houston, Penelope, *The Contemporary Cinema* (Harmondsworth: Penguin Books, 1963)

Huizinga, Johan, *Homo Ludens: A Study of the Play Element in Culture* (London: Routledge and Kegan Paul, 1949)

Jackson, Brian, *Working-Class Community: Some General Notions Raised by a Series of Studies in Northern England* (London: Routledge and Kegan Paul, 1968)

Jacobson, Howard, *Roots Schmoots: Journeys Among Jews* (London: Penguin Books, 1993)

Jarvie, G., and Walker, G. eds, *Scottish Sport in the Making of a Nation: Ninety Minute Patriots* (Leicester: Leicester University Press, 1994)

Jay, Kathryn, *More Than Just a Game: Sports in American Life Since 1945* (New York: Columbia University Press, 2004)

Kershaw, Ian, 'The Human Hitler', *Guardian (G2)*, 17 September 2004, 4–5

Kidd, A.J., *Manchester* (Keele: Keele University Press, 1993)

—— and Roberts, K.W. eds, *City, Class and Culture: Studies of Social Policy and Cultural Production in Victorian Manchester* (Manchester: Manchester University Press, 1985)

King, Anthony, *The End of the Terraces: The Transformation of English Football in the 1990s* (Leicester: Leicester University Press, 1998)

—— 'New Directors, Customers and Fans: The Transformation of English Football in the 1990s', *Sociology of Sport Journal*, 14 (1997), 224–40

Korr, Charles P., *The End of Baseball As We Knew It: The Players' Union, 1960–81* (Urbana: University of Illinois Press, 2002)

Krutnik, Frank, *In a Lonely Street: Film Noir, Genre and Masculinity* (London: Routledge, 1991)

Lambert, Gavin, *Mainly About Lindsay Anderson* (London: Faber, 2000)

Lanfranchi, P., Eisenberg, C., Mason, T. and Wahl, A., *100 Years of Football: The FIFA Centennial Book* (London: Weidenfeld and Nicholson, 2004)

Laski, Neville, 'The Manchester and Salford Jewish Community 1912–1962', *Manchester Review*, 10 (Spring 1964), 97–108

Lea, K.J., *A Geography of Scotland* (Newton Abbot: David and Charles, 1977)

Leader, Zachary ed., *On Modern British Fiction* (Oxford: Oxford University Press, 2002)

Lerner, Laurence, *The Frontiers of Literature* (Oxford: Basil Blackwell, 1988)

Lipman, V.D., *Social History of the Jews in England, 1850–1950* (London: Watts and Co., 1954)

Lodge, David, *Consciousness and the Novel: Connected Essays* (London: Penguin Books, 2003)

Lowerson, John, *Sport and the English Middle Classes 1870–1914* (Manchester: Manchester University Press, 1993)

Macintyre, Stuart, *A Concise History of Australia* (Cambridge: Cambridge University Press, 2004)

Malzahn, Manfred, 'The Industrial Novel', in Cairns Craig ed., *The History of Scottish Literature* (vol. 4; Aberdeen: Aberdeen University Press, 1989), pp. 229–42

Mandle, W.F., *Going It Alone: Australia's National Identity in the Twentieth Century* (Harmondsworth: Penguin Books, 1980)

Mangan, J.A., *Athleticism in the Victorian and Edwardian Public School: The Emergence of an Educational Ideology* (London: Frank Cass, 2000)

—— and Walvin, J., *Manliness and Morality: Middle-Class Masculinity in Britain and America 1800–1940* (Manchester: Manchester University Press, 1987)

Marwick, Arthur, *The New Nature of History: Knowledge, Evidence, Language* (Basingstoke: Palgrave, 2001)

—— 'The Arts, Books, Media and Entertainments in Britain Since 1945', in J. Obelkevich and P. Catterall eds, *Understanding Post War Society* (London: Routledge, 1994), pp. 179–91

—— '*Room At The Top*, *Saturday Night And Sunday Morning*, and the "Cultural Revolution" in Britain' , *Journal of Contemporary History*, 19 (1984), 127–52

—— 'Six Novels of the Sixties – Three French, Three Italian', *Journal of Contemporary History*, 28 (1993), 563–91

207

Marwick, Arthur, *The Sixties: Cultural Revolution in Britain, France, Italy and the United States, c. 1958-c. 1974* (Oxford: Oxford University Press, 1998)

Mason, Tony, *Association Football and English Society 1863–1915* (Brighton: Harvester, 1980)

Messner, Michael A. and Sabo, Donald F. eds, *Sex, Violence and Power in Sports: Rethinking Masculinity* (Freedom, CA: The Crossong Press, 1994)

Midwinter, Eric, *Quill On Willow* (Chichester: Aeneas Press, 2001)

Millar, Tom, 'Australia, Europe and Asia', *Australian Studies*, 1 (1988), 42–52

Millard, Kenneth, *Contemporary American Fiction* (Oxford: Oxford University Press, 2000)

Miller, Lucasta, 'The Human Factor', *Guardian Review*, 26 February 2005, 20–3

Ministry of Education, *The Youth Service in England and Wales* (London: HMSO, 1960)

Montrose, Louis A., 'Professing the Renaissance: The Poetics and Politics of Culture' in H. Aram Veeser ed., *The New Historicism* (London: Routledge, 1989), pp. 15–36

Moore, Andrew, *The Mighty Bears: A Social History of North Sydney Rugby League* (New South Wales: Macmillan, 1996)

Moorhouse, Geoffrey, *At the George: And Other Essays of Rugby League* (London: Sceptre, 1990)

Moorhouse, H.F., 'Repressed Nationalism and Professional Football: Scotland Versus England', in J.A. Mangan and R.B. Small eds, *Sport, Culture, Society: International Historical and Sociological Perspectives* (London: E.F. Spon, 1986), pp. 52–9

—— 'Blue Bonnets Over the Border: Scotland and the Migration of Footballers', in J. Bale and J. Maguire eds, *The Global Sports Arena: Athletic Talent Migration in an Interdependent World* (London: Frank Cass, 1994), pp. 78–96

Morton, Brian, 'Goodness in a Fallen World: The Fate of Robin Jenkins', *Scottish Review of Books,* 1:3 (2005), 8–9

Munslow, Alun, *Deconstructing History* (London: Routledge, 1997)

Murray, Isobel, and Tait, Bob eds, *Ten Modern Scottish Novels* (Aberdeen: Aberdeen University Press, 1984)

Naremore, James, *More Than Night: Film Noir and Its Contexts* (London: University of California Press, 1998)

Nathan, Daniel A., *Saying It's So: A Cultural History of the Black Sox Scandal* (Urbana: University of Illinois Press, 2003)

Oates, Joyce Carol, *On Boxing* (London: Bloomsbury, 1987)

Oriard, Michael, *Dreaming of Heroes: American Sports Fiction, 1868-1980* (Chicago: Nelson-Hall, 1982)

—— *Reading Football: How the Popular Press Created an American Spectacle* (Chapel Hill: University of North Carolina Press, 1993)

—— *King Football: Sport and Spectacle in the Golden Age of Radio and Newsreels, Movies and Magazines, the Weekly and Daily Press* (Chapel Hill: University of North Carolina Press, 2001)

—— 'From Jane Allen to *Water Dancer*: A Brief History of the Feminist (?) Sports Novel', *Modern Fiction Studies,* 33:1 (Spring 1987), 9–20

Orr, Linda, 'The Revenge of Literature: A History of History', *New Literary History,* 18:1 (1986), 1–22

Ortner, Sherry B., 'Introduction', *Representations,* 59 (1997), 1–12

Palmer, Melvin D., 'The Sports Novel: Mythic Heroes and Natural Men', *Quest,* 19 (1973), 49–58

Panayi, Panikos, *Immigration, Ethnicity and Racism in Britain 1815–1945* (Manchester: Manchester University Press, 1994)

Pronger, Brian, *The Arena of Masculinity: Sport, Homosexuality and the Meaning of Sex* (London: GMP Publishers, 1990)

Radic, Therese, 'The Song Lines of Waltzing Matilda', in R. Niles ed., *The Australian Legend and its Discontents* (Queensland: Queensland University Press, 2000), pp. 105–16

Redhead, Steve, *Post-Fandom and the Millennial Blues: The Transformation of Soccer Culture* (London: Routledge, 1997)

Reiss, Steven A., 'History, Memory and Baseball's Original Sin: The Telling and Retelling of the Black Sox Scandal', *Journal of Sport History,* 30:1 (Spring 2003), 101–7

Richards, Jeffrey, *Happiest Days: The Public Schools in English Fiction* (Manchester: Manchester University Press, 1998)

Roberts, Randy, and Olsen, James S., *Winning Is the Only Thing: Sports in America Since 1945* (Baltimore: Johns Hopkins University Press, 1989)

Rockwell, Joan, *Fact in Fiction: The Use of Literature in the Systematic Study of Society* (London: Routledge and Kegan Paul, 1974)

Roth, Philip, *The Facts: A Novelist's Autobiography* (New York: Farrar, Strauss and Giraux, 1988)

Rush, Ian, *My Italian Diary* (London: Arthur Barker, 1989)

Russell, Dave, *Football and the English: A Social History of Association Football in England 1863–1995* (Preston: Carnegie Press, 1997)

Russell, Dave, *Looking North: Northern England and the National Imagination* (Manchester: Manchester University Press, 2004)

Sahlins, Marshall, *Apologies to Thucydides: Understanding History As Culture and Vice Versa* (Chicago: University of Chicago Press, 2004)

Sammons, Jeffrey T., *Beyond the Ring: The Role of Boxing in American Society* (Urbana: University of Illinois Press, 1988)

Scott, Joan, 'The Evidence of Experience' in Gabrielle M. Spiegel ed., *Practicing History: New Directions in Historical Writing After the Linguistic Turn* (New York: Routledge, 2005), pp. 199–216

Searles, George C. ed., *Conversations with Philip Roth* (Jackson, MI: University of Mississippi Press, 1992)

Schwarz, Richard Alan, 'Postmodernist Baseball', *Modern Fiction Studies,* 33:1 (Spring 1987), 135–49

Segal, Lynne, 'Look Back in Anger: Men in the Fifties' in R. Chapman and J. Rutherford eds, *Male Order; Unwrapping Masculinity* (London: Lawrence and Wishart, 1988)

Showalter, Elaine, 'They Think It's All Over', *New Statesman*, 12 August 2002, 24–6

Sigal, Clancy, *Weekend in Dinlock* (London: Secker and Warburg, 1960)

Silet, Charles L.P., *Lindsay Anderson: A Guide to References and Resources* (London: George Prior, 1979)

Sissons, Ric. and Stoddart, Brian, *Cricket and Empire: The 1932-33 Bodyline Tour of Australia* (London: Allen and Unwin, 1984)

Smith, D. and Williams, G., *Fields of Praise: The Official History of the Welsh Rugby Union, 1889–1981* (Cardiff: University of Wales Press, 1980)

Spiegel, Gabrielle M., *Practicing History: New Directions in Historical Writing After the Linguistic Turn* (New York: Routledge, 2005)

Steedman, Carolyn, *Dust* (Manchester: Manchester University Press, 2001)

Sugden, J. and Bairner, A., *Sport, Sectarianism and Society in a Divided Ireland* (Leicester: Leicester University Press, 1993)

Taylor, A.J.P., *Essays in English History* (Harmondsworth: Penguin Books, 1976)

Taylor, Ian, 'Putting the Boot into a Working-Class Sport: British Soccer After Bradford and Brussels', *Sociology of Sport Journal,* 4:1 (1987), 171–91

Taylor, Rogan, *Football and its Fans* (Leicester: Leicester University Press, 1992)

Thomson, David, *The Whole Equation: A History of Hollywood* (New York: Little, Brown, 2004)

Tosches, Nick, *Night Train: The Sonny Liston Story* (London: Penguin Books, 2001)

Tygiel, Jules, *Past Time: Baseball As History* (New York: Oxford University Press, 2000)

Vakar, Nicholas P., *Belorussia: The Making of a Nation. A Case Study* (Cambridge, Mass.: Harvard University Press, 1956)

Voigt, David Q., *America Through Baseball* (Chicago: Nelson-Hall, 1976)

Ward, Stuart, *Australia and the British Embrace: The Demise of the Imperial Ideal* (Victoria: Melbourne University Press, 2001)

Weininger, Otto, *Sex and Character* (London: William Heinemann, 1906)

Whannel, Garry, *Media Sports Stars: Masculinities and Moralities* (London: Routledge, 2002)

—— 'Sport Stars, Narrativization, and Masculinities', *Leisure Studies*, 18:3 (1999), 249–63

Williams, Bill, *The Making of Manchester Jewry 1740–1875* (Manchester: Manchester University Press, 1976)

Williams, Charles, *Bradman: An Australian Hero* (London: Abacus, 1997)

Williams, Jack, *Cricket and Race* (Oxford: Berg, 2001)

Williams, Raymond, *Marxism and Literature* (Oxford: Oxford University Press, 1977)

Windschuttle, Keith, *The Killing of History: How Literary Critics and Social Theorists Are Murdering Our Past* (New York: First Tree Press. 1991)

Wootton, David, 'The Road Is Still Open', *London Review of Books*, 3 February 2005, 21–2

Wykes, Terry, *Public Sculpture of Greater Manchester* (Liverpool: Liverpool University Press, 2004

# Index

215